Cross-Cultural Conversation

(Initiation)

AAR
American Academy of Religion
Cultural Criticism Series

Cleo McNelly Kearns
Editor

Number 5

CROSS-CULTURAL CONVERSATION
(INITIATION)

by
Anindita Niyogi Balslev

Cross-Cultural Conversation

(Initiation)

by
Anindita Niyogi Balslev

Scholars Press
Atlanta, Georgia

CROSS-CULTURAL CONVERSATION

(INITIATION)

by
Anindita Niyogi Balslev

© 1996
The American Academy of Religion

Library of Congress Cataloging in Publication Data
Cross-cultural conversation (Initiation) / [edited by] by Anindita Niyogi Balslev.
    p.   cm. — (American Academy of Religion cultural criticism series ; no. 5)
    ISBN 0-7885-0308-1 (paper : alk. paper)
    1. Cultural relativism. 2. Multiculturalism 3. Communication and culture. I. Balslev, Anindita Niyogi. II. Series.
GN345.5.I55   1996
306—dc20   96-30768
                                        CIP

Printed in the United States of America
on acid-free paper

List of Contents

Preface by Anindita N. Balslev	7
Introduction by Anindita N. Balslev	9
Anindita N. Balslev Cross-Cultural Conversation: Its Scope and Aspiration	15
Richard J. Bernstein The Hermeneutics of Cross-Cultural Understanding	29
Don Howard The History That We Are: Philosophy as Discipline and the Multiculturalism Debate	43
Aziz Al-Azmeh Culturalism, Grand Narrative of Capitalism Exultant	77
Don Ihde Image Technologies and 'Pluriculture'	101
Lars-Henrik Schmidt Commonness across Cultures	119
Søren Christensen From the Native's Point of View – And Other Paradoxes of Cultural Relativism	133
Thomas M. Seebohm Literary Tradition, Intercultural Transfer and Cross-Cultural Conversation	145
Christopher Norris Postmodernizing Science: Against some Dogmas of the New Relativism	173
Carol L. Bernstein Interpretive Play: Masks, Bicycles and Heliotropes	197
Fred Dallmayr Modes of Cross-Cultural Encounter	211

Preface

(A Personal Note)

It is a matter of great personal satisfaction for me to be involved in the initiation and organization of a program on Cross-cultural Conversation and especially to see this volume, bearing the same title, getting ready to go to press. Studying various thought-traditions and actually living in different countries have been an intellectually rewarding and immensely enriching experience. In fact, this undertaking draws its chief incentive and impulse from the cumulative experience of awe and admiration, trials and tribulations that I have shared with men and women divided by 'boundaries' of various sorts.

Among other things, I also learnt early that at different phases and levels of self-understanding of a cultural tradition, there occurs various representations and constructions (..imperceptibly as it were, as these are not usually issues for debate among the members of a given culture, until a later, real-to-life encounter situation with 'others' makes all that was hitherto assumed appear questionable. .) about the 'otherness' of other cultural traditions that nourish the lives of people in diverse parts of the globe. Some of these construals can, perhaps, be considered to be useful (so I thought) , whereas some others badly require a correction, or at least merit a careful re-examination. The designation of 'otherness' in the frame of this coversation, is meant to serve - despite its grammatically singular form - as an umbrella term that stands for a cluster of issues. These issues vary and depend on who are these others' that we seek to converse with, by crossing the boundaries of race, gender, ethnicity, religious affiliation, political ideology and other various forms of group identity.

In course of time, I have come to feel strongly about the need for a forum for an open conversation within as well as outside the university campuses as an effective tool for correcting some of the assymetries between the diverse groups in a national as well as international context.

While considering the endeavor as an academic project, I became aware of the fact that it will not be possible even to get a glimpse of the wide range of issues that need to be addressed, step by step, if we are to grasp their ramifications both for theory and practice, without the collaboration of a group of scholars of various disciplines who will be willing to interact not only among themselves but eventually also with people of different walks of life. I, therefore, would like to express my sincere thanks to Lars-Henrik Schmidt (Docent, Institute of History of Ideas, Aarhus University), the present Director of the Centre for Cultural Research, for sharing with me my enthusiasm for this project. Without his active involvement at every step of the practical arrangements, the conversation among the contributors of this volume could not have begun.

I thank the Center for Cultural Research, Aarhus University for hosting the meetings which enabled the participants to converse freely and discuss the concerns of all the invited papers. It seems to me that one of the hopeful signs of the academic scene today, which is becoming more and more visible around the globe, is the creation of new centres for culture studies. These have made it possible for those concerned to draw attention to issues of crosscultural dimension which were previously underscored or simply ignored. I hope that this volume is only a beginning in this direction.

My thanks are also due to Inger Klausen, Secretary, Center for Cultural Research, whose careful work has made it possible to submit the manuscript in its camera-ready form.

While I record my friendship and appreciation for each of the contributors of this volume, I am also very pleased to acknowledge the sincere interest and co-operation from colleagues in both hemispheres that I have received so far for the promotion of this program.

Last but not the least, I acknowledge my debts to Erik Balslev (Professor, Institute for Mathematics, Aarhus University), my spouse. Sharing my life with him has been an important source of my awareness that the 'boundary' between cultures is to be understood and appreciated in the soft sense of that metaphor.

Introduction

Cross-Cultural Conversation at the university campuses is, no doubt, born of an academic awareness that we need to open new ground, create a new intellectual space and seek a tool informed by multiple disciplines in order to comprehend today's world - a world in which an unprecedented set of circumstances have been brought about by the remarkable feat of technology. The overwhelming experience of 'cultural, closeness and clashes - in all its ramifications - revealing the interchangeable status of strangers and neighbours - that living in a technological era has made it inevitable, had to have its impact on the academic program and curriculum. This means, to put it simply, time is ripe to recognize the legitimacy of all those questions that were previously ignored or underscored or in some cases could be granted relevancy as themes for ivory-tower academic deliberations. The willingness to face the challenge of the present situation - to engage ernestly in cross-cultural conversation is, I believe, the best we can do in our academic preparation for the twenty-first century.

Today we can only look back, sometimes almost with a sense of nostalgy, to those days when stories about distant cultures were part of our much treasured travellers' tales and which, of course, generated no philosophical worry. As steadily increasing facilities in communication made them not so distant any more, a grand vision was cherished viz. that all conceivable heterogeneities will be consummated in the harmonious vision of 'one world'. This reading in the face of diversity of cultures - the vision of 'one world' - now also seems to belong to humanities' past history. Recent developments clearly show the continued power of group-identities which resist cultural homogenization that previous theories predicted. Numerous questions come to our mind, such as: Does the interconnectedness of the various parts of the globe that we are experiencing today, along with the impact of the play of economic and political forces, point to an eventual cultural homogenization anyway ? Or, is it that despite an increasing sharing of a common technology, diversity of cultural traditions is here to stay ? In the latter case, will it be possible for us to foster a sense of human solidarity with no strings attached to monoculturalism? If not, what then?

The lesson that we have learnt in today's world is a complex one which can no more be expressed in simple, elegant extremism of one sort or another. We can no more hold high a banner glorifying the sense for an abstract or homogenized unity nor can we go to the other extreme, highlighting the sense for a radical difference to the extent that it weaves a story of utter incommensurability. It is precisely this shared awareness that prompts the participants of this conversation to focus on various issues of cross-cultural importance.

Culture is a loaded word. Leaving aside the questions of etymology or of philosophical analysis as to how we intertwine the various senses of the word to our advantage or to our peril, it seems obvious from the use of the word in our everyday language that it is impregnated with multiple meanings. In its widest sense, it can encompass just about anything and everything that human beings have created and are still creating - a sense that is reflected in such expression as 'culture versus nature'. In its narrow sense, the word may restrict its usage to a single aspect of human activity. In between these wide and restrictive uses, there are numerous other possibilities for which we need only to look into the books on citations and the works of cultural anthropologists.

If the concept of culture is such that it allows for a wide range of descriptions but defies a stable, rigorous definition that is acceptable to all concerned, it is perhaps because it refers to a phenomenon which is an ongoing, developing process. This is at least true when we speak of a living culture. We cannot draw a boundary, once and for all, in order to demarcate the range of its reach and treat it as a play field whose external limits can be fixed or imposed in one way or another, nor can we enumerate all its salient features. If we could, then - I believe - we are speaking of a dead culture that has exhausted all its possibilities.

It is precisely, therefore, that we need to try to understand what is it that we are seekig to cross' in involving ourselves in Cross-cultural Conversations? What is the implied sense of boundary which we have in front of us and whom are we expecting to meet on the other side of the boundary? Who are these 'others'?

This demands that the sense and significance of the metaphor of boundary is carefully grasped. The metaphor of boundary, if I may put it this way, can be said to have a soft sense as well as a strong sense. The soft sense of the metaphor is that it implies a separating line, a border that allows us, in the context of study of cultures, to recognize and to speak of a plurality of cultures. It is also this, as we shall see later, is what enables us to perceive the inner divergences, tensions within a culture. The strong sense of the metaphor of boundary signifies a barrier, a hindrance where 'crossing' is, as if, trespassing. It is about this second sense that we need to excercise caution as we venture to engage ourselves in this enterprise. It is here lies the veritable obstacles to cross-cultural communications.

Cross-cultural conversation, thus, call for a preparedness - a preparedness for seeking strategies that abstain from setting up boundaries that are barriers, avoid using cliches about the 'otherness' of the other. It calls for even a readiness when - if need be - 'we the interpreters' may have to perceive ourselves as 'us the interpreted'. This conversation is not a monologue 'set up' as a dialogue, nor is it a dialogue with an imaginary other. This is the new component in cross-cultural endeavor where the 'other' is a partner, a participant in this exchange. This encounter situation is not only enormously difficult and complex, sometimes it turns out indeed to be a. sensitive area of investigation.

Our present involvement with culture studies, for example, has made us aware that in our previous theory- making which had invariably important impact on actual policy-making, we have often neglected the fact that even in a seemingly homogenous frame of a single culture, there are differences, incoherences, there is much that are not shared. For the sake of theory, we have projected the story of the dominant group of a culture, we have forgotten those who have been in the periphery. In this sense, this new conversation also seeks to mediate between the marginalized and the dominant groups - pertaining to race, religion, ethnicity, gender, etc. - in diverse cultural contexts.

Thus, as I see it, one of the major tasks before the new centres for culture studies that are created today at various university campuses, is to bear the burdens of intellectual responsibility that the process of critical understanding demands from us as we strive to acquire a new identity as members of a multi-cultural global community. In short, the challenge and the concern that we have before us, we have them precisely because we have begun to perceive ourselves as participants in an enterprise which is of crucial significance for changing the environment in which we live. It takes more than simply repeating the hollow slogan of a 'new world order' . The participants of this conversation hope that in the process of these exchanges and interactions, debates and discussions, we will gradually gain deeper comprehension of the forces that are shaping our contemporary world, that we will detect many hitherto unexplored possibilities for building bridges which are lacking at present.

ii

Now a few words about the volume, the contributors and their contributions. This volume entitled, *[Initiation] Cross-Cultural Conversation* is a result of the contributions made by scholars who have visited the Centre for this purpose during the calender year 1994. While Lars Henrik Schmidt and myself had the opportunity of conversing at length with Fred Dallmyr in March, and with Richard and Carol Bernstein in October, 1994; I am pleased to note that it was possible for us to receive the rest of the contributors to this volume during the spring of 1994. The interactions have been stimulating for all and in some cases have influenced the final versions of the papers.

Given the enormous scope of this endeavor, which I further elaborate in my paper Cross-Cultural Conversation: Its scope and aspiration, must be read as an extension of the introduction and precisely for that reason is placed just after the introduction. Focusing on general trends in culture-studies and some of the shortcomings of those ventures where attempts have been made to situate cultural traditions in a global context, the paper pleads for a systematic continuation of this conversation that seeks to mediate between the marginalized and the dominant groups within and between cultures.

Richard Bernstein, New School for Social Research, New York, argues in his paper, entitled, The Hermeneutics of Cross-cultural Understanding that Gadamer's hermeneutics is relevant to some of the central problems of cross-cultural understanding, by focusing on the concepts of play, dialogue and conversation, traditions, prejudgements and prejudices, horizons and the fusion of horizons, finitude , openness and language. Drawing upon the criticisms of Habermas and Derrida, he explores the relevance of these criticisms for cross-cultural understanding.

Don Howard, University of Kentucky in his paper, entitled The History that We Are: Philosophy as Discipline and the Multicultural debate takes a critical look at the western cultural presuppositions in the way the discipline of philosophy has been defined since the beginning of the nineteenth century - by the way the history of philosophy is told as well as by the way the institutional boundaries are drawn between philosophy and other disciplines. His specific critical question would be to see whether there is a way to reconceive the discipline that would remove unwarranted impediments to serious multi-cultural conversations.

Aziz Al-Azmeh, St. Anthony's College, Oxford, lays before us in his paper, entitled Culturalism, Grand Narrative of Capitalism Exultant the current trends by drawing attention to a body of discourses celebrating a radical otherness. He will discuss some of the "tropes of romantic culturalism and nationalism" leading to "the revaluation and reclamation of Enlightenment universalism as the only possible means of counteracting" these phenomena.

Don Ihde, the State University of New York at Stony Brook examines a range of transformations in which cross-cultural phenomena have taken and are taking place with special emphasis upon the role of communications and imaging technologies. of particular importance will be examples of image perceptions in relation to 'others'.

Lars-Henrik Schmidt, Director of the Centre for Cultural Research, Aarhus University, in his paper entitled, Commonnes Across Cultures, emphasizes the idea of 'the socius as distinct from the concept of culture perceived as entity. He seeks to take a stand which is "beyond the appositional framework" proposed by the globalists and the localists.

Soren Christensen, Centre for Cultural Research, Aarhus University, in a paper entitled From the Native's Point of view and other Paradoxes of Cultural Relativism, focuses on issues that lead to intellectual disputes concerning cultural relativism. He argues that "every culture is capable of transgressing its own point of view."

Thomas M. Seebohm, the Johannes Gutenberg University, Mainz, describes in his paper entitled, Literary Tradition and Intercultural Transfer the methodologies that were used by the German philologists in classical antiquity for understanding their own tradition. He then points out the limitations of this approach as well the difficulties that are embedded in the philological-historical method of Dilthey, proposing a phenomenological approach for understanding the "possibilities of cultural contacts and transfer between cultural traditions".

Christopher Norris, Wales University, Cardiff, in his paper entitled Post-modernizing Science: Against some dogmas of the New Relativism, focuses on the philosophical inadequacies of such radical thinking whic seeks to promote an attitude of wholesale scepticism toward such values as truth, reason and critique'. This sort of relativistic outlook, he maintains would close off the very possibility of meaningful debate on issues of shared human concern.'

Carol Bernstein, Bryn Maur College, Philadelphia, in her paper entitled, Interpretive Play: Masks, Bicycles and Heliotropes maintains that one of the ways in which interpreters have approached the 'othernes' of cultures not their own has been through the 'artifacts' of those cultures: masks as forms of self-representation and as art-forms, industrial objects as bicycles, that are transformed into artworks, and metaphors that endow literal objects with distinct symbolical meaning. Drawing upon the writings of Levi-Strauss, Derrida, Geertz and Appiah, she examines the ways in which such objects acquire the burden of otherness and become the loci for interpretation.

Fred Dallmyr, University of Notre-Dame, exposes in his paper entitled, Modes of Cross-cultural Encounter, the various modes in which cross-cultural exchanges take place. He discusses these modes under several headings such as conquest, conversation, assimilation and acculturation, cultural borrowings, class struggle and dialogical engagement.

Anindita N. Balslev

Cross-Cultural Conversation:
Its Scope and Aspiration

As the twentieth century is merging into the twenty-first, thinking at the confluence of cultures is no more perceived as an ivory-tower speculation. Today if some of us have begun to speak of the 'global village, we know that it is made possible by the unprecedented march of technology. This, however, is not the same as saying that cultural distances have been traversed in matching with the spectacular achievement of 'killing the distance' in a geographical sense. Far from it ... It is this awareness that has contributed much to the present academic endeavors to take another look at our multicultural situation where neighbors and strangers seem to be interchangeable verities and get ready to pay a price for the sake of maturity.

The responses that reflections on the sway of the technological civilization have invoked are neither simple nor neutral. It is steadily causing us to perceive the ambiguous nature of technology itself, of the beneficient and questionable purpose that it can be made to serve. It is no exaggeration to say that we live in an era of unlimited hope and fathomless fear. It is this sense of ambiguity, embedded in our present conception of 'progress' and 'development', is also creating the urge to innovate new ways of thinking and providing the impetus to have us grow. In short, it is in this setting of anguish and expectations that we are to give up some of our old practices and search for new images, new metaphors in order to replace the stale, hackneyed ones that would help a novel comprehension of the current cultural configuration of 'Us' and They'. In a way, the situation seems to be just ripe to begin afresh an open-ended conversation which is decidedly cross-cultural.[1]

Living in a technological civilization, as we seek a higher level of critical self-understanding by placing ourselves in a progressively larger context, it inevitably involves an encounter with the otherness of other cultures and we cannot stop short of reaching the global context. However, this fact does not seem to entail that we can be said to have achieved a sense of a global community, more than in a rather remote meaning of that phrase. This is evident in the way we conduct and perceive ourselves in the public space. We can almost wonder about the fact that today when we in a matter of a few hours can travel from one hemisphere to the other, when resources and supplies get transferred with incredible speed and efficiency from one part of the globe to another, when an event taking place in a remote territory appears in the following day's newspaper - no matter where one is, why has it not furthered the cause for what it is to be members of a global community more than it actually has.

This could be ascribed to various reasons of which perhaps one of the principal ones is that we are not yet genuinely comfortable with the notion of a community which is pronouncedly multi-cultural in character. The existing structures of our educational, social and political institutions have not lived up to the challenge that living in a technological era demands. We are still not quite at ease with the thought that human solidarity does not ask for a homogenized or an abstract cultural unity. The myth of mono-culturalism legitimates, more often than not, actions that is geared to bring about human suffering. I cannot help sensing a conceptual vacuum that needs to be filled before the links between the idea of human solidarity and that of cultural diversity can be established in any genuine manner so that it can eventually influence our collective policy-makings in various areas of life.

Thus, it is not quite surprising when we come to read such an observation as the following:

The culture of a village in southern Italy may be different from that of a village in northern Italy, but both will share in a common Italian culture that distinguishes them from a German village. European communities, in turn, will share cultural features that will distinguish them from Arab or Chinese communities. Arabs, Chinese and Westerners, however, are not part of any broader cultural entity. They constitute civilizations. ... For the relevant future, there will be no universal civilization, but instead a world of different civilizations "...[2]

There is not much doubt in my mind that despite some slogans and catchy phrases, there remains a conceptual vacuum in our understanding, to repeat once more, about how to view the constellations of the diversity of cultural traditions in a global context. Granted that this situation can be seen as potentially volatile and can even be interpreted as dangerous, it is nevertheless regrettable that it can lead anyone to perceive the major cultures as basically antagonistic to the extent that to predict eventually a 'Clash of civilizations.'

This brings me to the three basic concerns of my paper: a) How to construe human solidarity in the face of cultural diversity, b) Must cultural diversity be necessarily seen as incommensurable with the rise of a global community? and c) How to make emerge a cross-cultural conversation that is perceived by the participants as mutually empowering. In what follows these concerns are not treated separately but are seen as intertwined with each other, having direct bearing on the question of how do we handle the multicultural composition of our so-called 'global village'.

Culture, to repeat what I said in the Introduction, is a loaded term, which is impregnated with assorted meanings. However, since the concern of this paper is not how to define culture but rather how to promote cross-cultural conversaion for the benefit of all concerned, it may be asked in this context, what is entailed in the idea of 'solidarity' (taking the most conventional and generally accepted use of the word) which is supposed to be shared by the members of a given culture? I ask this question, as I am inclined to believe that human solidarity - whether asuumed to have been achieved in a monocultural setting or imagined as a possibility in a multi-cultural global context - is not something which has been (or can be) just 'found' but 'made'. In all cases, it is or will have to be gradually constructed. How it is actually construed in its most rudimentary sense and what it takes to construct such a relation are themes which calls for lengthy discussions - not possible within the compass of this paper. But some useful and general hints can perhaps be obtained by asking the simple question: What is the prevailing atitude of a member of a given culture toward other members of what is perceived and identified as the 'same' culture? In a broad and open sense of the expression, perhaps the suggestion could be made that the members share a sense of community which they, generally speaking, do not quite share with the members of what is perceived as 'an-other' culture. This phenomenon calls for a critical analysis.

It needs to be stressed that even in a monocultural setting, the sense of partnership that members cherish for various purposes social, political and others must not delude us to accept a narrative of a monolithic culture. On the contrary, we need to note that individuals who have divergent perceptions, even conflicting opinions on various strategic issues, yet may still be said to have this sense of community. In other words, they recognize that there are shared bonds, shared interests. The partners engage each other freely in conversation concerning various issues without any pledge of having to hold the same view or recommend the same public policies or approve of the final decisions. In short, the sense of community understood in this open sense does not mitigate against the possibilities of disagreements and disparities amongst its members just as it does not outrule that on occasions it may demand the employment of devices to arrive at a concensus. This sense of community is obviously something which has been achieved by different human aggregates and which is perceived as something which needs to be guarded against all possible disruptive forces that seek to destroy the bond of civility that binds the members.

It has required, let us note, setting up of various institutions educational, social, political, legal etc. which launch programs that strengthen and sustain this sense of community. In brief, these are mutually reenforcing - the community sets up and supports the institutions and the latter empower the former. As long as this state of affairs prevails, the members are inclined to perceive differences, not as intimidating but perhaps as a valuable resource for keeping the culture alive, and consider it to be important for figuring out the common options that are available. When, however, the internal divergences are felt to be menacing, and the institutions are perceived as serving and favoring exclusively, let's say, only the dominant group, at the cost of others, the sense of community is in jeopardy and the culture in question is in crisis. In other words, the well-being of a culture is dependent on the sense of partnership that its members share, despite the fact that these individuals inevitably know of different group affiliations which do not see eye to eye in all matters. To perceive oneself as a member of a culture is to be aware of this constellation of various groups and of the interconnectedness that exists among them. No major culture is monolithic.

In other words, construed this way, a vitally important component for the construal of a sense of partnership seems to be the cultivation of an attitude, a way of looking at oneself and others belonging to various groups within a culture which is vigilantly guarded by the society at large through its various institutions. The question before us is whether it is possible to envisage that this attitude, with some luck, can be extended to members of other culture-groups who perhaps do not occupy the same space where one locates one's own culture. I suppose the answer depends on many factors. First of all do we have adequately functioning organizations and institutions that can empower the idea of a global community, which is multi-cultural to its core? This is exactly the question that we need to direct primarily to our educational institutions to-day as to whether these institutions are consciously fostering what I am describing as Cross-cultural Conversation. The bridge-building task is the foremost challenge of the coming century.

Promoting a sense of global community is striving to articulate the interconnectedness of cultures in ways that has been so far missing. The demand for a conversation, which is not merely talking to the other but with each other calls for a preparedness, a preparedness to learn from those occasions when 'we, the interpreters' would get transformed to 'us, the interpreted', when we may well be forced to look for an answer where we had not expected a question. This conversation is prompted by the awareness that no cultural tradition is so completely and rigidly fixed that it leaves absolutely no room for further self-examination or the dawning of new insights. Were it not so, it would tantamount to saying that the cultural tradition in question is incapable of further growth, that virtually it is no more alive.

Cross-cultural studies is not an independent, isolable area of enquiry. The themes that need to be addressed are not entirely new. However, the way these have been enframed in academic discussions deserve a critical examination. The attitudes and the assumptions that often govern these discussions are not always brought to the surface, the imageries that are in vogue are not always analyzed.

In other words, what we need is a more complex, a more intricate and nuanced understanding of the relations that exist among these large human aggregates. We require new stories about our collective past where success and defeat, growth and poverty, hunger and affluence will be told in a manner that their interconnectedness will come into focus, shaking the boundaries of the disciplines in our academic conversations by making the concerns of economics, politics, ethics and philosophy intersect each other. A search for this sort of complex understanding will gather momentum only when the intellectuals will not try to bypass these questions. This enterprise, which requires the collaboration of scholars of various disciplines now seems to be far-fetched, as it is never an easy task to change the trends in thinking, to examine questions that are still outside the ambit of our intellectual self-consciousness. It is tempting to observe that it is unlikely that there will be ever final answers to any of these questions but then, final answers are not what we are seeking. However, it does not seem altogether implausible that as we continue to struggle with these issues, we will in this process eventually learn to overcome the latest forms of tribalism. In the long run, the sense of global community, a phrase I use for want of any better expression, is to be seen as an antidote to all forms of tribalism, no matter in which guise it appears before us. It is a call to foster a sense of togetherness that the technological civilization alone can promote. No living culture today unfolds its life by maintaining a pristine distinctness without vigorously interacting with the otherness of other cultures. If understanding the other need not be construed as an unwarranted attempt to reconcile differences, it also does not entail an advocacy for overemphasizing differences that are trivial. It is tempting to imagine, in the name of human solidarity, a posterity which will know of new ways of resolving conflicts, which finds it obscene to waste intellectual and economic resources serving the cause of violence. This is undoubtedly a hope, but the hope to be able to transcend, to surpass and to overcome our present situation is what all human beings live by; to say this is not the same as indulging in any transcultural generality.

A strong sense of boundary in the context of diversity of cultures is that which obstructs the perception of the overlapping contents, the interrelation of the destinies of traditions and cultures and the countless manners in which these are nourished and impoverished by each other. Under these circumstances, to allow cross-cultural conversations - as a project - to remain in the periphery of the academic offerings of educational institutions is indeed a complicity with the status quo. It is an expression of an unwillingness to help emerge a new civil society that consciously strives for a more critical self-understanding, lets ethnic differences thrive for its own benefit while discouraging its fanatic expressions, deters domination and exploitation on every level and is fully supportive of new ways of thinking about the 'otherness' of the other.

No living culture is static hence effort must be made to understand that the direction of its growth is multi-dimensional. In this connection, let me observe that one device which is often employed in our theory-making is through the projection of a simplistic picture of a culture. This is often done by omitting the stories of those who are marginalized by the dominant group. The dominant group, let it be noted, does not necessarily mean the majority. It may be (more often than one suspects) a minority group of insiders or outsiders, given the power structure of a society at a specific phase of its cultural history. We tend to ignore the dissents, the protests of those who reside at the periphery of the powerstructure - note that these are not necessarily the minority groups of insignificant number - and fail to represent them adequately in our accounts. Thus cross-cultural conversation has to mediate between the dominant and the marginalized groups, cutting across ethnicity, gender, religious affiliations etc. etc. In our theory-making we often neglect the fact that even in a seemingly homogenous frame of a single culture, there are differences, incoherences, there is much that is not shared. For the sake of a theory, we have not often paid attention to those who in their constant interaction, even through their very refusal to accept the dictates of the dominant group, have influenced the course of a culture.

In this connection, another point that deserves critical scrutiny is the practice of projecting major cultures in a contrasting manner, sometimes even as if these are diagrammatically opposed to each other. One way of doing this is by describing a culture in terms of the forces of emancipation and ignoring those which are geared to oppression and the 'other' culture quite as simplistically in an antithetical. way. Let me give a few examples of the manner in which distinctions between East and West are made. The most extreme forms of contrast bearing on the East and the west echo the famous line "Never the twain shall meet". At the end of the nineteenth and the beginning of the twentieth centuries, it was commomplace to desribe the East as spiritual and the West as materialistic, then after the era of colonialism a self-critical posture of Western thinkers such as Roger Garaudy , the contrast sounds something like the West is 'sick' and others are 'deceived'; finally one could consider Richard Rorty's description where the West is a 'culture of hope' and the East is a culture of 'resignation'.[3]

A compilation of such characterizations of large culture-complexes in terms of such simple dichotomy almost make many of these renderings seem like ideological labels, glorifying one while underscoring the other. What we need is to unlearn some of these stereotypes and redescribe these cultures by bringing into focus those aspects and trends which can contribute toward fostering a sense of partnership. In other words, focus should be made on those aspects which have been so far, very largely pushed to the absolute periphery of our discourse on cultures in our eagerness to project them as diagrammatically opposed. I am inclined to believe that these components are present in all these culture-forms. and that it is worth a try to see closely in what way these can be helpful in checking the grotesque asymmetry in cross-cultural exchanges of all sorts. The most hopeful tone of our time is that the silence is broken and that there is no dearth of information. A better sharing of world pool of ideas will require that the educational system provides a general access to these for the future generation. The intellectual endeavor has to be toward what to learn and what to unlearn.

Living in societies which are plural in every sense, we are learning to watch out in theory or in practical policy-making what it is that is being compromised: Is it the differences that we regard to constitute our identity in the name of some abstract, unreal unity or is it the shared- bonds that are being shrewdly underplayed in the name of some trivial, irrelevant differences? In other words, we are gradually becoming aware of the subtleties of the game that is played in the name of cultural diversity/clash of civilizations or whatever.

Cultures, like sub-cultures within a so-called single culture, resist the forces that attempt to reduce them into a common, homogenous denominator. It is perhaps no exaggeration to say that no unique mode of self-understanding, no single perception of the otherness of the other can be found in any given culture, let alone of clusters of cultures of such enormity, as the East and the West. A culture which is perceived by some as a 'culture of resignation, is seen by others as a 'redemptive force'. These readings about cultures, it seems to me, are indicative of various trends and potentialities that are present within a culture. These cannot be captured in simplistic interpretations that tend to ignore the differences in the various strands of self-understanding and perception of 'otherness' of other cultures. There is often a tendency, for example, to describe the modern West as exclusively secular, to say that is to ignore the deep religious strands in the Western culture that stubbornly resists that.

Thus to promote cross-cultural conversation in the university campuses is not to introduce a totally separate field but to give a new direction to academic enquiry by attempting to bring together the expertise that the scholars of various disciplines already have about various cultures and sub-cultures. It is rather to be considered as a program having decidedly a contemporary slant in so far as it invites a multi-disciplinary approach for correcting some of the oddities resulting from certain configuration of power and knowledge. It will indeed make a difference when the politicians who are today the major players in cross-cultural games will have to live up to the challenge of the better informed academic communities that will raise new political issues which demand greater proficiency to handle. We are bound to arrive at a critical consensus which will help us better perceive what our common options are, where ought to be our priorities. It is only then that we will be better able to show that we no longer wish to be passive spectators of a scenario where the defeat and humiliation of a people or a tradition has been the story of glory and success of another. This program, therefore, has to draw from our past and must yet be forward-looking. What we need today are cosmopolitan thinkers who can teach us to think globally without demolishing local differences, who can fill in the gaps where our culture theories have been deficient, who can weave stories of the interactions between cultures and how these have shaped their destinies. In short, to be able to perceive ourselves as members of a multi-cultural global community is to discover that cultures are not merely juxtaposed in a public space but are related to each other in multiple ways, more today than it ever has been. To learn to appreciate that the idea of human solidarity is not better expressed by denying diversity but precisely the contrary is the price we pay for the sake of maturity

Dissemination of stories of cultures and sub-cultures, of their successes and failures, of their pain and hope may well turn out to be one of the most effective ways that our educational institutions can render service to the emerging global community. Perhaps as we will get more and more inputs, we will begin to see to what extent the plots and sub-plots of these stories interweave with those of other human aggregates who otherwise happen to claim a separate cultural identity of their own; perchance this will generate and augment a deeper level of sensitivity enabling us to register the overlapping, the interdependent character of our multi-cultural situation. More than theories, what we need are these narratives.

May be, as members of a multicultural global community, 'we' will become aware that the game is still going on, when 'otherness' of the other is used to legitimize the oppression and subjugation, be that in the name of group-identity where membership is not even voluntary, such as that of race and gender, or be it, at least in principle, a matter of choice such as that of religious denominations or secular fold of divergent political ideologies. The tensions and anxieties that we bear as members of distinct groups are now to be seen in their interconnectedness. To the extent that a social theory ignores or glosses these features of our contemporary situation, that are increasingly making our interdepedence prominent, it loses its exlanatory power.

However, it is no easy task. It is indeed difficult to fight a battle whose goal is not to defeat any one but rather that nobody is defeated. The battle is to be waged against a system that produces the oppressors and the oppressed, the exploiters and the exploited, the winners and the losers, cutting across race, gender, nationality or any other form of collectivity. It is indeed hard to make emerge a discourse that reflects a new description of a society which can do without these stereotypes. A critical look at various disciplines, as several conscientious scholars in recent times have revealed it to us, makes it evident that some of our professed neutralities are nothing but disguises for discriminations of one sort or another. These assumptions, let it be noted, cannot be treated as just simple, remote-from-life depictions that are there only in some abstract, theoretical level which need not perturb us seriously. On the contrary, these are assumptions that eventually come to play decisive roles in the manner we shape our self-images and project images of 'otherness' of the others, influencing our attitudes and actions as we go about in our transactions of daily life.

The question before us in the educational context is not, as I see it, whether to implement some changes in our curriculum or not but rather how do we enlarge or modify our curriculum so that a new picture may gradually emerge, instead of the one that brings out the present asymmetry in cross-cultural exchanges. The challenge before us is not to validate a heritage or a culture at the cost of another but to perceive cross-cultural conversation as a mutually empowering dialogue that raises the consciousness of all the participants involved. Thus, thinking of the cross-cultural dimension of the vast area of study such as philosophy, I am inclined to believe that the more philosophers of the different parts of the globe will become familiar with each other's traditions, it would show that the geographical dimension of human thinking such as German idealism, French existentialism, American pragmatism or Indian Vedanta need not be taken as territories where a native can have proper access and others can contemplate only from outside. As a matter of fact, even if there are not very many, still it is not difficult to find some good examples to demonstrate the point when a scholar has shown profound understanding of a tradition which is not his native. If there are not many such examples, I suspect, it is perhaps because the educational program does not always open up possibilities that is geared to acquaint students with the philosophical tradition of other cultures. It seems to have been very largely a matter of private initiatives.

In this connection, it is useful also to recall the view that today in the modern West, philosophers are largely university professors. The "institutionalization of universities into departmental structures"[4] play an important role in the cultural life of the West. This is precisely why when these departments do not represent the intellectual traditions of the East, they are not simply silent but that they are helping to perpetuate the image of a mythical, mysterious, non-rational East.

On the other hand, it is tempting to observe, taking the example of India as representative of the East, that it will be advantageous to perceive that whatever the historical circumstances that introduced Western thought to India, it is here to stay. Thus, while a genuine involvement with the sources, the methodologies and the concerns of Indian thought is indispensable for a creative advancement of the Indian intellectual tradition, the encounter with the West is to be seen as an opportunity for going beyond the tradition's already achieved self-understanding. What is needed is not to get stuck with a static image of the West. It is important to realise that a simple, neatly-told narrative of by-gone past or a spectacular parade of hallowed figures is not enough. It is necessary to get a glimpse of the various reactions and responses of the contemporary, living Western philosophers to their past and to know the story of how the main currents of thought have split into tributaries and nourish the soil that keep the West alive.

What philosophers can do is to lay bare before our critical gaze the assumptions, the cliches that block communication. How can philosophers do their part in this urgent task if they are themselves unwilling to speak differently about intellectual traditions across cultures, holding on to images of East and west, as if these are rigid, fixed, monolythic structures imperme-able to change. As an insider or as an outsider to a specific tradition, the philosopher's critique is welcome, not as a design to obliterate differences but as a help to foster a conceptual world where options for our future deliberations with regard to various issues, in a global context, can be discussed.

In this connection, let me also draw attention to the fact that the practice of setting up cultural traditions against each other has been almost fatal with regard to the question of religion. one such example, which I have disussed at length elsewhere, pertains to the theme of time. The cliche that the Indo-Hellenic conception of time is cyclic as opposed to the Judeo-Christian understanding of linear time has been repeatedly used wherever attempts have been made to place the conceptual experience of time in major thought-traditions in a global context. It was almost disturbing to see, that not only these are inadequate for comprehending the great variety of views with regard to this theme but how these metaphorical descriptions gradually cease to be simple time-metaphors and get associated with the idea of progress, that of history and even that of salvation.[5] When the presuppositions of such schemes continue to go unexamined, the final result of it is that it severely blocks inter-religious exchanges.

In other words, some addition to or modification of the existing curriculum in these areas, as the case may be, is long overdue. These are only a few examples. I am sure that scholars in other disciplines who are themselves teachers have insights into such omissions in their respective domains and that they themselves can best judge as to how such neglected themes can be incorporated into the curriculum. In short, by urging that we need to break away from the old habit where the educational program failed to represent the diversity that we come across in the world at large, the point I am trying to make is that it is depriving us of that valuable support which is required to place ourselves in the global context. Our academic curriculum needs to reflect the realities that the technological civilization has created for us.

As we stand in the last decade of this century, we know that several moves have already been tried out in the in the face of diversity. Some have perceived cultural differences in a manner that resulted in setting up of a hierarchy and have looked at the other culture "as earlier stages of the evolution of the self".[6] Some, on the other hand, have projected the vision of 'one world' where in course of time all heterogeneity will eventually be dissolved. Some adopted a theological stance and hoped that a theory of Transcendence will come to our resue and still others have reminded us of the essence of human nature. This is not all. We have also witnessed that recognition of diversity has led some to accentuate 'ethnocentrism' of a sort - a view which others suspect to be a disguised form of cultural imperialism.

As one goes through these wide range of possibilities which have been used as philosophical presuppositions for the promotion of human solidarity - one realizes the challenges that are there to be dealt with, both for the sake of theory and practice by the participants engaged in cross-cultural conversation. However, it is indeed remarkable that in recent times the theme of human solidarity has again captured the imagination of thinkers, no matter what might be otherwise be their philosophical bents and political inclinations.[7]

While reflecting on this important theme, a word of caution may be inserted. If unity is not the other name of homogenization, a call for domination of one culture -form over others, the emphasis on diversity is not to be seen as an opportunity for creating an atmosphere of separatism, division in society or to promote ethnic chauvinism. If that is what is sought, the entire purpose of this battle is then lost in its very inception. For this battle is not about who should be excluded but about how do we innovate a system, create a community that will allow us to participate in each others' traditions.

I am inclined to believe that as cross-cultural conversations continue, it will be possible to uncover the overlapping contents without underplaying the deviations, the divergences. It is in this process we help emerge a partnership that does not get put off by the talk of radical difference or gets thwarted at the thought of the highly unlikely prospect of a dissolution of serfhood. Thus, a sense of community in the global context does not need to bank on the melting-pot metaphor even though it does call for a renewed effort to represent the intricate plots by interweaving the themes of power and poverty, wealth and oppression, freedom and knowledge. A redescription of human interrelationships in this track is not merely a re-interpretation but a way of changing the environment in which we live, by giving it a different sense of direction than what it has at present.

---

1   cp. my *Cultural Otherness: Correspondence with Richard Rorty*, Shimla/Delhi, 1991

2   cf. paper entitled, A Clash of Civilizations? by Samuel P. Huntington, Director of Olin Institute for Strategic Studies at Harvard university, 1993. He also maintains that "World politics is entering a new phase.... It is my hypothesis that the fundamental source of conflict in this new world will not be primarily ideological or primarily economic. The great divisions among humankind and the dominating source of conflict will be cultural."

3   Richard Rorty, "Intercultural comparison", presented at the Sixth East-West Philosophers' Conference, Honolulu, 1989

4   Cf. essay by Ninian Smart in *Interpreting Across Boundaries: New Essays in Comparative Philosophy*, Princeton,1988, eds. Larson + Deutsch.

5   See my paper in *Religion and Time*, E.J. Brill, Netherlands, 1993, eds. Balslev + Mohanty.

6   cf. Ashis Nandy, *Traditions, Tyranny and Utopias*, Oxford University Press, Delhi, 1987.

7   Thus, even while decrying the idea of human essence or that of an ahistorical human nature in all its versions, Rorty writes in his *Contingency, Irony and Solidarity*, Cambridge University Press, New York, 1989,: "There is such a thing as moral progress. (which) is indeed in the direction of greater human solidarity. But that solidarity is not thought of as a recognition of core self, the human essence, in all human beings. Rather it is thought of as the ability to see more and more traditional differences (of tribe, religion, race, customs and the like) as unimportant when compared with similarities with respect to pain and humiliation - the ability to think of people wildly different from ourselves as included in the range of us".

Richard J. Bernstein

The Hermeneutics of Cross-Cultural Understanding

I want to begin by sketching a caricature of recent debates concerning what has been called "multiculturalism." A caricature requires simplification and exaggeration. But it must also be "truthful" -- it must bear some striking resemblance to what is being caricatured. Like Wittgenstein's famous example of the duck-rabbit, my caricature is open to a double interpretation -- the "same" caricature can be seen from radically opposing polarities. Consider the following narrative sketch about the Enlightenment legacy and the problem of incommensurable and conflicting cultures. The Enlightenment aspirations which have shaped so much of modernity appear to be noble and high-minded. Opposing entrenched political and social hierarchies, the Enlightenment thinkers -- the *philosophe* and the *Aufklarer* -- affirmed the dignity and intrinsic worth of all men. They proclaimed the universal *Rights of Man*. They initiated what Charles Taylor felicitously calls "the politics of dignity." These thinkers also believed that if Reason were allowed to flourish and be publicly disseminated then there surely would be social and moral progress. They envisioned a future in which the rights of every man would be protected and where enslaving superstition and myth would come to an end -- where human beings would be autonomous, free, enlightened and rational.

    Although these ideals, aspirations, and hopes appear quite laudable, they have actually hidden and obscured a much darker, uglier and more brutal reality. These "noble" ideals are little more than an ideological veneer that has masked violent oppression, ruthless imperialism, and brutal colonialization. When stripped of its false pretensions, this ideology turns out to be an instrument for control and marginalization, an instrument of power for the dominant class or group. The so-called Enlightenment ideals are not --

and never were -- universal; they are Eurocentric and patriarchal. They have been used to destroy and suppress cultural differences and identities. The Rights of "Man" -- despite their alleged universality -- have excluded women, people of color, and other ethnic and religious minorities. Even if we set aside the more blatantly ruthless forms of imperialism, racism, sexism, and class oppression which have been the real historical forces of modernity, and focus our attention on more moderate enlightened forms of liberalism, we find the same "logic" at work in more subtle but no less pernicious ways. Liberals have never been able to recognize the value of conflicting radical cultural differences. The very idea that a historically concrete culture or group (as distinguished from abstract individuals) might have collective rights has been anathema to a liberal mentality. The liberal says: "I am tolerant, I am open-minded, I am willing to accept individual differences in life styles -- as long as you basically act and talk like me -- as long as you suppress your group identity and cultural differences and behave like a 'good' liberal."

During the twentieth century we have been witnessing a protest and revulsion against the hypocrisy and mystification of this liberal ideology -- an ideology which fosters a bland cultural homogeneity. Today what is needed is an affirmation and a genuine recognition of the integrity and worth of radically different cultures -- where we fight against all forms of demeaning stereotypes. What is needed today is not a politics of pseudo-dignity of abstract atomic individuals, but a serious politics of cultural difference and identity. We are not faceless isolated human beings; "we" are many different -- and sometimes conflicting and overlapping -- we's. We are gays, lesbians, Afro-Americans, Chicanos, women of color, etc. We demand our rights not merely as members of these groups, but as individuals whose historical identities are constituted and defined by the cultural groups to which we belong. We (members of different cultural groups) need to be wary of the liberal talk about tolerance -- which can mask a deeper unspoken intolerance. For this language has become thoroughly contaminated and politically corrupt. Every culture, no matter how alien, "other," strange or threatening it may appear from the perspective of the dominant hegemonic culture, deserves recognition and respect for its own intrinsic worth and identity.

I said earlier that the polarities of this caricature can be reversed. By this I mean that without calling into question its underlying (and unacknowledged) presuppositions and conceptual distinctions, we can reverse our rhetoric and our value judgments. A defender of the Enlightenment liberal legacy will accuse his multicultural critic of proposing a distorted and mistaken diagnosis of our current situation. For such a critic fails to appreciate the dangers -- indeed the disastrous consequences -- of what he is affirming. A true liberal will not only concede but insist that there has been and continues to be an enormous disparity been liberal *ideals* and actual political, social and economic *reality*. But this is no indication of what is wrong with liberalism. On the contrary, this disparity shows how much more needs to be done if these ideals are to be realized or even approximated in everyday practices. The point of enunciating and debating liberal ideals and principles is not to *describe* existing reality, but to *prescribe* what ought to be done in order to bring about a more just society. It is not liberalism but the "new" politics of cultural difference and identity that needs to be exposed for what it really is. Despite the seemingly high-minded rhetoric of calling for the celebration and recognition of cultural differences, this "new" ideology turns out to be nothing but an aggressive form of cultural relativism and nihilism. Behind the facade of claiming that every culture is worthy of recognition and respect, it is really saying that there can be no legitimate cross-cultural norms or judgments. Each and every culture ought to be accepted for what it is -- no matter how perverse its beliefs or practices may be. This means that one ought to accept such practices as female circumcision, infanticide of female children, or the varieties of fanaticism that advocate murdering those who hold opposing beliefs. All of these are practices of actually existing cultures. So under the banner of radical plurality -- recognizing the worth of incommensurable cultures -- the advocate of multiculturalism is really calling for ever more stringent forms of separatism and segregation. Instead of what the multicultural critic facilely calls "Eurocentrism," we have an ideology calling for the proliferation of fragmented "centrisms." Taken to its "logical" extreme -- an extreme that can no longer be thought of as a mere fantasy -- the "logic" of multiculturalism turns out to be a "logic" of ethnic cleansing!

Although, at the beginning of this essay, I said that I was going to sketch a caricature, the sad truth is that what I have just presented comes very close to being an accurate representation of the polemical debates that are now taken place. Before critically probing the unexamined presuppositions of these debates which continue to fuel such strong oppositions, I want to indicate briefly what I take to be the "truth" which gets distorted in these heated controversies.

Anyone who has experienced the pain, suffering and humiliation of belonging to a group that has been persecuted, victimized or marginalized by a dominant group can well understand why there is so much skepticism about the Enlightenment liberal legacy. Despite reiterated claims concerning universal human rights, political equality, human dignity and equal justice for all citizens, modern history has been largely a history of racism, sexism, class oppression, and mass genocide. Cultural hegemony has been a much more manifest reality than the mutual respect for cultural, ethnic and religious differences. What is most troubling and alarming is that oppression and marginalization have been carried out -- over and over again -- in the very name of the so-called Enlightenment ideals. Liberalism with its soothing images of the "melting pot" or the "harmonious society" where all differences are happily reconciled has obscured the real violence of conflicting cultural differences. Even the new liberal attempts to develop multicultural curricula in our schools and colleges do not really break with the reassuring illusions of liberalism. For these new curricula are all too often like those hurried packaged tours of foreign lands where one rushes from place to place taking snapshots of quaint natives -- and then returns safely to the comfort of one's own ethnocentric biases.

On the other hand, those who are alarmed by the shrill rhetoric of a politics of identity and a politics of difference cannot be simply dismissed as Neanderthal reactionaries or dogmatic neo-conservatives. There are all too real dangers of fragmentation, the break-up of societies, and bizarre forms of separatist doctrines and practices. There is a danger that a politics of cultural difference slides into a politics of cultural animosity where no serious mutual understanding is even ventured. There is a danger of a "clash of absolutes" where cultural and ethnic groups treat each other as threatening enemies.

If we are to break the stalemate of the polemical extremes, then we need to probe more deeply into the presuppositions and conceptual distinctions that keep these debates seesawing back and forth. I want to try to make some progress in doing this by drawing upon the relevant insights and claims of the hermeneutic tradition -- as it has been elaborated by Hans-Georg Gadamer. Gadamer's primary focus has been the "happening" of understanding, especially in regard to art, history, tradition, and classic texts. Gadamer himself has often been accused of being Eurocentric in his understanding of tradition. But as I hope to show, Gadamer's hermeneutics can be extremely fertile and illuminating when applied to current issues concerning cross-cultural dialogue. As I proceed I will also point out some of the inadequacies and weaknesses of hermeneutics which have been highlighted (from radically different perspectives) by Habermas and Derrida.

Until now, I have been speaking about "culture" and "multiculturalism" without specifying what I mean by "culture." One is tempted to say today about the word "culture" what John Dewey once said about "experience": it is a weasel word. It seems to function as a cipher that takes on whatever meaning is assigned to it -- even conflicting and contradictory meanings. Without falling into the traps of a false essentialism or arbitrary stipulation, I want to underscore some of the prominent characteristics that have been foregrounded in recent controversies. Perhaps what is most striking, especially in the new burgeoning discipline of "cultural studies," is the way in which "culture" is now being used to designate what -- not so long ago -- was thought to be the opposite of culture, the "other" of culture. For "culture" was once used to single out high or elite culture -- what the Germans call *Bildung*. This is the idea of cultured person, the one who has been properly educated in the liberal arts -- whose taste and judgment has been refined through the rigorous process of an "elitist" education. The opposite of the cultured person was the philistine, the lover of kitsch. But today there is an almost joyful deliberate transgression (frequently most vehemently advocated by those who have benefited by an "elitist" education). All distinctions between high and low culture, the culture of the few and the culture of the masses, high modern art and kitsch, even art and entertainment are transgressed and obliterated. Studying the cultural significance of Madonna is deemed just as important (and by some it is considered more important) as studying Shakespeare -- who after all is just another dead white male. So we hear talk about the "culture of soap operas," the culture of the film noire," "the new rap or hip-hop culture," etc. And this new "democratic" extension of "culture" has definite political implications. For it is intended to transgress and disrupt accepted cultural and political hierarchical orderings. We have a new kind of politics -- "cultural politics."

There is another aspect of the new popularity of talking about radically incommensurable cultures which is also germane to my argument. Here we touch on one of those tacit presuppositions that is shared by many defenders and critics of multiculturalism. This is the tendency to think that a culture is somehow a complex integrated "whole" of beliefs, attitudes, and practices that cannot be properly understood or evaluated by someone who is "outside" the culture -- someone who does not actually participate in it. We are told that the plurality of cultures are incommensurable with each other. It is this alleged incommensurability that is given as the primary reason why a culture cannot and should not be judged by the standards and norms which are not intrinsic to the culture. Any cross-cultural evaluation is thought to be illegitimate -- an illegitimate imposition from the outside that violates the integrity of a distinctive culture. So, for example, a "connoisseur" of rap music -- one thoroughly immersed in this culture -- can discriminate between good and bad examples of rap. But to condemn rap as a vulgar or despicable form of "art" -- as not measuring up to the standards of Mozart or Keats -- is to pass off one's ethnocentric biases as if they were universal norms for making such judgments. This is the same "logic" that is a work when white Europeans condemn or patronize so-called "primitive" societies.

One of the great ironies of twentieth century philosophy is that the language of "incommensurability" and "incommensurable paradigms" which is so often used uncritically to characterize different cultures was originally introduced by Thomas Kuhn to deal with a very limited problem. In *The Structure of Scientific Revolutions,* Kuhn's main objective was to understand what are the distinctive characteristics of the *natural sciences*. This is what led him to speak about paradigms. And in bringing out the distinctive character of scientific revolutions it was important to understand the sense in which competing paradigms are incommensurable. Kuhn's book, for all its enormous popularity and widespread influence, never really had much influence on the actual practices of working natural scientists. But it did have a profound -- and not always a beneficial -- influence on humanists and social scientists. Kuhn's language has been appropriated and used (or rather *misused)* to reinforce what Wittgenstein calls a "picture" that has mesmerized us and holds us captive. This is the "picture" of a language game, a paradigm, a framework, or a culture that is self-contained and incommensurable. According to this *sense* of "incommensurability " there are no common inter-paradigmatic standards or norms. Consequently, to evaluate a given culture A by the standards appropriate to an incommensurable culture B is to do violence to culture A. There are even those (mistakenly thinking that they are drawing upon Kuhn) who maintain that we cannot even rationally compare two different incommensurable cultures because what is meant by "rationality" is itself dependent upon and relative to a given culture. This is what Karl Popper once called the "myth of the framework" -- that we are prisoners locked within our own languages, paradigms and cultures. And although I think Popper is mistaken when he claims that Kuhn is guilty of perpetuating this myth, I do think Popper's criticism is applicable to many who facilely use the language of incommensurability.[1]

It is precisely here that Gadamer can be so helpful. He shows us a way of escaping from the "myth of the framework" without assuming that there is some universal ahistorical framework or language into which we can translate all competing and rival claims. He shows us how we can recognize genuine -- even incommensurable -- cultural differences, and yet how we can mutually understand each other. We can make legitimate cross-cultural judgments without violently imposing alien standards and norms. Gadamer argues that we are "always already" shaped by the traditions to which we belong -- traditions that are the sources of our cultural identity. Furthermore, he argues that it makes no sense to think that we can abstract ourselves from all finite traditions and cultural backgrounds. This is *ontologically* impossible because our being-in-the-world is itself constituted by the prejudgments and prejudices that are handed down to us. Although Gadamer seeks to overcome what he calls "the Enlightenment's prejudice against prejudice," he also emphasizes the ways in which we can enlarge our finite horizons and (mutually) come to understand what initially strikes us alien, strange, and foreign. There is no horizon that is ontologically closed. Gadamer shows us the intrinsic openness of all language and experience. Given the intrinsic ontological openness of all natural languages, there are always the linguistic and imaginative resources within any horizon that can enable us to extend our horizon and achieve a "fusion of horizons." Cultures do not stand to each other like self-enclosed windowless monads. Insofar as all cultures are linguistic, they are porous -- open to understanding. Gadamer is certainly aware of how difficult it can be to achieve a genuine fusion of horizons -- one that does justice to what is distinctive about the tradition or culture we are seeking to understand. For we have to learn to listen, to be responsive to the claims upon us made by the tradition or culture that we are seeking to understand. He knows how easy it is fail to make the effort to understand. But this failure to understand is a practical moral failure -- not an ontological impossibility. This is one of the primary reasons why Gadamer thinks of hermeneutics as belonging to the great tradition of practical philosophy which was initiated by Aristotle. Potentially we can always understand if we are willing to make the effort to understand and have developed the necessary talents and virtues required for hermeneutical understanding. If such understanding is to be achieved, then it requires the cultivation of a hermeneutical sensibility -- a willingness and ability to move beyond our limited finite horizons. We should not think that such a fusion of horizons means uncritically accepting the claims of a tradition or culture. Every hermeneutical encounter is critical. Understanding a tradition or a culture is like a conversation where "when we have discovered the other person's standpoint, his ideas become intelligible without our necessarily agreeing with him."[2] Gadamer eloquently characterizes what he means by openness when he describes what is involved in a hermeneutical understanding of an I-Thou relation.

In human relations the important thing is. . . to experience the Thou as a Thou -- i.e. not to overlook his claim but to let him really say something to us.

Here is where openness belongs. But ultimately this openness does not exist only for the person who speaks; rather anyone who listens is fundamentally open. Without such openness to one another there is no genuine human bond. Belonging together always also means being able to listen to one another. . . Openness to the other, then, involves recognizing that I myself must accept some things that are against me, even though no one else forces me to do so. (p. 361)

Consequently, coming to understand another culture is not like gazing at a curious object from the outside. Understanding requires that I open myself, listen and respond to what the culture really says to me. This itself presupposes a moral receptivity in which I believe that there is something that I can genuinely learn from my encounter with the "other" culture -- something which can enlarge my own limited horizon. Gadamer tells us that "to acquire a horizon means that one learns to look beyond what is close at hand -- not in order to look away from it but to see it better, within a larger whole" (p.305). This last point is crucial. It is not idle curiosity or intellectual voyeurism that motivates hermeneutical understanding. On the contrary, by reaching out and imaginatively seeking to understand what is "other" and different -- by responding to something that makes a claim upon me -- I come to a better understand of myself, my culture, and my finitude. It is only through the imaginative encounter with what is genuinely different that we can come to self-understanding.

Gadamer is acutely aware of the extremes to be avoided in achieving a fusion of horizons. One extreme is the hubris of thinking that our own culture is the standard for translating, judging and evaluating whatever we encounter. This is the hubris of a type of ethnocentrism that refuses to listen, that refuses to acknowledge that there is something to be learned from other cultures, that pretends to be open when it is really closed. The other extreme is to deceive ourselves into thinking that we can "go native" i.e., we can suspend *all* our own prejudgments and prejudices, and by some sort of empathetic leap we can completely identify ourselves with an alien tradition or culture. It must be reiterated that there is and can be no understanding without activating our prejudices.[3] These prejudices are what enable us to understand. There are those who think that if we can never "escape" from our own traditions, from our own inherited prejudgments, then this means that we can never really understand another tradition or culture as it is in itself. But the fallacy here is to think that understanding can only be achieved if there is complete and total identification. Gadamer is particularly insightful in exposing this fallacy -- in showing us that even when we attempt to understand our own history and traditions, we are always understanding from our perspective, from our changing historical horizon. Against those who think this is what *prevents* "true" understanding, Gadamer argues that it is precisely what *enables* understanding.

But there is a serous problem that must be squarely faced at this point. Gadamer has claimed that as finite human beings we are always shaped by the prejudgments and prejudices handed down to us and which constitute our being-in-the world. Furthermore it is clear that he wants to distinguish those prejudgments that are legitimate and enabling -- that make understanding possible -- from those prejudgments that turn out to be blind and limiting prejudices. It is precisely here that we come to the most central feature of Gadamer's hermeneutics -- the practice of authentic dialogue.

Drawing on the philosophic tradition that goes back to Socrates, Gadamer calls our attention to the to-and-fro play of dialogue. Dialogue exhibits the rhythm of play where play itself has ontological primacy over the players. So in a genuine dialogue, the dialogical partners are not merely "subjects" speaking to each other, but *participants* in the dialogue. The practice of dialogue is an art that must be cultivated. It requires learning to listen and to respond, and a willingness to understand the other's point of view in its strongest possible light. In is in the to-and-fro movement of a dialogue that we learn to sort out our blinding and enabling prejudices. For in seeking to understand, we must "project" hypotheses about what is being said. This is true not only when we are in the presence of another living human being, it is also true in seeking to understand a tradition or another culture. When we actively listen to what the other is saying, then we may first discover that we don't quite understand what is being said. We discover that our prejudgments don't quite fit the meaning of what is being said. We must revise our prejudgments, modify our hypotheses, and then listen again. In this to-and fro movement in which we (mutually) seek to understand each other, the dialogic partners cultivate the *art* of the hermeneutical circle. This is the way in which we learn to enlarge our horizons and achieve a fusion of horizon. This dialogical encounter is eminently fallible and never achieves "absolute" finality, but as we come to understand another culture and the ways it challenges us, then we become more aware of those prejudices which can distort and inhibit understanding.

Gadamer self-consciously appropriates the Platonic-Socratic tradition of dialogue, but he blends this with a distinctive interpretation of Hegelian dialectic. Against Hegel, Gadamer categorically rejects the very idea of "absolute knowledge." According to Hegel "the dialectic of experience [*Erfahrung*] must end in that overcoming of all experience in absolute knowledge" (p.355). But Gadamer tells us that "the truth of experience always implies an orientation toward new experience . . .the dialectic of experience has its proper fulfillment not in definite knowledge but in openness to experience" (p.355). Hermeneutics, and the type of dialogical encounter it encourages, is not only non-dogmatic: it is essentially anti-dogmatic.

It may be objected that this conception of hermeneutics is itself Eurocentric. Gadamer himself is deeply immersed in the "Western tradition"; whenever he refers to tradition, his examples are typically drawn from Western culture. I don't want to deny (and I don't think that Gadamer himself would deny) that he draws his illustrations from the traditions that he knows best. Furthermore we must always be careful about the danger of reifying tradition -- making it into something that is more permanent and unchangeable than it really is. In this time when there is so much controversy about canons and what constitutes a canon, we ought to recognize the historical fact that in any living tradition canons are always in the process of being remade and reformulated. A living tradition can almost be defined as an ongoing contest about what constitutes its canonical texts and how they are to be interpreted. But we must also beware of the opposite danger which is all too prevalent today -- what Eric Hobsbawn has called the "invention of tradition" where this is done for various ideological purposes. Even when all this is acknowledged, I fail to see any reason why Gadamer's understanding of dialogical hermeneutics is or should be restricted to any one tradition. On the contrary, its distinctive power is that it enables us to see how we can genuinely enlarge our horizons and achieve a fusion with radically different traditions and cultures. But it might again be objected that the very emphasis on openness and dialogue itself reflects typical Western biases which fail to understand that there are other traditions and cultures that don't share these biases. In response it should be noted that a belief in "absoluticity" is not unique to any culture. It is ethnocentric to think that Western cultures are somehow more open and tolerant than other cultures. Openness (as well as closure) can take many different forms. There is nothing about hermeneutics that necessitates the uncritical acceptance of all beliefs and practices -- especially those which are grossly intolerant. Hermeneutics is not a type of relativism that refuses to make any sort of judgment about an alien tradition or culture. This is just the sort of historicism and nihilistic relativism that Gadamer strongly opposes. Hermeneutics doesn't bracket all cross-cultural judgments: it shows us how we can (mutually) make *reasonable* judgments without making claims to absolute finality.

I have been trying to show how hermeneutics -- as developed by Gadamer -- can enable us undercut some of the stale polemic that characterizes recent debates about multiculturalism, and how fertile it is when applied to questions concerning cross-cultural dialogue. But I have also indicated that it has its weaknesses and needs to be supplemented . This is not the occasion for a full scale exploration of the points of agreement and disagreement among Gadamer, Habermas, and Derrida. But I can give a brief indication of some of the ways in which Habermas and Derrida are relevant.[4]

Gadamer enables us to understand what is involved in the mutual understanding and interpretation of cultures. He also argues that hermeneutics is the heir to the tradition of practical philosophy that "originated" with Aristotle. Although I am extremely sympathetic with Gadamer's "retrieval" of the concept of *phronesis*, I do not think that he has an adequate conceptual understanding of what stands in the way, blocks, and distorts authentic cultural understanding in the contemporary world. Gadamer is not primarily a social and political thinker. We will not find in his hermeneutics a developed notion of how power, force, and violence actually work in contemporary societies. Gadamer sometimes writes as if it is always possible to engage in undistorted dialogue. But here I think Habermas has been much more realistic and penetrating about "systematically distorted communication," and "the colonization of the life-world by systems rationality." It is Habermas who stresses the social and political conditions that are required if we are to engage in the type of hermeneutical understanding of different cultures. Furthermore, I sometimes think that in his battle against "the Enlightenment prejudice against prejudice," Gadamer -- at times -- slips into his own prejudice against the Enlightenment. For the Enlightenment cannot be identified with a naive belief in abstract universality and reason. At times, Gadamer fails to acknowledge that the Enlightenment legacy itself constitutes a living tradition. Furthermore, this legacy contains a truth that ought to be acknowledged and appropriated -- the demand for universal emancipation and freedom. There is also good reason to be skeptical about the abuse of appeals to traditional authority. Although there is a place for legitimate authority and the role of tradition in our lives, we must never fall into the nostalgic trap of thinking that all traditions are desirable. There are sexist, racist, and other oppressive traditions. Gadamer, of course, knows this. But I do not always thinks that he squarely confronts a question that is uppermost for Habermas: What norms, indeed what *universal* norms, are appropriate for critically evaluating competing traditions, and completing cultural claims? It is all very well to point out -- as Gadamer does -- that every genuine encounter with a tradition or with another culture is *critical*, but we can legitimately ask for a clarification (and justification) of the standards and principles of critique.

From a very different perspective, Derrida also points out some of the weaknesses of Gadamerian hermeneutics. Just as Habermas focuses on issues of societal conflict, violence and power which are not always in the foreground of Gadamer's hermeneutics, Derrida makes us painfully aware of how rare and difficult it can be to achieve the type of understanding that Gadamer envisions. Sometimes Gadamer makes the "fusion of horizons" seem a bit too easy and smooth. Furthermore Gadamer doesn't sufficiently focus and on the inner tensions, double-binds, and double readings that we discover when we seek to understand and interpret any cultural tradition. Derrida, as I read him, is *not* saying (or implying) that understanding is never possible -- or that all understanding is misunderstanding. Rather his distinctive "genius" is to show us how much can go wrong in our attempts to understand; how fragile any such understanding really is; how much indeterminacy there really is when we think we understand each other or another culture. Derrida is a master at showing how, even with "good will," we unreflectively impose hierarchical biases -- what Gadamer calls "blind prejudices" -- on what we are seeking to understand with "openness." He warns us about how much violence there can be in our invitation to engage in open dialogue.

I want to conclude by returning to the question of *praxis*. Even those who think that the project of modernity is still an unfinished project must admit that one of the gravest defects of the original Enlightenment thinkers was their lack of a deep understanding about the devastating significance and role of nationalism and chauvinism in the modern world. Over and over again, we have experienced the weakness of universal normative claims when confronted with the varieties of "tribal nationalism." Mutual understanding, openness and respect are not common realities; they are rare and fragile. One of the most painful realizations of a post-Communist world is how -- despite all the high rhetoric about democracy and freedom -- old (and new) rivalries have broken out with an explosive violence. We are experiencing just how difficult it is for any society or nation --- East or West -- to accommodate itself to the new forms of multiculturalism that are becoming increasing prevalent. Hannah Arendt was prophetic when she suggested that our century might become best known as the century of the stateless, the refugees, and the homeless. It begins to look as if the most serious social and political problems of the next century will continue to focus on the ways in which different cultures can not only learn to live with each other (without violence and killing), but can live together in ways in which they can genuinely learn from each other. We have learned -- or should have learned -- from history that there is no grand "solution" to these intractable problems -- that one never quite knows when there will be new eruptions of violent conflict. But without exaggerating or denigrating our role, "we educators" have a modest but important role in fostering the idea and, even more important, the *practice* of ongoing, open, engaged, imaginative, pluralistic dialogue; the type of dialogue that respects differences and seeks commonalities.

---

1   For a detailed discussion of the meanings of incommensurability as well as the use and abuse of Kuhn , see Richard J. Bernstein, *Beyond Objectivism and Relativism* (Philadelphia: University of Pennsylvania Press, 1983); and "Incommensurability and Otherness Revisted" in *The New Constellation* (Cambridge: M.I.T. Press, 1992) .

2   Hans-Georg Gadamer, *Truth and Method*, Second Revised Edition, trans. revised by J. Weinsheimer and D. G. Marshall (New York: Crossroad, 1989), p.305 (All page numbers in this text refer to *Truth and Method.*)

3   I have translated the German word "*Vorurteil*" as "prejudgment" and "prejudice". Gadamer himself uses the provocative English word "prejudice" to convey his meaning. He tells us: "If we want to do justice to man's finite, historical mode of being, it is necessary to fundamentally rehabilitate the concept of prejudice and acknowledge the fact that there are legitimate prejudices" (p.277).

4   For a fuller discussion of the fertile tensions among Gadamer, Habermas and Derrida, see *Beyond Objectivism and Relativism* and *The New Constellation*.

Don Howard

The History That We Are: Philosophy as Discipline and the Multiculturalism Debate

1. *Introduction*

A few months ago I received a flyer from Lakehead University in Ontario announcing the establishment of a new program in "Native American Philosophy." My initial, unreflected reaction was, I am embarrassed to say, much like what I surmise was the reaction of many of my philosophical colleagues upon first hearing such expressions as "African philosophy," namely, to think it virtually a *contradictio in adjecto*, an oxymoron. Religion, yes; mythopoeisis, perhaps—but not philosophy. African and Native American thought may have something in common with Greek and Egyptian mythology, with the creation stories like those found in the Babylonian creation epic, the *Enūma Elishu*, or the Book of Genesis. But as we were all taught in our own introductory courses, and as we all now teach our beginning students, philosophy is different in kind from poetry and myth. Born in the Greek settlements of Ionia in the sixth century B.C., philosophy seeks to understand nature, both human and nonhuman, not in terms of the actions of the gods and the giants, but in terms of abstract metaphysical principles like Anaximander's τὸ ἀπειρον or the atom and the void of Leucippus and abstract moral principles, like justice and the form of the good. Moreover, philosophy is unlike religion in the antidogmatic, critical posture that Socrates taught us to adopt with respect to all received opinion. And, perhaps most importantly, the philosopher's characteristic concern with the critical distinction between true knowledge and mere opinion is not to be found in "traditional" or "primitive" systems of thought. Neither poet, nor sophist, nor carping moralist, the philosopher is a lover of wisdom. There may have been a Hesiod among the Tlingit or a Homer among the Hausa, but there has been no African Aristotle and no Plato of the Pueblo, just as there has also been no African Shakespeare, as Saul Bellow tiresomely insists.[1]

"African *philosophy*."— Not all such appositions strike us as being quite so oxymoronic. For while I speak here—need it be said?—the language of prejudice and stereotype, it is not simply a white, Western prejudice, which would be too easy a target. We do not stumble at the thought of there being an "Indian philosophy" (in the sense of the Indian subcontinent); nor does the expression "Jewish philosophy" give us much pause. The more generous souls among us will permit, as well, the expression, "Chinese philosophy," though the more anthropological term "Chinese thought" is clearly preferable; and in some quarters one may even be allowed to speak of "Arabic philosophy," especially if one agrees to confine one's attention to long and safely dead thinkers like Ibn-Sina and Ibn-Rushd.[2]

Why is this so? Why do the authors of the Vedanta, domesticated by Schopenhauer and Deussen, already have a reservation at the philosophers' *Stammtisch*? Why do we so easily imagine ourselves in the heaven for which Socrates yearns in the *Phaedo*, conversing with Maimonides about ακρασια, as easily as we might converse with Descartes about the soul or with Kant about the categories, whereas it has long been much harder to imagine a properly *philosophical* conversation with Chuang-tzu about *Tao* (even before the *Tao-te-ching* became the New Age bible), much less a conversation with a Navajo *hataali* about *hozro* and "walking in beauty"?

That this is so should give us pause when we pretend, as philosophers, to engage in cross-cultural conversations. For the measure of our aversion to expressions like "Native American philosophy" is the measure of our inability, *as philosophers*, to engage in such conversations, the point being that the felt sense of aversion reflects our having defined ourselves, *as philosophers*, in such a way as to beg many of the most important questions that should be at issue in those conversations, leaving us, as philosophers, no stance but that of condescension toward those cultures that have failed to evolve a properly philosophical culture.

From another point of view, what is going on here is that cultural boundaries have been inscribed as disciplinary boundaries. Looking out from within a department of philosophy, it is impossible for me, as a philosopher, to talk with the Ibo about their creation stories. That is a job for the anthropologist or the student of comparative religion. We can have a properly philosophical conversation only if we first persuade ourselves, as we succeed in doing in the case of the Vedanta in India, that the culture in question incorporates a genuinely philosophical tradition. But we may well be suspicious—surely it is a clue to what may really be going on—when we find a leading authority like Louis Renou writing in the *Encyclopædia Britannica:* "The Vedic religion was brought to India by the Aryan invaders when they invaded the upper Indus basin sometime around 1500 B.C."

2. *Constructing the Discipline of Philosophy*

The hypothesis that I want to put forward here is that the conception of the "philosophical" underlying this state of affairs does not correspond to a timeless Platonic form, but that it is instead a *construction* undertaken in a specific cultural context, at a specific historical moment, for some very specific reasons, not all of which have to do with the love of wisdom. The time is the end of the eighteenth and the beginning of the nineteenth century. The place is northern Europe, chiefly, though not exclusively, Prussia and Hanover. The reasons have to do, among other things, with the development of industrial capitalism, the onset of a period of European colonial expansion, and the rise of the secular state and the consequent need to train bureaucrats for careers in civil administration.

The construction was carried out in two main ways: First, there was a new way of telling the history of philosophy, one that valorized what was now, for the first time, claimed to be a distinctively Greek and Aryan philosophical impulse and emphasized, as rarely before, a distinction between religion and secular philosophy. Second, a new form of organization was imposed on university faculty and curricula. Departments of philosophy were for the first time clearly distinguished from other faculties, most importantly the faculties of theology or religion and psychology, while the thought and literature of other cultures—aside from those of ancient Greece and Rome, now assigned to the central new field of classics—was made the object of mere anthropological and philological investigation.

Let's begin with the new way of telling the history of philosophy. A few ancient and Renaissance precedents notwithstanding, the very idea of writing history from a synoptic point of view is an invention of the eighteenth century. We had earlier had lives of the saints, narratives of the conquests of princes and kings, and half-fanciful history in the guise of epic poetry. But the eighteenth century was the century in which the modern attitude toward history was invented. It was the century of the first great philosophies of history, those of Bossuet, Condorcet, Rousseau, Voltaire, Diderot, d'Alembert, Turgot, Montesquieu, Burke, Mendelssohn, Lessing,

Herder, and Kant (see Beck 1963, pp. xii-xv). It was the century that first gave us history as a story with a beginning and an end, history governed by a theme, a principle, or telos, history with a meaning or purpose, moral or otherwise. It also first gave us history as science, in the portentious modern sense of the term, that is, history pretending to tell an objectively true story, bound by the claims of evidence. Of course the pretense to objectivity made these histories all that more effective in advancing the larger cultural projects in whose service they were written. It was precisely because they could pose as disinterested historical truth that Hume's *History of England* (1754-1762) was so successful in helping to construct the modern conception of Great Britain as a nation and Gibbon's *Decline and Fall* could serve as moral map and compass for the architects of the British empire.

The writing of such histories had to await the coming of the Reformation and even more so the secularizing tendencies of the Enlightenment, for they presume that peoples and nations can have careers of their own, not dictated, at least not in every detail, by divine plan. One might still interpret a nation's triumph over its adversaries as a sign of God's blessing—one thinks of England marching to empire to the strains of "Onward Christian Soldiers"—but the human actors are now seen as agents in their own right, whose hopes, motivations, and behaviors are thought worthy of record.

Histories of philosophy followed a similar course. In the Renaissance and the early modern period, the first histories of philosophy continued the ancient doxographical style of Theophrastus and Diogenes Laertius, starting with Walter Burleigh's 1470 re-edition of Diogenes, *De Vita ac Moribus Philosophorum*, up through Thomas Stanley's 1655 *History of Philosophy*. Those few histories that attempted a more synthetic understanding did so, however, from a Christian perspective, as in the case of Georg Horn's 1655 *Historiæ Philosophicæ de Origine, Successionis, Sectis et Vita Philosophorum ab Orbe Conditio ad Nostram Ætatem Agitur*, which takes the aim of the history of philosophy to be the rediscovery, through Christian revelation and clues contained in the Old Testament, of a true, unitary, pre-lapsarian philosophy, the philosophy that was known to Adam before the fall led to the emergence of multiple philosophical sects.

In the early seventeenth century, Francis Bacon called for a different kind of history that would do more than just list the names and opinions of the philosophers (Bacon 1623), but this call was not to be answered for over a century, not until the publication of Jakob Brucker's five-volume *Historia Critica, a Mundi Incunabulis ad Nostram usque Ætatum Deducta* (1742-1767), which served as a standard for many decades, both in its original

Latin version and in William Enfield's free English adaptation, *The History of Philosophy* (1791).

For all its influence, however, Brucker's history is still not what we would today expect from a critical history of philosophy, for the critical perspective it adopts remains a Christian one, the various thinkers and schools being praised or castigated depending upon the degree to which their views either advanced or hindered the cause of Christianity. What distinguishes the new histories of the late-eighteenth and early-nineteenth centuries is, in part, precisely their rejection of a religious standard in favor a purely secular, philosophical one, and their assumption that philosophical problems and projects have careers of their own, independent of any divine plan.

This secularization of the history of philosophy is for a purpose. For one thing, it makes possible the characteristically Enlightenment distinction between religion and philosophy that is appealed to starting at the end of the eighteenth century in order to denigrate as "merely religious" those contributions that non-Greeks may have made to the intellectual traditions out of which modern philosophy is said to have developed. Simultaneously, the secularization of philosophy makes possible claims on behalf of philosophy to an independent place in the new kind of university then being created in places like Göttingen and Berlin for the purpose of training young men for careers in civil administration in service to a state that is to become a center of power distinct from the church.

The two most important exemplars of this new Hellenized secular history of philosophy are Dietrich Tiedemann's *Geist der speculativen Philosophie* (1791-1797; 6 vols.) and Wilhelm Gottlieb Tennemann's *Geschichte der Philosophie* (1789-1819; 11 vols.). Tiedemann, especially, insists as no one before him on a distinction between religion and secular philosophy, but his history also exemplifies the new philosophical temperament in being the first history of philosophy to insist, in a thoroughly modern fashion, that philosophy proper is born among the Greeks in the sixth century B.C., that there is something new and different about the way thinkers like Thales, Anaximander, and Pythagoras approached the understanding of nature, something that distinguishes this Greek, philosophical way of thinking, with its celebration of the ideal of reason, from the mythopoeic thought and dogmatic religion of other cultures.[3]

Even before Tiedemann, Brucker had argued that there was something distinctively new in the thought of the pre-Socratics and Socrates himself, especially in the latter's turn to moral philosophy. But like many of his contemporaries, including Montesquieu, and like Isocrates and many other ancient Greeks themselves (Bernal 1987, p. 104), Brucker still recognized the existence of important elements of continuity between Greek philosophy and the thought of both its predecessors and other contemporary cultures, most importantly the religious culture of Egypt, this particularly in his attack on Plato (Bernal 1987, p. 197). Tiedemann is the first of the new historians in whose work the alleged novelty of the Greek way of philosophizing and its alleged discontinuity with the other intellectual traditions of its time and place are both elevated to the level of principle and made part of the very definition of what it is to be a philosopher.

In thus insisting on the unique and novel philosophical moment in Greek high culture, and denying its links to Egypt, Tiedemann is representative of the time in which he worked, a time when the modern European identity was being born. With the Ottoman Empire safely in retreat, with the prospect before it of a new period of colonial expansion in Africa and the Orient, Europe was for the first time becoming aware of itself as a geographical and cultural entity. The very concept of the "West" as we know it today was being created. As a part of this process, European intellectuals were revising their understanding of the roots of their own culture. This was the period when a pan-European Aryan racial identity was being forged. It was the period when an Indo-European family of languages was first invented. And it was the period when a secular European high culture was being constructed around a newly Aryanized ancient Greek cultural heritage. It was a period of Hellenomania. Historians of philosophy, like Tiedemann, were the Winckelmanns of the mind, employing the new scientific tools of philology and source criticism to unearth the "real" Plato, as opposed to the figure of myth and legend who was earlier believed to have learned the basic tenets of his philosophy from the priests of Egypt.

The Tiedemann model, emphasizing the distinctively Greek beginnings of philosophy, quickly entrenched itself as the paradigm for succeeding generations of histories of philosophy. Here, for example, is how George Henry Lewes introduces his 1845 *Biographical History of Philosophy:*

Having to trace the history of the mind in one region of its activity, it is incumbent on us to mark out the countries and epochs which we deem it requisite to notice. Are we to follow Brucker, and include the Antediluvian period? Are we to trace the speculations of the Scythians, Persians, and Egyptians? Are we to lose ourselves in that vast wilderness the East? It is obvious that we must draw the line somewhere: we cannot write the history of every nation's thoughts. We confine ourselves, therefore, to Greece and modern

Europe. We omit Rome. The Romans, confessedly, had no philosophy of their own; and did but feebly imitate that of the Greeks. Their influence on modern Europe has therefore been only indirect; their labors count as nothing in the history of Philosophy. We also omit the East. It is very questionable whether the East had any Philosophy distinct from its Religion; and still more questionable whether Greece was materially influenced by it. True it is, that the Greeks themselves supposed their early teachers to have imbibed wisdom at the Eastern fount. True it is, that modern oriental scholars, on first becoming acquainted with some of the strange doctrines of the Eastern sages, have recognised in them strong resemblances to the doctrines of the Greeks. But neither of these reasons are valid. The former is attributable to a very natural prejudice, which will be explained hereafter. The latter is attributable to the coincidences frequent in all speculation, and inevitable in so vague and vast a subject as Philosophy. Coincidences prove nothing but the similarity of all spontaneous tendencies of thought. Something more is needed to prove direct filiation. (Lewes 1845, pp. 12-13)

The "prejudice" inclining the Greeks to assume Egyptian origins for philosophy is explained in Lewes's discussion of the legend of Pythagoras' having studied with the priests of Egypt and having borrowed from them the very concept of philosophy, Pythagoras being credited with having introduced the term itself. According to Lewes, this prejudice is simply a result of the universal human inclination to regard "no man as a prophet in his own land," meaning, Lewes says, that the Greeks, like all of us, could not accept the possibility of home-grown genius and so invented foreign sources for Pythagoras' learning (see Lewes 1845, p. 50). After sufficient repetition, in ever more histories such as this, the idea that philosophy is a peculiarly Greek invention becomes axiomatic.

Tiedemann was trained at the University of Göttingen, which brings us to the question of the place and the institutional setting in which the new histories of philosophy were written. Established in 1734 by George II, King of England and Elector of Hanover, Göttingen was the first of the new German universities, more than any other the place where the new model of "professional" academic life was pioneered.

As befits a university distinguished by its modern focus on the sciences, the first philosophers at Göttingen tended to reject Christian Wolff's rationalistic conception of philosophy as the "science of the possible" and to follow, instead, Christian Thomasius' way of breaking with Scholasticism, both in emphasizing a critical, practical conception of philosophy as a species of wisdom concerned with the happiness or welfare of all humankind, and in asserting a purely secular role for philosophy. Thus, Samuel Christian Hollmann, the first occupant of the chair of philosophy at Göttingen, lectured until 1784 not only on logic, metaphysics, and moral philosophy, but also on the natural sciences, his *Einführung in die Naturwissenschaft auf der Grundlage der Erfahrung* (1742) going through four reprintings by 1765. The definition of philosophy that he gave in his 1727 "Institutiones Philosophicæ" was very much in the tradition of Thomasius by virtue of its emphasizing an instrumental role for philosophy (see Schneiders 1985, pp. 63-65, 85-86; Kleinert 1985, p. 241).

Johann Georg Heinrich Feder, who joined Hollmann in Göttingen in 1768, was more a follower of Wolff. Still, he too stressed the instrumental role of philosophy, defining it in his *Grundriß der Philosophie* as the "science of general and useful truths of reason," and adding in his 1769 *Logik und Metaphysik* that philosophy concerns itself with the most important pieces of knowledge "that can be discovered by the mere employment of reason for the knowledge of nature and the general laws by means of which it acts" (as quoted in Schneiders 1985, pp. 86-87).

Along with this practical conception of philosophy, Hellenophilia was much in evidence in Göttingen. One of the founders of the university was the philosopher Christoph August Heumann. He wrote as early as 1715 in the newly established scholarly journal, *Acta Philosophorum*, that, Isocrates notwithstanding, the Egyptians were not "philosophical," that philosophy arose in Greece "because it could not flourish in climates that were too hot or too cold; only the inhabitants of temperate countries like Greece, Italy, France, England and Germany could create true philosophy" (quoting from the paraphrase in Bernal 1987, p. 216).

Philosophy was, however, only one of many disciplines being professionalized in Göttingen by the end of the eighteenth century, where one finds a disturbing association between professionalization and racial and cultural concerns. For example, the Göttingen natural historian, Johann Friedrich Blumenbach, was pioneering the "scientific" study of races with his 1775 *De Generis Humani Varietate Nativa*, the 1795 third edition of which first introduced the term "Caucasian" in its modern racial sense. Historical linguistics was being pioneered in Göttingen by August Ludwig Schlözer, who anticipated the later concept of an Indo-European family of languages with his attempt to construct a "Japhetic" family of language, Japhet, the third son of Noah, being regarded as the ancestor of the Europeans (Bernal 1987, p. 220).

History at Göttingen was being turned into a "science" in the hands of the philosopher, Christoph Meiners, who, in the 1780s, developed both a scientific theory of *Zeitgeist* as a category for historical understanding, this presumably independently of Vico, and the concept of "source criticism," whereby one discriminates among historical sources according to the degree to which they evince the "spirit of the age" in which they were written (Bernal 1987, p. 217). The technique of source criticism was picked up, in turn, by Christian Gottlob Heyne, one of most influential Göttingen intellectuals of the late-eighteenth century and one of the founders of classical philology or *Altertumswissenschaft*. True to his Romantic Hellenism, Heyne employed source criticism to attack those ancient authors who asserted the Egyptian roots of Greek high culture (Bernal 1987, p. 220), in this way prefiguring the employment of the same "scientific" technique for impeaching the authority of ancient authors by Tiedemann, Tennemann, and subsequent generations of Hellenophile historians of philosophy (see also Muhlack 1985).

Even more important than Göttingen in advancing the new model of the secular, scientific university in the service of the state was the University of Berlin, which was founded in 1809. When we think of philosophy at Berlin, we think, of course, of Hegel, who succeeded Fichte in the chair of philosophy in 1818. Hegel was, if anything, even more strident than were his immediate predecessors in insisting upon the original character of the Greek philosophical temperament and in denying to the soon-to-be-colonized peoples of the Middle East and Africa not only any claim that their ancestors may have influenced the development of what is now defined as philosophy, but even any capacity to do philosophy. Indeed, in Hegel we witness a turn from the earlier Romantic Hellenism to something more akin to outright racism. Consider, for example, the following particularly troublesome passages from the introduction to Hegel's *Vorlesungen über Philosophie der Weltgeschichte*, which were delivered in Berlin five times from 1822 to 1831:

Generally speaking, Africa is a continent enclosed within itself, and this enclosedness has remained it chief characteristic. It consists of three parts, which are essentially distinct from one another. . . . The first of these is Africa proper, the land to the south of the Sahara desert. . . . The second is the land to the north of the desert, a coastal region which might be described as European Africa. And the third is the region of the Nile, the only valley land of Africa, which is closely connected with Asia.

North Africa lies on the Mediterranean Sea and extends westwards along the Atlantic. . . . It could be said taht this whole region does not really belong to

Africa but forms a single unit with Spain, for both are part of the same basin. . . . This portion of Africa, like the Near East, is orientated toward Europe; it should and must be brought into the European sphere of influence, as the French have successfully attempted in recent times.

Egypt . . . is one of those regions which we have described as constituting a focus, as destined to become the centre of a great and independent culture.

Africa proper is the characteristic part of the whole continent as such. . . . It has no historical interest of its own, for we find its inhabitants living in barbarism and savagery in a land which has not furnished them with any integral ingredient of culture. From the earliest historical times, Africa has remained cut off from all contacts with the rest of the world; it is the land of gold, for ever pressing in upon itself, and the land of childhood, removed from the light of self-conscious history and wrapped in the dark mantle of night. (Hegel 1975, pp. 173-174)

In this main portion of Africa, history is in fact out of the question. Life there consists of a succession of contingent happenings and surprises. No aim or state exists whose development could be followed; and there is no subjectivity, but merely a series of subjects who destroy one another. . . . We shall now attempt to define the universal spirit and form of the African character. . . . This character, however, is difficult to comprehend, because it is so totally different from our own culture, and so remote and alien in relation to our own mode of consciousness. . . . The characteristic feature of the negroes is that their consciousness has not yet reached an awareness of any substantial objectivity—for example, of God or the law—in which the will of man could participate and in which he could become aware of his own being. The African, in his undifferentiated and concentrated unity, has not yet succeeded in making this distinction between himself as an individual and his essential universality, so that he knows nothing of an absolute being which is other and higher than himself. . . . All our observations of African man show him as living in a state of savagery and barbarism, and he remains in this state to the present day. The negro is an example of animal man in all his savagery and lawlessness, and if we wish to understand him at all, we must put aside all our European attitudes. We must not think of a spiritual God or of moral laws; to comprehend him correctly, we must abstract from all reverence and morality, and from everything which we call feeling. All this is foreign to man in his immediate existence, and nothing consonant with humanity is to be found in his character. For this very reason, we cannot properly feel ourselves into his nature, no more than into that of a dog, or of a Greek as he kneels before the statue of Zeus. Only by means of thought can we achieve this understanding of his nature; for we can only feel that which is akin to our own feelings. (1975, pp. 176-177)

We shall therefore leave Africa at this point, and it need not be mentioned again. For it is an unhistorical continent, with no movement or development of its own. And such events as have occured in it—i.e. in its northern region—blong to the Asiatic and European worlds. Carthage, while it lasted, represented an important phase; but as a Phoenician colony, it belongs to Asia. Egypt will be considered as a stage in the movement of the human spirit from east to west, but it has not part in the spirit of Africa. What we understand as Africa proper is that unhistorical and undeveloped land which is still enmeshed in the natural spirit, and which has to be mentioned here before we cross the threshold of world history itself. (1975, p. 190)[4]

Africa proper is incapable not only of philosophy but even of having a history, in Hegel's special sense of the term. That part of Africa that at least had a history—Egypt and North Africa—did so only in its role as a cultural appendage of other parts of the world, principally Europe. World history, for Hegel, belongs to "the realm of the spirit" (1975, p. 44), which is "self-sufficient being" (1975, p. 48), or, in another guise, self-consciousness and freedom. World history therefore comprises only the world-historical peoples, starting with the Greeks, among whom there first arose the consciousness of freedom, and culminating in "the Germanic nations," who "were the first to realise that man is by nature free, and that freedom of the spirit is his very essence" (1975, p. 54). It was because the Germans were the first to realize this that Hegel would assert: "The German Spirit is the Spirit of the new World. Its aim is the realization of absolute Truth as the unlimited self-determination of Freedom—*that* Freedom which has its own absolute form itself as its purport" (Hegel 1900, p. 341).

When set in the context of an evolving self-understanding of philosophy as something uniquely European in origin, passages such as this cannot be dismissed as peripheral to Hegel's project or as merely reflecting the polite racism of the age. Hegel's insisting, thus, on non-European peoples' *incapacity* for philosophy must be seen instead as an essential moment in the construction of the concept of philosophy then underway. Just how successful this construction was is evident from the unblanching way in which, at the end of the century, Wilhelm Windelband could write in his influential *Geschichte der Philosophie* (1892), a history written very much in the spirit of Hegel: "*The History of Philosophy is the process in which European humanity has embodied in scientific conceptions its views of the world and its judgments of life"* (Windelband 1892, p. 9). Why is this only a European cultural project? Windelband explains in words that echo Hegel's emphasis on the "freedom" characteristic of the European mind:

If by science we understand that independent and self-conscious work of intelligence which seeks knowledge methodically for its own sake, then it is among the Greeks, and the Greeks of the sixth century B.C., that we first find such a science,—aside from some tendencies among the peoples of the Orient, those of China and India particularly, only recently disclosed. The great civilised peoples of earlier antiquity were not, indeed, wanting either in an abundance of information on single subjects, or in general views of the universe; but as the former was gained in connection with practical needs, and the latter grew out of mythical fancy, so they remained under the control, partly of daily need, partly of religious poetry; and, as was natural in consequence of the peculiar restraint of the Oriental mind, they lacked, for their fruitful and independent development, the initiative activity of individuals. (Windelband 1892, pp. 23-24)

Another moment in this construction of the concept of philosophy is revealed in the connection that Hegel and many of his contemporaries saw between training in philosophy and the training of future bureaucrats for careers in civil administration in the emerging Prussian state (see Derrida 1986), which connection provides additional reasons for stressing the secular character of philosophy and for giving philosophy a place in the organization of the university and even the gymnasium distinct from that occupied by those charged with responsibility for religious instruction. If the state is to become a center of power in its own right, independent of the church, it needs a class of civil servants equipped with the intellectual tools necessary to legitimate and rationalize the state's claim to an authority separate from that of the church.

This idea finds its purest philosophical reflection in the celebration of human reason as the chief instrument for combating dogmatism—a recurrent theme in the Enlightenment—and in the valorization of the study of philosophy itself as the best training and discipline of our rational capacities. But what starts out as the celebration of reason in its emancipatory role, soon evolves into a celebration of philosophically-trained reason in the service of the secular state, each university-trained member of the civil administration being, therefore, a kind of miniature copy of Plato's philosopher-king. So it is not surprising to find Kant, in his *Streit der*

Facultäten (1798), defending the freedom and prerogatives of the "lower" philosophical faculty as against the claims of the "higher" theological faculty, and to find Fichte, the first rector of the University of Berlin and Hegel's predecessor in the chair of philosophy, arguing shortly thereafter that philosophy, as the queen of all the sciences, should be given a leading role in the university (see Hamlyn 1992, p. 89).

While most of the examples so far adduced involve German thinkers and institutions, it should not be inferred that the developments being sketched are confined to Germany. Local differences from one country to another may have affected the pace and character of the secularization, Hellenization, and professionalization of philosophy, as in England where philosophy was slow to win for itself a secure place in university faculties (see Hamlyn 1992, pp. 92-93), but similar tendencies are certainly to be found in Scotland, where philosophy enjoyed a secure place in the curriculum from early in the eighteenth century (see Hamlyn 1992, pp. 83-87) and where by the late eighteenth century Hellenophilia was at least as well advanced as in Germany (see Bernal 1987, pp. 206-210). Such tendencies are also to be found after the revolution in France, where an indigenous Hellenophilia was reinforced by the Scots influence, as this was mediated by Victor Cousin—student of Reid, friend of Humboldt, and translator of Tennemann (Tennemann 1829)—whose efforts at curricular reform helped give the new conception of philosophy an institutional home in French education as he championed the importation of the Prussian model (see Bernal 1987, p. 319).

Of course, not all non-European peoples were denied the capacity to philosophize, the most notable exception being the peoples of India. Thanks to the efforts of thinkers like Schopenhauer and, later, Paul Deussen, the Vedantic tradition especially was held to evince a genuinely philosophical impulse (see Schopenhauer 1844 and Deussen 1883). But this is the exception that proves the rule, for it was arguably only because of the discovery of a racial link between Europe and India that the capacity to philosophize could be accorded the Indian people. Even Hegel, no special friend of Indian philosophy, was impressed by this connection: "It is a great discovery in history—as of a new world—which has been made within rather more than the last twenty years, respecting the Sanscrit and the connection of the European languages with it. In particular, the connection of the German and Indian peoples has been demonstrated, with as much certainty as such subjects allow of" (Hegel 1900, p. 60).

The struggle to separate religion and philosophy proceeded unevenly for well over a century in German universities, continuing in some places, especially in Austria, well into the twentieth century (Gadol 1982, pp. 31-35). In some respects, the secularization, Hellenization, and professionalization of philosophy proceeded more rapidly in North America after the new German model of university organization was imported in the later nineteenth century. For in spite of the inherent religiosity of American culture, a strict separation between religion and philosophy was easy to enforce at least in publicly-funded universities, where the constitutionally-mandated separation of church and state had to be observed. And in both public and private universities, the drive for professionalization could be turned to advantage in legitimating the distinction between religion and philosophy. Finally, as in Cousin's France, the Hellenizing Scots influence on nineteenth-century American philosophy faculties should not be underestimated, this in spite of the possibly more famous pragmatist and idealist tendencies in evidence at institutions like Harvard. For in the American heartland, where the Scots-Presbyterian influence was strong during the late-eighteenth and early-nineteenth century first phase of trans-Appalachian settlement, Scots common sense philosophy set the intellectual tone, Sir William Hamilton's *Lectures on Metaphysics and Logic* (1865-1866) being required reading in many colleges and universities (see Hamlyn 1992, p. 86), including my own. Tellingly, my home-town of Lexington, where Transylvania University was established by the Presbyterians in 1783, fancied itself in the early nineteenth century the "Athens of the West."

One very revealing symptom of how deeply entrenched the separation of philosophy and religion had become by the middle of the nineteenth century is provided by the Catholic reaction to modernism and the Enlightenment. Theorists of the new church then emerging from the *Kulturkampf* and the battle over Papal infallibility, such as Joseph Kleutgen and Alfred Stöckl, sought to defend the church against assaults from the side of "modern" philosophy not by straightforwardly reasserting the claims of faith over reason, but instead by inventing a medieval "philosophy" subservient to the aims of the church and capable of opposing the anti-religious tendencies of the Enlightenment, a "philosophy" now asserted to have found its highest development in the work of Aquinas. In fact, Aquinas had insisted that philosophy had died with the Greeks, to be replaced by the purely spiritual concerns of a people striving for salvation. Only a "philosophy" could now oppose a philosophy, theology by itself no longer enjoying the cultural legitimation necessary to oppose the forces of secularization (see Inglis 1993).

The secularization, Hellenization, and professionalization of philosophy is rich with consequences for the way philosophers, *as philosophers*, must approach questions of cross-cultural communication. If we *define* philosophy, by the way we tell its history, as something that begins with the Greeks and reaches its apotheosis in Hegel, if we *define* philosophy as something of which non-European peoples (excepting perhaps those of India) are incapable, then, clearly, there are severe constraints on the degree to which, *as philosophers*, we can engage in cross-cultural conversations. At a very deep level, the boundaries of our discipline coincide with the boundaries of the European cultural world that many of us would like to think we are trying to transcend, so that from within a department of philosophy the only posture we can adopt with respect to most other cultures is one of condescension.

The secularization of philosophy was but one of two major changes in the self-understanding of philosophy and its consequent institutional definition in the nineteenth century. The other, somewhat later one was the final separation of philosophy from psychology. Even in Britain and North America, where at least the term, "natural philosophy," remained in use longer than on the continent, the separation of the natural sciences from philosophy was effected quite early, certainly by the end of the eighteenth century. And from their inception, the other social sciences, including anthropology, sociology, and political economy, were more or less clearly distinguished from philosophy and accorded a distinct institutional home. But psychology, the science of the mind, long enjoyed a more intimate connection with philosophy. It was only toward the end of the nineteenth century and the beginning of the twentieth that philosophy and psychology began to go their separate ways, the break being induced from the side of philosophy by the explicit anti-psychologism of a wide variety of thinkers from Russell to Husserl, and from the side of psychology by its self-conscious adoption of empirical methods (see Boring 1950, pp. 275-456). As late as 1900, it was still hard to tell into which category to put a thinker like William James, and we should remember that Baldwin's influential turn-of-the-century *Dictionary* was in fact entitled *Dictionary of Philosophy and Psychology* (Baldwin 1901-1905). Eventually, however, the two fields did separate, each settling into its own departmental and disciplinary home.

Though later in coming, the distinction between philosophy and psychology was only marginally less important for the issues under discussion here than that between philosophy and religion. For when psychology was at last driven out of the temple of philosophy, the last taint of the empirical was removed from a philosophy that could now further defend its disciplinary identity by proudly asserting its a priori foundational role in culture. That means, however, that when we, as philosophers, now approach the discussion of cross-cultural questions, we cannot, *as philosophers*, avail ourselves of the empirical tools of psychology, biology, comparative linguistics, or cultural anthropology. The past few years have witnessed a resurgence of interest in "naturalistic" approaches, at least in epistemology and the philosophy of mind, but naturalism remains still decidedly a minority position. So, *as philosophers*, the only questions we can address and pretend to answer are those that admit a priori answers. For us, questions of objectivity, communication, and morality are all questions of principle, unapproachable on the basis of contingent, empirical fact. This circumstance, too, will prove to be a severe constraint on the way in which we philosophers can participate in cross-cultural conversations.

3. *Reconstructing the Discipline of Philosophy*
In choosing to lay bare and emphasize the aspect of construction in our conception of the philosophical, especially in the way we tell the history of philosophy, I do not mean to imply that there is, for that reason alone, something wrong with this conception of the philosophical, that it should be jettisoned, that our departments of philosophy should be dissolved, their faculties set to more honest work. I am no flagellant postmodern ascetic who, having discovered the original sin of construction sets about, vainly, trying to purge himself and his community of all taint of evil. We are all, unavoidably, sinners, and construction is the sin we live by.

Indeed, one measure of the strength of a culture is its ability to construct convincing stories about itself and its origins. We know not who we are without a story about whence we came. "We are the children of '76." "We are the people who came over the mountains." "We are the descendants of those who emerged from the earth." "We are the world, we are the children." Even if the "we" is one cobbled together for some present end, as opposed to one given by biology or a profession of faith, we need a narrative whereby to draw the boundary between "us" and "them," not for the purpose of exclusion, at least not for that purpose alone, but more importantly simply for understanding who we are as individuals and as members of a community.

Given this need, the story that we commonly tell about Thales, Pythagoras, Socrates, and Plato may not be so much worse than others we could have told. After all, the Englightenment ideal of universalism was seized upon by at least one long-suffering people, the Jews, to rationalize their claim to an equal place in a larger European cultural project (see Rotenstreich 1984). In any case, the task we face is therefore not simply that of subverting or deconstructing the old story, but rather that of choosing which story we wish to tell, assuming, of course, that we first determine that something like philosophy should continue to exist in the academy and the culture at large.

I also do not mean necessarily to impute to all of those responsible for constructing our modern conception of philosophy a conscious intent to serve the needs of the nascent Prussian state, industrial capitalism, or colonial expansion. Some may have understood better than others whose interests were being served—Hegel, I think, had a fairly clear grasp of what he was about —but ordinarily a long historical view is necessary to appreciate the purposes served by such constructions, and to separate out the rhetorical moment from whatever bit of "truth" might lay at the core. How many of us today, for example, really understand what cultural project is served by the prejudices that lead us, instinctively, to condescend to those more "backward" universities where religion and philosophy still coexist in one department and to rail against bookstores that insist on shelving books on philosophy and religion in the same section. One of the ways that the cunning of history most clearly expresses itself is in its capacity to enlist for even the most damnable ends otherwise well-meaning people who are sincerely convinced that they do what they do for only the most high-minded, noble reasons.

That should induce a wee bit of modesty is those of us who might set about today to demolish or reconstruct our conception of philosophy for the purpose of facilitating cross-cultural conversations. For however noble our intentions, however pious our sentiments, who know not always who or what we really serve.

Contemporary, faddish, liberal multiculturalism is a case in point. The farther to the postmodern academic left we stand, the more we like to think of ourselves as being engaged in a campaign to subvert the structures of power and the hierarchies of dominance—male/female, north/south, east/west, rich/poor, high culture/low culture, etc.—that undergird the manifold forms of oppression in the world of the late twentieth century. This is all well and good, for oppression is usually a bad thing. Moreover, it is touching to find even those who flaunt their alienation from the academy indulging, nonetheless, in the illusion that a merely intellectual critique of modernity can really alleviate the suffering of the tragic victims of neo-colonialism in Biafra, Cambodia, El Salvador, the Sudan, and Rwanda. But when we assert our solidarity with the oppressed of this earth by the way we dress, speak, and decorate our homes, when we mount a radical critique of the universities that pay our salaries because of their complicity in the exploitation of women, minorities, the working class, and third-world peoples, when we do all of these things, what masters do we really serve?

We would like to say that emancipation and empowerment are the results we seek. But is this what actually happens? The campaign for democracy in South Africa, the impetus for which arose from within the Black South African cultural and political life, will most probably turn out to be, on the whole, for the best, even though campaigns to force American universities to divest their South African holdings had little effect in bringing about this transformation. But are ordinary Haitians well-served by economic boycott and the threat (or the reality) of military invasion for the purpose of imposing democratic political structures that have no organic roots in Haiti's own past? Or consider a Mexican village weaver who now makes rugs not for sale or trade to her fellow villagers but for decorating the living rooms of North American liberal academics. She probably enjoys a modest, if temporary, improvement in income and standard of living, and from the vantage point of a century hence we may look back upon this moment as the first step on a long road of cultural and economic transformations that eventuated in her grandchildren's enjoying a style and standard of life in no way inferior to that of the grandchildren of her former North American customers. But what happens when the next swing of fashion eliminates the market for "authentic" peasant crafts, this after our weaver, through producing for export, has lost her place in the traditional village economy?

One could adduce many examples of liberal white European and North American good intentions causing more harm than good. Think of the green revolution that leaves millions still to starve because marginal land once devoted to subsistence farming can now be made to yield a profit through production for export. Or think of the Body Shop, which advertises beauty-aids based on traditional formulations made with ingredients from third-world sources, but whose very success requires export production on an industrial scale that brings in its train massive social and economic dislocations.

The world can be a better place, but academic posturing will not make it so. For every Rigoberta Menchú who is made the darling of Parisian literary circles, there are a hundred peasant leaders, struggling for peace and better land, who still fall victim to the death squads, all the more conveniently forgotten precisely because we gave Menchú the Nobel Prize. It is not the interests of the oppressed that are served in this fashion.

No, in my darker moods I fear that multiculturalism really serves only the God of Mammon in his incarnation as Visa, God of international commerce and industry, attended by his herald and crier, CNN. This is multiculturalism as the legitimating rhetoric of multinational corporate capitalism; it was Coca-Cola, after all, that marketed itself a few years ago with the jingle, "I'd like to teach the world to sing in perfect harmony." There are at least two ways in which this happens.

First, because of the inauthentic mode in which it appropriates cultural values, academic multiculturalism tends to abet the commodification of those cultural values, both in a figurative sense as units of exchange in the academy—organizing a conference on clitoridectomy in central Africa will help earn you tenure just as well as designing a new general studies course on narratives of displacement in Native American legend—and in a literal sense, concretized in weavings, woodcarvings, recorded music, and recipes marketed to consumers around the world. Once these cultural values are thus commoditized, they are forever after deprived of any power they may once have had as bearers of cultural meaning, as sources of inspiration, and as foci of resistance to forces of change pressing from without. Once market my gods in a mail-order catalogue and I can no longer oppose or even thoughtfully manage the coming of Coca-Cola and McDonald's.

Second, the postmodern evangelists of multiculturalism have targeted for a most vigorous assault those very intellectual resources within the Western tradition that have long served as effective weapons in the fight against certain forms of oppression. I have in mind the concept of *theory*, which, because of its unavoidably universalizing aspect—its postmodern critics would say its "hegemonizing" aspect—cannot survive the particularizing and relativizing skeptical logic of postmodernism. Even the Frankfurt School notion of "critical theory" is debased in the postmodern intellectual world, surviving in vestigial form as nothing more than irony.

There is still enough of the Marxist left in me to fancy that even though I don't control the forces of capital, I nevertheless control something at least as important, namely, a critical, theoretical understanding of the world sufficient to enable me to do battle against the forces of injustice. Of course, this may also be just an aging intellectual's fantasy, but it's a comforting fantasy, and, I suspect, something more than that, to judge by the unions, the parties, the armies, and the people who, for better or for worse, have marched under its banner.

I have no desire to defend Marx; if anything, I find myself drawn more to Edmund Burke these days. But I do desire to defend theory. For I cling to the belief that the concept of theory that has developed in the Western intellectual tradition has value, that some kind of theoretical understanding of the world is necessary if we seek the betterment of the human condition. What's left of theory in the postmodern library is the history of theory and the critique of theory. There's this theory and that theory, one wrong for reason x, one wrong for reason y; and isn't it precious the way silly people once believed such things. It's as if theories too survive only in the commodity form, to be bought and sold in the academic marketplace. But without a robust concept of theory, I don't know what it means to be an intellectual at all, and by extension, I don't know what it means to be a public intellectual. Once market my theories in a mail-order course catalogue and I can no longer oppose or even thoughtfully manage the coming the New World Order.

Which brings us back to the question of the story we should tell about who and what a philosopher is. For I would like to find a story to tell that leaves us, as philosophers, open to conversation with the other cultures of this world without constraint or condescension. But I would also like to find a story to tell that leaves us with a significant role to play as public intellectuals.

The story will be a history, meaning that it's not simply an invention, like a fairy tale we tell our children at bedtime. As history, it will pretend to a measure of truth and objectivity, whatever those may turn out mean at the end of this story. As history, it will also submit to evidential control, though in its construction we may well choose to dispose of the evidence in a manner unlike that of our forbears who invented the Hellenized, secularized history of philosophy.

In particular, it will avoid the error of prematurely invoking source-critical methods for the purpose of discounting those reports of historical actors themselves and contemporary witnesses that fail to accord with our prejudices concerning what must have happened. If Herodotus and Isocrates agree that an historical Pythagoras learned the principles of his philosophy from the priests of Egypt, then let us not, like Lewes, discount the story on the preposterous argument that the Greeks invented this story only because they could not countenance the emergence of such genius from within their own culture. Let us, instead, take this story seriously enough for it to be a basis for further historical research. That is not to say that the authority of earlier authors should go unquestioned; far from it, their histories are most likely as thick with invention as our own. But we should not let the difference in kind that we need to find between Greek thought and the thought of their Mediterranean neighbors become a "fact," and then a premise in an argument for the impossibility of Greek borrowings from elsewhere.

Difference being easy to find, there is, of course, a difference between philosophy as it developed among the Greeks and the myth and religion of Egypt, and this difference's being there made a difference, if only because we chose once before to let it make a difference. The question is not, therefore, whether there is difference; the question is what, now, to make of it. The history that I want to tell would make far less of it than do the histories we have written since the Enlightenment.

Having no reason to fear a dark racial taint from Egypt, Nubia, and the farther reaches of Africa, I choose to tell a history that celebrates continuity as much as difference. I choose to tell a history that can comfortably accommodate the possibility (and for now nothing more than that) that the high priests of Egypt were the models for Plato's guardians and philosopher-king, and that the knowledge of the form of the good that we seek as we ascend the divided line corresponds to the esoteric wisdom that only the initiates were permitted to acquire, which is, after all, how neo-Platonic Hermetic mysticism long viewed the situation (see Yates 1964). And if further research indeed reveals that the Egyptians, in turn, borrowed their religion from Nubia, so be it.

It follows that I also choose to tell a history that recognizes continuity, as much as difference, between philosophy and religion. This is, perhaps, the most important moment in a revisioning of the history of philosophy if, as philosophers, we want to reopen, say, a conversation about the good life with Muslim fundamentalists, a move that requires our acknowledging a continuity between the Islam of Ibn-Rushd and the Islam of Sheik Abdul Rahman, or a conversation with a Native American religious leader over whether or not the land that is the sacred abode of ancestral spirits has a moral standing comparable to that of the humans whose activity on the land threatens the peace of those ancestral spirits.

Most of us would no doubt agree that it is easier to countenance the thought of a continuity between religious and philosophical ways of viewing the world in realms of metaphysics and morality, than in the realms of method and epistemology. After all, how much difference in *kind* is there, really, between the Plato of the *Timæus* and the nameless authors of the Book of Genesis, or between the doctrine of the first nine books of the *Nicomachæan Ethics* and the Navajo doctrine of "walking in beauty"? The real difference is not so much in the content of these doctrines as in the way we come to sanction them. Religion is dogmatic; philosophy is critical. Philosophy respects the claims of logic and evidence; religion sweeps them aside if they threaten the articles of faith. This was the locus of the medieval debates over reason versus faith, and the focus of the Enlightenment critique of religious dogmatism. This is what Galileo and Bellarmine argued about in the early seventeenth century and what creationists and evolutionists argue about in the late twentieth. In urging that we now valorize continuity along with difference in the relationship between religion and philosophy, do I not invite a retreat to the epistemological Dark Ages? I think not.

To begin with, all its posturing notwithstanding, philosophy is no stranger to dogmatism. It is, for example, one of the sweeter ironies of the history of modern philosophy that the very same Kant who celebrated reason as a tool for combatting religious dogma in essays like "What is Enlightenment" (Kant 1784b) was also the inventor of the most subtle form of philosophical dogmatism, the transcendental argument.

But rather than defend dogmatism—something I have no desire to do, since too many examples of the dangers of dogmatism lie ready at hand, from the Inquisition to the Vatican's continuing opposition to birth control—let me instead suggest that the appearance of such a difference in principle between religious dogmatism and the critical philosophical spirit depends both upon a willful caricature of the religious temperament—Bellarmine, after all, was not such a bad fellow—and, more importantly, upon our uncritical acceptance of certain logical, semantic, and epistemological notions that moved to the center of the philosophical stage in the wake of the secularizing and Hellenizing tendencies of the late-eighteenth and early-nineteenth centuries. I have in mind such notions as "truth," "objectivity," and "reality."

Time is too short on this occasion to permit the thoroughgoing historical deconstruction and philosophical analysis of these notions that my argument requires. That is all the more unfortunate because I do not want to create the misimpression that I am endorsing all of the sometimes silly things one reads today by way of critique of these notions on the academic left. Instead, let me just sketch the alternative point of view from which I approach questions of knowledge and method.

My position is, broadly speaking, that of Pierre Duhem, whose aim, unlike mine, was unfortunately the defense of dogma (see Duhem 1905-1906, 1906). That is to say that I start from the premise that the choice of a theoretical representation, in whatever domain, is underdetermined by both logic and empirical evidence. One's choice among the resulting rich multiplicity of theories equally compatible with the claims of logic and evidence has, therefore, the status of a convention. The claims of logic and evidence are not discounted, on this approach, but their capacity, in principle, to settle all disputes is denied.

If theory choice is, thus, underdetermined, then our received notions of truth and reality are rendered problematic. In place of one truth, one reality, there are many. If theory choice is, thus, underdetermined, then we must abandon those simplistic, progressivist models of inquiry that imagine the history of scientific inquiry to be a history of steady approach to a unique ultimate truth. The history of thought can, instead, have many outcomes, depending upon the contingent choices made by the various communities who contribute to that history. It is in appreciating how those choices are made that we find our opening from philosophy to religion and to manifold other cultural interests as well. For while the range of theories from among which we may choose at any one juncture in history is not limitless—remember that we are not discounting the claims of evidence and logic—it will, nevertheless, typically be more than large enough to discomfit Enlightenment prejudices and more than large enough to provide a place for even the most diverse religious and cultural agendas. This is an epistemology of tolerance and accommodation, an epistemology of generous compromise, acknowledging that there are many ways to make sense of the world. It was this epistemology to which Osiander appealed in trying to preserve the peace between Copernicus and the Church, and to which Bellarmine appealed when he proposed a compromise that would have allowed Galileo to do his science without forcing the Church to condemn him. The point is not, of course, that the Church was right and Galileo wrong, that science should always bow to scripture. The point is, instead, that the possibilities for rapprochement are far greater than the self-image of philosophy and reason that we have inherited from the Enlightenment permits us to acknowledge.

It must be stressed that this is not an epistemology uncongenial to science. I am, myself, a philosopher of science, trained in physics, most of whose work concerns the history and philosophical foundations of physics. It is, moreover, an epistemology that has informed some of the most important scientific projects of our century, Einstein, for example, being only one of many students of Duhem (see Howard 1990).

Indeed, it is interesting to see just what it was that a thinker like Einstein found so attractive about Duhem's epistemology. For one of its chief virtues—emphasized by Duhem himself and prized by Einstein—was this epistemology's capacity to *empower* theory. If theory choice were to be determined univocally by logic and experience, then it would not be clear what real role there was for theory, aside from its being a convenient bookkeeping tool, as it was for a thinker like Ernst Mach or twentieth-century instrumentalists. If, by contrast, we premise an ineliminable element of free choice in theory, we provide ourselves with the very kind of robust conception of theory that I earlier said I wanted to save in order to make sense of our role as public intellectuals. If theories are, as Einstein called them, "free creations of the human spirit," if theories are not simply forced upon us by logic and experience, then free intellection is necessary in our encounter with the world. Moreover, precisely that aspect of theory that most frightens the postmodern temperament—its universalizing, totalizing, hegemonizing character—is mitigated by the very arguments that hereby empower theory. For while theory still pretends to universal import, there is not merely the hope but the guarantee that many different theories, reflecting many different interests, can coexist happily with one another. In other words, the universalizing moment in theory need not be read as an exclusionary moment.

As with science, so too with history. Duhemian underdeterminationism helps us to understand what's at stake in the kind of rewriting of history that I am urging upon us. In history, as in physics, logic and evidence still constrain us, but they do not dictate in every respect the story we choose to tell. They leave us free to choose a story that conduces to ends rather more salubrious than those served by the Hellenophile histories upon which you and I were raised.

The Duhemian epistemology also offers hope for repairing the other main defect in the self-understanding of philosophy that I lamented above, namely, its willful divorce from the empirical sciences. For if theory choice is underdetermined by logic and experience, then we philosophers, as we have long conceived ourselves, can give no principled epistemological explanation for why one theory was, in fact, chosen over another. Why did Boyle choose the vacuum and Hobbes the plenum in the late seventeenth century (see

Shapin and Schaffer 1985)? Why did quantum physicists choose the Copenhagen interpretation of the quantum theory over the de Broglie program in the late 1920s and early 1930s (see Cushing 1994)? A full explanation necessarily involves appeal to contingent empirical facts about the individuals and communities making those choices. The philosopher who wants to do epistemology will have to do some psychology, sociology, anthropology, and maybe some history as well.

The advantage thereby gained is considerable. When philosophers, as philosophers, enter debates about cross-cultural conversations, we are inhibited by one serious problem, which is that if once we do give up the various foundationalisms that have defined us since the Enlightenment, then we seem to have no answer to the threat of radical relativism. If I give up the Enlightenment notion of truth, for the sake of an opening to other peoples and other cultures, then how can I be assured that, when the need arises, I can persuade others to join me in doing what is right? If there is no truth in politics and morals (not to speak of science, for the moment), how do I oppose the Hitlers and the Idi Amins of this world? How do I block the descent to an anything-goes radical relativism?

The answer is that there is no guarantee, and that it is only a philosopher's intellectualist fantasy that there should be one. But once we permit or oblige ourselves, as philosophers, to learn enough by way of contingent facts about other cultures, we are at once impressed by circumstance that virtually any two cultures have enough in common to serve as a starting point for a meaningful conversation. I share virtually none of the religious beliefs of a Sikh militant, but we both know the pain that accompanies the sudden loss of a loved one. I abhor the actions of those who are destroying the Amazon basin, but we live on the same planet, breath the same air, and need both to feed our children a minimally adequate diet. I do not share the politics of Helmut Kohl, and I wish that he and the CDU would do more to combat the rise of neo-Nazism, but we are both children of the Enlightenment.

One might worry, finally, that an epistemology that traces its origins to the writings of a right-wing, reactionary, French Thomist philosopher of science who was hailed as an apostle of the "new positivism" will, of necessity, be so culture-bound as not to capable of playing the role here projected for it by way of promoting tolerance while avoiding the slide into radical relativism. It might be argued that the very formulation of the underdeterminationist thesis presupposes culture-specific conceptions of theory and evidence, and a distinction between the two so strict that even hard-nosed philosophers of science doubt its cogency, so that there is no hope of employing this epistemology to make sense of cross-cultural encounters. Such doubts amount to nothing more, however, than another version of the genetic fallacy. Weaken the concepts of theory and evidence as you will; blur the distinction between them; talk of "stories" rather than "theories." The central "Duhemian" point remains unaffected: Given a common starting point—be it a body of evidence, a set of shared beliefs or feelings, or just the need to face common environmental challenges—there will be many stories or theories that we can construct on that basis, no one of these stories being privileged a priori, while some stories just will not work. It may take an effort of good will to find or construct the starting point, but an epistemology of tolerance makes the effort worthwhile, offering hope both that a common starting point can be found and that, having found it, we can reach a practical consensus in spite of the different stories we tell about what we are doing and why we are doing it.

Changing the self-image of philosophy in the way I here recommend will mean changing as well the way we organize our universities. The current boundaries of the disciplines date only to the early nineteenth century. There is no reason they should survive into the twenty-first. Perhaps we should welcome religion back into our midst. The trend in North America is still further to segregate, to drive religion out of the academy, the University of Pennsylvania, for example, having only this year abolished its highly-respected religious studies program. But if we both read Augustine, Aquinas, and Luther, why must we continue to do it under two roofs rather than one. Perhaps we should also rethink our relations to the sciences, especially the human and cultural sciences, the *Geisteswissenschaften*, to use the lovely older German term. Let's take philosophers, anthropologists, and literary theorists and put them together in social theory programs. Let's take classics, and semitics, and Egyptology, seasoned with some philosophers specializing in Plato, Aristotle, and Maimonides, and put them together in programs of ancient Mediterranean cultural studies.

Most importantly, however, we need to write a new history of philosophy, a history intended to serve a new set of ends. As sanction for writing such an "intentional history," if I may coin a phrase, let me quote that theorist of an older history, Immanuel Kant:

It is strange and apparently silly to wish to write a history in accordance with an Idea of how the course of the world must be if it is to lead to certain rational ends. It seems that with such an Idea only romance could be written.

Nevertheless, if one may assume that Nature, even in the play of human freedom, works not without plan or purpose, this Idea could still be of use.... That I would want to displace the work of practicing empirical historians with this Idea of world history, which is to some extent based upon an a priori principle, would be a misinterpretation of my intention. It is only a suggestion of what a philosophical mind (which would have to be well versed in history) could essay from another point of view. Otherwise the notorious complexity of a history of our time must naturally lead to serious doubt as to how our descendants will begin to grasp the burden of the history we shall leave to them after a few centuries. They will naturally value the history of earlier times, from which the documents have long since disappeared, only from the point of view of what interests them, i.e., in answer to the question of what the various nations and governments have contributed to the goal of world citizenship, and what they have done to damage it. To consider this, so as to direct the ambitions of sovereigns and their agents to the only means by which their fame can be spread to later ages: this can be a minor motive for attempting such a philosophical history. (Kant 1784b, pp. 24-27)

4. *A Concluding Story*

Since we've been talking about telling stories, let me end with one. It's actually a story about a story, or about my reading a story. And the story this story is about is, by intention, a piece of low-brow, pop-culture fiction.

About the same time that the flyer concerning the Lakehead University Native American Philosophy project landed upon my desk I chanced also to be reading for relaxation a detective story by Tony Hillerman, a current favorite of mine whose two main characters, Jim Chee and Joe Leaphorn, work for the Navajo Tribal Police on the Navajo reservation in Arizona, New Mexico, and Utah. Chee is the more traditional of the two. Though he is supposed to have studied for a while at Arizona State University, and he uses all of the modern technology of law enforcement that his underfunded police force can afford, he is now also studying to be a *hataali*, a singer or medicine man, if you will, who performs days-long ritual chants, like the Blessing Way, that are supposed to cure a variety of ills. Moreover, he believes in the Navajo moral and character ideal of "walking in beauty," where the aim is always to be in a state of *hozro*, a kind of balance with the natural order. He is not quite sure about the literal truth of the Navajo creation legend, having to do with an ancestral people that emerged from a hole in the earth, but like all traditional Navajo he does believe that the universe is an ordered whole, wherein nothing is accidental, unconnected, or random, this belief serving him well in his police work, where it functions like a principle of sufficient reason, driving him always to solve the crime in question, secure in the knowledge that there is a solution, if only he is patient and determined enough to find it.

I find myself drawn powerfully to the character of Jim Chee. He is not always comfortable living in the cusp between two worlds, all the more so when falls in love with a *belagana* school teacher from Wisconsin. But he survives, and even thrives, in no small measure because tries to understand how both his people and the *belagana* think about the world. It's a silly fantasy, of course, but I delight in imagining myself riding with Jim Chee over the high desert plateau, on the long drive from Shiprock to Gallup, with my telling him about Schopenhauer's *Fourfold Root of the Principle of Sufficient Reason* and his telling me how the Blessing Way restores one's balance with nature. I know that, as a philosopher, I would find it an interesting conversation.

Why do I find myself concluding the present discussion by talking thus about a piece of pulp fiction? Well, it is very good pulp fiction, and it is unusual, in its genre for its cultural setting, which is very sympathetically represented, though Hillerman is himself not a Navajo. Perhaps it also has something to do with the fact that the literary form of the detective novel, or any type of novel for that matter, recommends itself by eschewing the categories of both the philosophical and the anthropological in favor of the particularity and immediacy of a fully evoked human character. Anthropology necessarily distances the object of its descriptions as something other in kind from the anthropologist, while the categories that have defined the philosophical tradition for over two hundred years necessarily nullify any claim that Navajo religion might make to being taken seriously as a philosophy. Somehow one's first coming to know the person of Jim Chee makes the distancing of the anthropologist and the discounting of the philosopher seem, well, unjust. The dignity of the person secures the dignity of the philosophy.

One final moment in the construction of the self-image of philosophy in the eighteenth and early-nineteenth centuries should therefore also be stressed. Along with a new way of telling its history and a new institutional structure, the new philosophy also created for itself new literary forms, the most sigfnificant new form being the scholarly journal. Only certain kinds of texts can claim philosophical legitimacy through publication in such forms. These include the systematic treatise, the essay review, and the short analytic argument. They do not normally include the epic poem, the ritual chant, or the diary (let alone the detective story), which makes it all the more likely that the voices of many cultures cannot be heard with philosophers' ears.

ENDNOTES

REFERENCES

Bacon, Francis (1623). *De Dignitate et Augmentis Scientiarum.* London.

Baldwin, James Mark, ed. (1901-1905). *Dictionary of Philosophy and Psychology,* 3 vols. New York: Macmillan.

Beck, Lewis White (1963). "Editor's Introduction." In Kant 1963, pp. vii-xxvi.

Bernal, Martin (1987). *Black Athena: The Afroasiatic Roots of Classical Civilization.* Vol. 1, *The Fabrication of Ancient Greece 1785–1985.* New Brunswick, New Jersey: Rutgers University Press.

Blumenbach, Johann Friedrich (1795). *De Generis Humani Varietate Nativa,* 3rd ed. Göttingen: Vandenhoek et Ruprecht.

Bordo, Susan (1994). "Curricular Politics: Beyond the Polarities in the Pursuit of Truth." Typescript.

Boring, Edwin G. (1950). *A History of Experimental Psychology,* 2nd ed. New York: Appleton-Century-Crofts.

Brucker, Jakob (1742-1767). *Historia Critica, a Mundi Incunabulis ad Nostram usque Ætatum Deducta,* 5 vols. Leipzig: Bern. Christoph. Breitkopf.

Buhle, Johann Gottlieb Gerhard (1796-1804). *Lehrbuch der Geschichte der Philosophie,* 8 vols. Göttingen: Vandenhoek und Ruprecht.

Burleigh, Walter (1470). *De Vita ac Moribus Philosophorum.* Cologne.

Cushing, James T. (1994). *Quantum Mechanics: Historical Contingency and the Copenhagen Hegemony.* Chicago: University of Chicago Press.

Derrida, Jacques (1986). "The Age of Hegel." In *Demarcating the Disciplines: Philosophy, Literature, Art.* Samuel Weber, ed. Minneapolis: University of Minnesota Press, pp. 3-43.

Deussen, Paul (1883). *Das System des Vedanta. Nach den Brahma-Sutra's des Badarayana und dem Commentare des Cankaraber über dieselben, als ein Compendium der Dogmatik des Brahmanismus vom Standpunkte des Cankara aus dargestellt.* Leipzig: F. A. Brockhaus.

Duhem, Pierre (1905-1906). "Physique de Croyant." *Annales de Philosophie Chrétienne* 155: 44-67, 133-159.

___ (1906). *La Théorie physique. Son objet et sa structure.* Paris: Chevalier & Rivière.

Enfield, William (1791). *The History of Philosophy.* London. [English adaptation of Brucker 1742-1767.]

Feder, Johann Georg Heinrich (1767). *Grundri_ der Philosophie.*

___ (1769). *Logik und Metaphysik. Nebst der philosophischen Geschichte im Grundri_e.* Göttingen: Johann Christian Dieterich.

Fülleborn, Gerog Gustav (1791ff). *Beiträge zur Geschichte der Philosophie.* Züllichau.

Gadol, Eugene T. (1982). "Philosophy, Ideology, Common Sense and Murder—The Vienna of the Vienna Circle Past and Present." In *Rationality and Science: A Memorial Volume for Moritz Schlick in Celebration of the Centennial of His Birth.* Eugene T. Gadol, ed. Vienna and New York: Springer-Verlag, pp. 1-35.

Gibbon, Edward (1776). *The History of the Decline and Fall of the Roman Empire.* London: W. Strahan and T. Cadell.

Hamilton, Sir William (1865-1866). *Lectures on Metaphysics and Logic,* 4 vols. Edinburgh: W. Blackwood.

Hamlyn, D.W. (1992). *Being a Philosopher: The History of a Practice.* London and New York: Routledge.

Hegel, Georg Wilhelm Friedrich (1900). *The Philosophy of History*, rev. ed. J. Sibree, trans. New York: P.F. Collier & Son. English translation of *Vorlesungen über die Philosophie der Geschichte*, 2nd ed. Karl Hegel, ed. Berlin.

_____ (1975). *Lectures on the Philosophy of World History. Introduction: Reason in History*. H.B. Nisbet, trans. Duncan Forbes, intro. Cambridge: Cambridge University Press. English translation of *Die Vernunft in der Geschichte*, 5th ed. Johannes Hoffmeister, ed. Hamburg: F. Meiner, 1955.

Hollmann, Samuel Christian (1742). *Einführung in die Naturwissenschaft auf der Grundlage der Erfahrung*.

Horn, Georg (1655). *Historiæ Philosophicæ de Origine, Successionis, Sectis et Vita Philosophorum ab Orbe Conditio ad Nostram Ætatem Agitur*. Leiden.

Howard, Don (1990). "Einstein and Duhem." *Synthese* 83: 363-384.

Hume, David (1754-1762). *The History of England, from the Invasion of Julius Caeser to the Revolution of 1688*. London: A. Millar.

Inglis, John (1993). "Aquinas and the Historiography of Medieval Philosophy: A Reevaluation." Ph.D. Dissertation. University of Kentucky.

Kant, Immanuel (1784a). "Beantwortung der Frage: Was ist Aufklärung?" Page numbers and quotations taken from Lewis White Beck's English translation as "What is Enlightenment?" In Kant 1963, pp. 3-10.

_____ (1784b). "Idee zu einer allgemeinen Geschichte im weltbürgerliche Absicht." Page numbers and quotations taken from Lewis White Beck's English translation as "Idea for a Universal History from a Cosmopolitan Point of View." In Kant 1963, pp. 11-26.

_____ (1798). *Der Streit der Facultäten. In drey Abschnitten*. Königsberg: F. Nicolovius.

_____ (1963). *On History*. Lewis White Beck, ed. Indianapolis and New York: Bobbs-Merrill.

Kleinert, Andreas (1985). "Mathematik und anorganische Naturwissenschaft." In Vierhaus 1985, pp. 218-248.

Muhlack, Ulrich (1985). "Klassische Philologie zwischen Humanismus und Neuhumanismus." In Vierhaus 1985, pp. 93-119.

Rotenstreich, Nathan (1984). *Jews and German Philosophy: The Polemics of Emancipation.* New York: Schocken Books.

Schneiders, Werner (1985). "Der Philosophiebegriff des philosophischen Zeitalters. Wandlungen im Selbstverständnis der Philosophie von Leibniz bis Kant." In Vierhaus 1985, pp. 58-92.

Schopenhauer, Arthur (1844). *Die Welt als Wille und Vorstellung,* 2 vols., 2nd ed. Leipzig: F. A. Brockhaus.

Shapin, Steven and Schaffer, Simon (1985). *Leviathan and the Air-pump: Hobbes, Boyle, and the Experimental Life.* Princeton, New Jersey: Princeton University Press.

Stanley, Thomas (1655). *History of Philosophy.* London: Humphrey Moseley and Thomas Dring.

Tennemann, Wilhelm Gottlieb (1789-1819). *Geschichte der Philosophie,* 11 vols. Leipzig.
_____ (1829). *Manuel de l'histoire de la philosophie.* Victor Cousin, trans. Paris: A. Sautelet.

Tiedemann, Dietrich (1791-1796). *Geist der speculativen Philosophie,* 6 vols. Marburg.

Vierhaus, Rudolf, ed. (1985). *Wissenschaften im Zeitalter der Aufklärung. Aus Anla_ des 250jährigen Bestehens des Verlages Vandenhoeck & Ruprecht.* Göttingen: Vandenhoeck & Ruprecht.

Windelband, Wilhelm (1892). *Geschichte der Philosophie.* Freiburg: J.C.B. Mohr. Page numbers and quotations are taken from the English translation of the 1900 second edition: *A History of Philosophy, with Especial Reference* to the Formation and Development of Its Problems and Conceptions, 2nd ed. James H. Tufts, trans. New York and London: Macmillan.

Yates, Frances (1964). *Giordano Bruno and the Hermetic Tradition.* Chicago: University of Chicago Press.

---

[1] For Bellow's denial of this allegation, but with a defense of the distinction between literate and preliterate cultures, see his recent column, "Papuans and Zulus," *New York Times*, 10 March 1994.

[2] For example, Richard Walzer's article on "Arabic Philosophy" in the 1971 edition of the *Encyclopædia Britannica* simply assumes that anything philosophical in Arabic intellectual history starts and ends in the middle ages; it begins with this sentence: "Medieval Arabic philosophy represents a case of the adaptation of Greek philosophy to a different civilization and to a new language."

[3] Two other important early histories are those by Fülleborn (1791ff) and Buhle (1796-1804).

[4] I want to thank Susan Bordo for drawing my attention to this passage; see Bordo, 1994, pp. 10-11.

Aziz Al-Azmeh

Culturalism,
Grand Narrative of Capitalism Exultant

> "Nous les pouvons donc bien appeler barbares eu égard aux règles de la raison, mais non pas eu égard à nous, qui les surpassons en toute sorte de barbarité"
>
> *Montaigne*

I should like to question, and radically to question, the theme of cross-cultural conversations[1]. This is not because I wish there to be eternal incomprehensibility between peoples, or because I wish to promote xenophobia, and encourage ethnic cleansing and correlativ acts of barbarity. It is, rather, because I believe that the notion of cross-cultural conversation rests upon an unreflected assumption of the fixity and finality of the interlocutors in this conversation which, even at the hands of seriously philosophical authors, tends to devolve to the tritest statements on common maxims of etiquette[2]. It is this very same assumption of fixity and irreducibility underlying the etiquette of interculturalism, of multiculturalism as a form of conservative etiquette, that I see to be the apparently paradoxical correlative of the sorts of assumptions about others -- other *ethnoi*, other religious groups, and so forth -- that prepare the grounds, in the realms of conception and imagination, for the entire range of possibilities, extending from the correlative boundaries of rapturous fascination with the exotic at one extremity, to genocidal demonization and bellicose dehumanization of the Other on the other.

The other consideration that leads me to question the theme of cross-cultural conversations is the culturalism it subtends. By culturalism I understand the view that regards an entity termed "culture" to be the determining moment in the history and present condition of an historical mass. An historical mass, in this sense, is one whose imputed distinctiveness, individuality, and indeed whose very name -- the West, Islam, etc. -- is taken to subtend a culture so specific and irreducible as to be in itself constitutive of both the history and the present condition of this mass, or at the very least the element that overdetermines its elements and totalizes them as mere manifestations. Culturalism is consequently the view that regards conceptual and imaginary representations to be the ultimate and irreducible constraints at work in the life of the historical mass in question, despite the fact that social and historical life demonstrates to us daily that not all social and historical constraints are conceptual, and that although cultures are in a certain sense genetically transmitted and do indeed use genetic traits -- ethnographic detail, real or imagined, encoded in a genealogy and in a pseudo-history of uniqueness and continuity, of the West or of Islam for instance -- as symbols and markers, yet this is not sufficient ground for asserting that societies, or historical masses, are perpetuated by cultures[3]. Still less is it legitimate to assert that what are imprecisely known as cultures have an absolutely determinant role in setting the constitution of this mass, or that culture is in itself a sufficient defining element in this mass, or that culture overdetermines a given history to such an extent that it is in itself not only the chief iconic marker of this mass, but is also substantively representative of an inner nature ascribed to it [4]. While much historical and sociological writing that conceives itself as post-modern or post-structuralist protests, sometimes legitimately, that culture is not merely that which is remaindered after accounting for society and the economy, the crude transition to culturalist determinism is normally seen somewhat naturally to flow as a corollary of this protest[5].

That which invariably comes to pass in this connection is that, both for native votives of the cult of authenticity and for foreign priests of the cult of Difference, visible tokens of ethnographic distinctiveness, of dubious reality, pervasiness, and consequence, are taken for iconic markers not only of a totalizing ethnographic description, but also of ethnological typification, that is, of insertion into a genealogical and taxonomic lore used by the protagonists of culturalism. Ethnography is thus replaced by ethnology, and this latter is ever captive to the *topoi* of what I should follow a recent precedent and designate by the name "culturalist differentialism"[6]. Most salient in the enunciations of this differentialism are stigmata of otherness, of iconic character, that purport visibly to represent the culture in question in its entirety: examples of this are the head scarf, the saffron string, or the repudiation of grand narratives. Far from being treated with the circumspect fascination with which it should, this coquette of the spirit, referred to as culture, is a term rather thoughtlessly applied to objects poorly apprehended and regarded with the eyes of sheer exotism. The perspective which today renders culturalism an epistemological and normative imperative, is an aesthetic of difference and of otherness, in which matters of otherness are perceived as either the objects of enthusiastic fascination, or the occasions of disagreeable sensation of varying degrees of intensity.

This trope of radical otherness sustains two complementary practical positions, the one heterophobe and the other heterophile. These are both possible variants of the differentialist stance; the former affords the sustenance of a policy of distanciation with regard to others, the other renders possible a libertarian communalism claiming roots in sympathy rather than in the antipathy and xenophobia that animate the exclusivist position. In both cases, we are supposed to use this culturalism to "correct asymmetries", to stem "the suppression of diversity"[7]. Heterophiles emphatically add that this perpective guards against the "arrogant, intolerant, self-aggrandizing rational subject of modernity", by "resurrect[ing] the virtues of the fragmentary, the local, and the subjugated in order to unmask the will to power that lies at the very heart of modern rationality and to decenter its epistemological and moral subject"[8].

This position, with its legion representatives, is linked to more than anti-imperialist revindication. It embodies what is perceived, and not for the first time, as a crisis in the supposed excess of Cartesian reason, and encompasses a correlative shift from the innocent naturalness of reason to reclaiming an innocent naturaleness of desire, need, locality, fragmentariness. In order to describe this position I shall borrow from Umberto Eco the delightful expression "new Cartesianism of the irrational"[9]. Thus, for example, from the motto "different cultures, different rationalities" is derived the possibility of dissolving reason by its dismissal as "hyperrationality", and the ridiculous construal of myth as "so-called myth"[10]. We shall see later that this celebration of sheer otherness in the context of an undisciplined liberal discourse is really the result of the political domestication 'post-colonial' discourse[11]. To the same discursive and ideological universe belong the reiteration of notions of ecological and environmental integralism, nature romanticism, including the adulation or adoption of exotic religions with varying degrees of New Age tropes: very much like the weariness of reason and of modernity, forms of romantic rusticism were prevalent in European and non-European thought in other periods of crisis, namely the 1920s and 1930s in the waske of the Bolshevik Revolution, and previously in the wake of the French Revolution. Now as previously, notions of a return to natural innocence, to the recovery of immediacy and of subjectivity, and disenchantment with abstraction in thought have always come together as a bundle, and it is as such that they will be treated in what follows.

There is not very much need to dwell at length on the heterophobe variety of culturalist differentialism, but I do nevertheless propose briefly to highlight some of its major features before I get on to the sympathetic differentialism with which I should like to take issue, and before I examine the common bases shared by these two positions and indicate the precise historical, conceptual, and political concordances and genealogies they share. Heterophobe differentialism is an essentialist system of social perception premised on a notion of a pregiven culture which, although like race it lacks a sociological definition, is yet coined to schematize without precision an indeterminate reality[12], and to regard this object of the imagination as a predetermined boundary of natural sympathy. Overdetermined by a social instinctivism, this position, so prevalent in public discourse in Western Europe today and the mainstay of anti-immigration arguments, is in no need to present itself is terms of racialism or of racial hatred. It has in the last two decades modified its terms, deployed a discursive deracialization, and underpinned its terms and its socio-political consequences of exclusivism by "arguments from genuine fears" premissed on the supposed authority of "common sense"[13]. By arguments stemming from considerations such as these, xenophobia is not only legitimized, but also naturalized on a par with Fate itself.

I need only add briefly that arguments from "predetermined boundaries of sympathy" appear in the public mind to be sustained by recent sociobiological thinking with its genetic engineering associations. Although eugenics is very much out of fashion, molecular biology has engendered a renewed confidence in physicalist interpretations[14]. Sociolbiological notions of gene-culture coevolutionary circuits, and the sweeping links between gene-pools and cultures envisioned by very widely read sociobiologists like Richard Dawkins and E. O.Wilson are reviving associations between human collectivities and the notion of stocks with predetermined characteristics -- and indeed, qualities and deficiencies -- and naturally correlative boundaries of natural sympathy. Thus cultures become natures, and the history of human masses becomes a natural history. This is a point to wqhich a return shall be made below.

I now come to the celebration and positive valorization of difference. This is taking place at the confluence of many discourses and their correlative social and political positions. There is on the one hand the communalist social philosophy, or the philosophy of communal democracy, associated with various tendencies ranging from the medievalism of Alisdair Macintyre through to thinkers of the post-modernist era like Richard Walzer. There is also the perfunctory post-modernism of ethnicist, religious, and gender communalism, and the self-conscious nihilism of demotic post-modernism one encounters in mediatic and even in high-minded presentations of this term. These represent a curious blend of radically conservative social philosophies, with the remnants of a left-wing libertarianism disassociated and disoriented, and with an anti-Communism consolidated by the demised of 'actually existing socialism' as a viable global contestation. They subsist in an international scene marked by the revival everywhere of right-wing ideologies, racism, and bigotry, associated with the resuscitation of reactionary philosophies of the not too distant past, and their parading as beacons of ellightenment, here regarded as the destruof the supposed illusions that Communist made posible Such is for instance the resuscitation, not only by the Right, and the central positioning in Germany of Ernst Jünger, in France of Emmanuel Levinas and others, throughout the world of Nietzsche and Heidegger -- not only as the high priest of Being and of its revelations, of the will to will, of Verworfenheit, but also as the philosophical mate of the Earth with the blood and earth it immediately produces, as the pursuer of idyllic milestones in the Black Forest, the rustic speaking in philosophical tongues: all bereft of any consideration as to the non-textual parameters of their work which will have overdetermined even the most complex philosophical speculation, and radically deprived them of the innocent illumninationism attributed to them[15].

This celebration of diference and rediscovery of the wholesome also bespeaks conditions of post-Keynesian social fragmentation and involution. This was again, in its turn, a consequence of the dieappearance of the Soviet bloc, and the dissolution, most particularly in the United States, of notions of citizenship for those of ascriptive and savage identitiers, of ethnic and religious origin and of gender. There is also -- and this is very germane for our purposes -- the treatment of countries of the South as if they were recoverable within the register of North American notions, a treatment which describes societies of the South in terms of the communalist democratic tropes used by self-constituting pressure groups arising out of North American conditions, and using the same politically correct vocabularies of empowerment, of recovering local and regional histories, and so forth. The net effect of these vocabularies and tendencies, again of North Americal origin duly globalized by the intelligentsia as by Non-Governmental Organizations, is to assist the process of upward social mobility sat the top of these groups, and confirm systemic disadvantage at the lower end. These have now devolved to naively-adopted shibboleths that accrue from a systemic conformism that recalls notions of repressive tolerance put forward by Herbert Marcuse three decades ago, and carried further into arguments of mediatic manipulation of consent by Noam Chomsky. Thus arguments from North American conditions are universalized by the setting of universal agendas according to North American perceptions. These matters are associated with certain forms of appropriating (and I think frequently misappropriating) the anti-orientalist theses of Edward Said, and the historical theses of Martin Bernal: in this was, orientals, most particularly those who describe themselves as post-colonial, re-orienalize themselves radically when they speak of re-gaining their authenticity and singularity. Thus arises a traffic in mirror images between re-orientalized orientals speaking for authenticity, and post-modernists speaking for Difference.

I will try to show that, despite libertarian pronouncements, this is profoundly detrimental both to the perception and to the actualization of projects for liberation and self-empowerment. All of these, in their different ways, premise their presumptions on what they perceive to be the bedris of a modernity which not only manifestly failed but also deserved to fail. This is especially true with reference to the triumphalist tonaliy associated with the chiliastic transcendence implied by the prefix "post": post-modernity, post-coloniality, post-Enlightenment, even post-historicity, and their cognates, reminiscent all of them of finalist prophecies throughout the 19th and 20th centuries, one of the most recently memorable of which is perhaps the eminently ideological notion of the "end of ideology", the thesis propounded by Daniel Bell in the early 1960s to designate an ideological moment in the Cold War waged against the Communist block which, in this perspective, was the only ideological formation.

The trouble with this fetishized prefix is that it indicates little beyond fixing a point in time. Post-modernism appears as a transcendence of modernism, but is in fact a cluster of rococo glosses on themes of a modernity accomplished with the exultant triumph of capital, just as this self-same capital in its countries of origin is being in large sectors dissociated from processes of production. In other words, post-modernism and associated notions appear to me to indicate not so much the transcendence of modernity in any serious or consequential sense, but rather a series of movements within the regime of modernity which abdicate the social, political, and very frequently, normative and aesthetic consequences and correlates of modernism. The mechanism whereby this abdication is actualized is by the censorship of history, the positing and organization of an amnesia, an insensibility to history -- i.e. to social and cultural reality -- grounded in a sense of well-being which relegates history to those who might have need of it, and Heidegger's ideas to deconstructive *jouissance*. For historical reality, and for the position within modernity of post-modernism, are substituted virtual realities of the present, of the past, and of the Other, among which stands out the virtual reality of collective well-being in a West riven with structural crises, unemployment, and social stresses sublimated in a triumphalism of the moment.

Ultimately, all these posterior conditions celebrated in post-modernism, post-Enlightenment, post-coloniality, and so forth appear, in the perspective of history, to be no more than gullible, hasty, and rather thoughtless redactions of post-Communism, or rather, the collapse of the Socialist block after the end of the Cold War. This made possible the economics of deregulation, the acceptance of large-scale unemployment and of the economic values of the Victorian era, all of these premised on the collapse of the Keynesian consensus which regulated socio-economic life in the wake of the Second World War and in the light of events that preceded it, and which resulted in immiseration and social involution in lands of the North, and the correlative ejection, in the South, of notions and policies of development and their replacement by notions of structural adjustment. Yet Western triumphalism marking the end of the Cold War was given the sense of conveying the end of an era. It is to mark a particular major conjunctural event that the thesis of the End of History is propounded, and it is herein that is to be found the locus of variations spun on the theme of posteriority. But the amplitude of the event is not such as to merit an epochal or even an eschatological regard as is presumed for it by the End of

History thesis and its spinoffs[16], most particularly if we regard the end of the Cold War as a reconfirmation -- not the disappearance -- of the vigour of one side to this great conflict and of the defeat of the main contestant. The war against Iraq does not mark a new era, but a continuation of one that has been with us for two centuries, and is one which, anthropologically speaking, could be regarded in its major forms of representation[17] as the performance of a ritual sacrifice marking the reconfirmation I have spoken of.

I need make no apologies for bringing in facts of contemporary history into this discussion, as the terms of our theme -- cross-cultural conversations and the conceptual and imaginary grounds on which it stands -- is inseparable from conjunctural conditions. The presumption of posteriority, and the positing of this posteriority as a break, as the provision of a *tabula rasa* upon which the writ of transcendence is inscribed, has taken the form of an antithetical discourse : it is not only asserted that modernity has been transcended, but that it has been overcome, and it is not only claimed that the Enlightenment has been fortunately reduced to its true proportion as an historical episode in an absolute and irrevocable past, but that we are now living in conditions that render largely invalid the intellectual equipment ascribed to the Enlightenment. This is not least so because of the preposterous claim that the Enlightenement is the progenitor of all the acts of European barbarity in the twentieth century -- it will emerge later that these acts, associated with Fascism (associated in the general mind with Germany; commentators normally forget the Balkans, Vietnam, Palestine, and the thermonuclear attacks against Japan) were performed under the ideological signature of anti-Enlightenment doctrines. Finally, it is suggested that, instead of studying cultures -- ours and those of others -- in terms of universal ethnographic, sociological, and historical concepts, we are to yield to a notion of individuality so irreducible that the multiplicity of historical masses is conceived in terms of "incommensurability". Thus post-objectivism, post-rationalism, post-historism, post-metaphysical anti-foundationism, are taken far too readily to yield positions antithetical to objectivism, to rationalism, to historism, and to foundationism, and all of these are postulated as antitheses of an entity known as modernism. In this respect, we are told of the need to decenter structural interpretations of cultures in favour of interpretations in phenomenological terms such as "meaning"; we are urged to look at cultures as trans-historical masses in which change is inessential and continuity constitutive, and we are enjoined to look at these cultures not as structured historical units subject to the changes and mutations that occur in all histories, but as absolute subjects that found history and constitute its massive and glacial presence in an enormous movement of self-reference, of irreducibility, of essential otherness to all that is not in essence its own.

I wish to claim an historical corrective to these stances and to speak against culturalism by contesting the strongly foundationalist premises on which it stands, just as the notion of an end of history is contested, among other things, by indicating its firm enracination in classical philosophies of history[18] -- although one must bear in mind the cautionary note concerning the cultural analysis of new forms struck by Raymond Williams in the statement that it is extremely difficult to determine "whether these are new forms of the dominant or are genuinely emergent" in view of the relation between innovation and reproduction[19]. What can be unambiguously stated, is that culturalism as a mood of historical ans social analysis was at its inception, in Germany, intimately connected to the recession of liberalism and the reinforcement of conservatism after the revolutionary waves of the early nineteenth century [20]; it is also clear that culturalist analysis has almost invariably been associated with social conservatism and reaction, anti-colonialism notwithstanding. The notion of culture on which culturalist claims stand is, I submit, firmly grounded in an organismic metaphysics[21], in which historical masses are regarded as entities defined by analogy to biological systems, and in which culture is conceived in terms of a bacteriological model. This vitalistic figure, whose metaphorical rhetoric founds the discourse of culturalism, is of course one which has always been associated with romantic notions of history, society, and polity, and these in turn have always been associated with right-wing political movements in Europe and with retrograde anti-modernism subsisting within the interstices of subaltern nationalisms and within populism[22] (which, I should like to emphasize, given a common misconception, is distinct from being popular: populism is a mode of claiming full representativity of a people --which could correspond to a nation, but does not necessarily conceive the people as a nation-- and of suturing what is claimed to be a disjunction between a people and a state, of bringing state and people into full correspondence, on the assumption that the agency claiming this representative character does so by embodying the essence and inner being of this people: some Russian populists at the end of the 19th century decided the Volksgeist to be iconically realized in the *obshchina*, Hindu and Muslim fundamentalist populism regards this to reside in certain tokens of religious and social observance. In all cases, stress is laid on the exceptionalist nature of a given people which is accounted for by a certain golden age which preceded the fetishization of modernity, capitalism, and reason, and this primitivism is regarded as an atopia to be reappropriated within the social and political programme of populism[23]). The fact that these philosophies of history, society, and politics do not figure prominently in standard textbooks of these subjects seems to stem from an organized collective amnesia, a rewriting of cultural history consequent upon the Second World War, and to some extent account for the prevalent ignorance about the intellectual roots of the present anti-Enlightenment positions.

Yet this ignorance is by no means absolute, most particularly in the field of literary theory which, in some quarters, celebrates its irrationalist roots in Romanticism and in American Pragmatism[24]. The all-important nihilistic epistemology resulting from these positions is also informed by a profound seam of scepticism, most particularly cultivated in the Catholic anti-positivist polemic of the nineteenth century[25]. The "persistence of certain rhetorics of disbelief"[26], including, as we shall presently see, the elision of subject-object boundaries and thre ascendancy of language-game theories, is of course not a direct replication of Romantic discourses, but neither is it independent of them.

In social and political theory -- our main concern here --these Romantic notions had been most fully developed in counterposition to the politics fostered by the Enlightenment. In Germany France, and England, these were associated with figures such as Herder, Bonald, Gobineau, Renan, Le Bon, Spengler, Burke, Coleridge and others, and formulated in terms both of culture-nation and of race. Thus Burke, for instance, spoke of the "method of nature", of an historical mass as a "permanent body composed of transitory parts"[27], in order to indicate an instinctivist of the historical mass conceived as a nature. The far more systematic formulations of Herder fully deployed the organismic metaphor and conceived historical masses to be powered by Kräfte, vital genetic forceseffected by but not determined by ecological and other factors. Further, and within the same medieval conception, he conceived the constitution of an historical mass -- the nation -- to consist of a permanent condition of perfection, an entelechy, whose maintenance by internal vital powers is the condition for historicalk stability, indeed for abiding historicity[28]. Nations or cultures are therefore utterly and irreducibly individual, according to a naturalistic morphology of history described, with reference to the roughly congruent conception of Spengler as "a deliberate and painstaking attempt to extrude from history everything that makes it historical"[29]. History therefore becomes a vast space for the classification and tabulation of ethnological individualities in a manner that joined together Romantic philosophies of history with nineteenth century anthropology[30].

The same tropes and figures thus employed to theorize race are the ones that have, since the end of the Second World War, become employed in the theorization and celebration of cultural diversiy, a development to which British cultural anthropology made a decisive contribution[31]. Such were and still are its high-cultural expressions. But it must also be said that these are closely tied to demotic and even primitive images of *Gemeinschaftlichkeit,* and the tribal idiom employed in demotic conversation, and in the demotic modes of the modern media, endow the luxuriance of high-cultural culturalism with immediate perceptive inflexions which telescope the social perceptive field and produce immediate tokens of difference and of antipathy (blacks, Muslims, Algerians, Ausländer, and so forth) -- even of direct action against the objects of antipathy as in organized social and political movements which mobilize on principles of culturalism conjugated with a variety of other matters: such as the new Right in Europe and Serbian nationalism, Jewish fundamentalism (which construes culture in direct correlation with race and religion), Hindu communalism (which construes it in direct relation with religion and its social, caste correlate), and cognate phenomena.

Be that as it may, the fact remains that the rhetoric culturalism, a rhetoric of identity which views difference as antithesis, can only subsists naturally in the context of a revivalism. So also post-modernism: I have tried to indicate that the profound ambiguity of post-modernism resides not only in the play of virtuality against reality, in such a way that posteriority of post-modernism inscribed in its name is postulated as absolutely novel, whereas it in fact it is grounded in particularistic, vitalist, and irrationalist body of notions traditionally associated with right-wing politics, although not all strands of post-modernism partake politically of organismic nationalist mythologies[32] .It resides also in a naive body of reference to pasts of which it partakes liberally, for it presents itself, in the field of social observation and commentary as distinct from literature, as the repository of things **recovered.** There is at work a sort of conceptual irredentism, which claims to be recovering matters occluded by the falsity of actual history, the history of modernity, of the Enlightenment, and of the world. Matters such as identity, indeterminacy, subjectivity, authenticity, asserted in the spirit of *revanchisme,* often by former Marxists settling accounts with an erstwhile philosophical consciousness. It is, finally, this same revanchisme which some third-world intellectuals are reclaiming as a sort of saviour, a continuation of nationalism by other means; hence the positive assessment of exclusivist social retrogression, under the title of 'recovering inwardness', that is expressed in the propensity of subaltern nationalisms to defer questions of soial progress, most particularly the emancipation of women, to the realm of inwardness, as a token negotiable in the process of resistance to colonialism, a sort of primal virtue preserved[33]. What is normally absent from this celebration of primal innocence is the fact that its mode of expression and articulation is so much part of modernity.

I shall turn now to what I claim to be an objective complicity between the three sides that sustain the culturalist rhetoric, Western heterophobia, post-modernist heterophilia, and xenophobic, retrograde nationalisms and para-nationalisms in Eastern Europe and countries of the South, and in these I include political Islamism and Hindu communalism. This is an objective complicity between exotism and the rhetoric of identity and authenticity. By objective complicity I refer not only to their contemporaneity, their intersection at a given point in time, but also to a conceptual concordance, which I shall take up forthwith, and to a global political and structural complementarity, which will be taken up later.

There are a number of salient features that need to be brought up as essential, constitutive structural elements in this discourse of culturalism. It is certainly true that progressivist conceptions of history and of society were insensitive to the material force, indeed, the ontological weight of matters cultural and national, in the broad sense, matters "impervious to theoretical debunking"[34]. It is also the case that anthropological research, among other fields for the production of knowledge, is entangled in a web of textual, poetical, and conceptual conventions which re-formulate 'others' along a manner which is 'inadequate' to their reality[35]. What anthropological self-reflection has not taken on board is the degree to which its objects of study, who may be savage but are certainly not stupid, play to the anthropological gellery. But all this this is a far cry from deriving what is in effect a nihilistic ontology from the impossibility of absolute knowledge, and from the assumption that knowledge of others is thus rendered radically questionable and confined to a self-expressive intuitionism, indeed, a solipsism, and the use of molluscar notions such as 'cultural ontologies'[36].

We find in the assumptions of epistemological relativistic life-worlds of the spirit, first of all, an epistemological element deriving from the notion of *Verstehen* [37] which founded, first of all, certain elements of biblical criticism with Schleiermacher in the early part of the nineteenth century, then made its way through the sociologistic irrationalism of Dilthey, on to its diffusion, through various phenomenological and ethnographic procedures and pathways, into the mainstream of post-modernism, some of which were indicated in preceding paragraphs. This epistemological elements propounds implicitly a social version of the innate ideas concept, regards knowledge to be bounded absolutely by the immediate social and conjunctural conditions of its emergence, and postulates a certain correspondence, therefore, between thought and its social object, in such a way that being and knowing become, in principle, indistinct [38]. This implicit conception is constitutive of all rigorous privileging of the "subject-position", of all ethnographies that pretend to allow natives to speak for themselves, of all fetishizations of 'incommensurability' and positive mystification of 'others'. The indistinctness of knowledge here is such that Reason, in this Lebensphilosophie, becomes construed as life, which is at once subject and object of knowledge, such that "history is life realized, and life is potential history"[39]. Reason thus becomes multiple, and knowledge of self which constitutes self-expression -- of the social self, the historical self, or whatever other definition of subjective identity is preferred -- is reduced to a solipsism. Trans-cultural communication becomes problematized as one requiring an act of **sympathy** which alone, according to this conception, allows access to a meaning which is, ultimately and in principle, inaccessible, it being the sense apprehended by an irreducible subject. And of course, such is only to be expected when using the organismic, vitalist metaphor of organic self-possession and self-enclosure.

When highly theorized, this stance is expressed in terms of the notion of incommensurability, which I regard as a highly inappropriate surveyors' metaphor. I also consider the linguistic modelling of this question current in Anglo-Saxon philosophy (and its extensions beyond Anglo-Saxon domains) inappropriate, for languages are untranslatable only if they are entirely private, in which case their description as languages will no longer be apposite. Communication, between individuals as between collectivities, takes place through the medium of vocabularies, of regional vocabularies -- social, historical, philosophical, erotic, ceremonial, and so forth. Thus political Islamism is perfectly expressible in French and entirely accessible in the medium of Danish, and I believe we should be extremely wary of the relativistic temptation consequent upon the mystification of otherness: cross-cultural knowledge does not have conditions distinct from the conditions of knowledge in general and, further, a cross-cultural epistemology is not possible epistemologically, except in so far as it stands on the perception of othernesses both radical and virtual, and I will claim that this renders it undesirable. For the consequence and main instrument of cross-cultural epistemology is classificatory in quite a primitive sense, as it consists in the main of tabulating discrete differences and of classifying ethnogpraphic detail into that emanating from the self-identical Ego, and that arising out of an other, into sheer alterity, in terms of a language of the self taken as the exclusive metalanguage of cultural typology[40] whose elements are generically closed because they are constituted on the assumption of self-referential selves and self-referential others. The result of this is an antithetical discourse, whose elements in the description of others is constituted by inverting notions of the self : this is what constitutes the analytics of orientalist discourse, for instance[41]. Ultimately, this position arises from a moral relativism, and transcribes this into a cognitive relativism into which its holders argue themselves: an aesthetic problem which is not theoretical and can have no theoretical protocol, but one which is sustained by the will to an identitary rhetoric[42]. This position yields not only a relativism, but a correlative exceptionalism, which regards others as being beyond the remit of the normal procedures and constraints of human histories, societies, polities, and cultures. In the final analysis, we have in the discourse of culturalist individuality a radical scepticism, as we have indicated above, effecting areas stretching from natural science (Feyerabend, for instance) to history, a scepticism unthinkable without the Ro,mantic heritage, but equally disenchanted with objective knowledge because it is not absolute, as are certain strands of scepticism disenchanted with natural science because it is probabil;istic, given to complexity and other forms of non-linearity, and does not have the occult determinism and certainty and magic. The question has been asked in ethnography, whether

Culturalism, Grand Narrative of Capitalism Exultant 91

with the disappearance of the possibility of 'true' interpretations the possibility of musinterpretation las also vanished, and whether with the disappearance of notions of certitude the notion of error has also vanished[43]. The same question is equally legitimately asked today in other fields of human and social sciences.

I turn from the epistemological constituent of identities and cultures to their ontological constituent, to the description of the substances and essences which constitute cultures, identities, selves, subjects. I have already discussed this matter in describing vitalism and organism, which form the grounds of this discourse on identity, subjectivity, and culture. The constituent notion[44] of this substance, as was indicated briefly above, is that of an historical subject which is at once self-sufficient and self-evident, which is self-identical over time, whose rhythm and tempo are prescribed by internal organismic mechanisms of system maintenance and essential continuity. History is therefore the domain of the merely contingent, the inessential, and all change that is perceptible and which might appear consequential is not relegated to any proper notion of historicity, but is conjugated with the neo-Platonic metaphysical notion of materiality as privation. Time becomes the material element, whereas the essence -- often confused with the textual or historico-mythological as in the discourse of religious and national fundamentalism -- becomes the spiritual, whose diminution can never result from the inside, but is ever caused by heteronomous interference. Thus -- to think along in organismic metaphors -- we have historical masses construed as individual states or permanent conditions of phylogeny. They are conceived as supra-historical masses which speak in the tones of a chronophagous discourse. Thus societies and nations rise and fall, but do not change in any serious sense, and the wheel of fortune is animated, quite literally, by internal, intransitive, self-subsistent preumatic impulses (Herder's *Kräfte*) and which together can be described by the term *Volksgeist* . The term is wonderfully apposite, certainly, but unconvincing, not only on account of ahistorical vitalism replete with associations with medieval notions of somatic composites sustained by the *anima* which is said to make possible the realization of the very materiality of an historical mass, but also with regard to the psychologistic metaphor of the individual according to which the collective self is construed as individual subject[45]: if I am allowed to think analogically, I might apply to this notion the recent considerations of a psychoanalyst regarding the notion of personal identity [46], and I would maintain that the unconscious -- the analogon for structured and mutable historicity -- ruins the notion of an unified ego and by consequence the very notion of an individual, for the ego is not a subject and can only be analytically defined in relation to its conditions. So also with collective identities: not only do these have no exclusive, absolutely and fully self-reflexive psyches, but such psyches, even if we admit them hypothetically, do not constitute subjects. This is not to exclude altogether, however, forms of behavioural coherence that might episodically display traditionalist regression and similar phenomena[47], or that might have a wider anthropological salience[48]. What needs emphasis is that this social-psychological theme is often taken for self-evident, when in fact it requires clarification and proper elaboration.

As for the tongue with which the suprahistorical subject of Romanticism speaks, it is none other than the rhetoric of authenticity: a rhetoric structured in antithesis, a classificatory topos, which is in reality not the unmediated voice of the nature of a particular history or culture, but rather the recherché self-presentation of this or that social force seeking hegemony; authenticity is highly inauthentic and presents, as described by Adorno in another context, a *für-andere* masquerading as an *an-sich*. [49]. And we can clearly see how this works when we look at the representations of authenticity in countries of the South[50], where we witness the wholesale invention of vestimentary, ethical, and intellectual traditions amongst Islamist ideologues, or the deification of the Buddha in Sinhala nationalism, or again the invention of Hinduism and, subsequently, what has been termed the Semitization of Hinduism in the use of the God Ram by the Hindu Right. In all cases, we witness an effervescent culture of classicization and of folklorization which, together, produce tangible tokens, or icons, of authenticity, read history through them, and posit their realization as the political programme to establish a utopian order, a Shangri-La where everyone is authentic, where all is essence fulfilled, and where everyone smiles in contentment.

Fundamental to this conception of culture is an implicit assumption of homegeneity. The Other has a Geist, a soul, a genius, a totalizing notion whose appellation as 'culture' was inaugurated by Tyler, but which has also taken various other names, such as 'pattern', value, meaning[51], the latter one of the least meaningful notions in the cultural sciences. With the transitions from notions of society to those of representation, from evolutionism to incommensurability, sight was lost of a number of fundamental facts concerning social reality. Not the least of these facts is that knowledge and representation, even in small-scale societies, is distributed and controlled, that cultures are webs of mystification no less than of signification, and that local diversity renders questionable notions of 'shared meaning', a notion which is also compromised by the surface pragmatism of daily life. Facts such as these invite the inversion of the Geertzean thesis that ideology be a cultural system into the assertion that cultural systems be ideologies[52]. The notion of culture as an unmodifiable system to which novelties are impurities and in which all disturbances lead to crises -- of 'identity' -- has no justification in social reality[53]. Often construed partly as a result of linguistic and other technical forms of incompetence on the part of even some of the most authoritative social scientists[54], this notion of culture makes certain unreflected assumptions about autochtonous utterances on tradition, including assumptions about a certain primacy given to discursivity. This is also grounded in an implicit causal hypothesis that utterances and actions arise from and are held together by some underlying intellectual project, so that the conservation of 'traditions' is regarded as an observed property of events rather than "a hypothesis put forward [by the anthropologist -- and by extension, the cultural scientist and historian -- no less than by those who are taken for authentic speakers] in order to account for their actual repetition"[55].

I need not dwell very much on this authentic correlate of exoticism, and I need only make a few comments. The first is that the discourses of authenticity in the South are utterly heteronomous in origin, contrary to what is claimed, and equally autonomous. By this I mean that the tropes and notions of political and social thought available today form a universal repertoire which is inescapable, a repertoire which, though of Western origin, has in the last century and a half become a universal patrimony which constitutes the limits beyond which poltical and social thought is inconceivable, except very marginally. This was the result of a universal acculturation which has filtered through modern state structures, forms of discourse and communication, educational and legal systems, terms of political life, and much more, which have become globalized, and have become native not only to their points of origin, but worldwide. This repertoire has been described by another author in a slightly more restricted context as "modular"[56].

As against this, the discourse of authenticity reaches back into a re-worked and re-elaborated past by means of a deliberate primitivism and nativism. This primitivism consists of two distinct elements, the one symbolic and specific to each group (like Sanskritism, the notion of the Shari`a, or the medieval insignia, coiffure, and songs of Serbian nationalists), the other universal, being the form of social and political thought which is bounded by the universally and, for all practical purposes, uniquely available modules of social and political thought, of which organismic culturalism is one form, freely available, and liberally used. No authentic social science or social philosophy is therefore possible, not only because its formal and institutional elements are no longer historically available, but also because what it implies is the collapse of knowledge into being in the monotony of solipsism and of sheer self-reference, the incommunicative perpetual nirvana of an Aristotelian god. All that actually exists of the latter is a clamorous celebration of some sentiment of transcendental narcissism, in a language, nevertheless, almost exclusively heteronomous.

It goes without saying that the language of primitivism subtends a project of cultural hegemony and of primitivist social engineering, and substantive examples of this can be multiplied virtually at will. Desirous of creating conditions of novel and anti-modernist (but only ambiguously so) conditions of social, cultural, and intellectual life, fascistic political groups in the South propound a culturalism which is consonant with their political formation and renewed elite formation, and which is simultaneously consonant with the international information system as it has come to be in the last two decades: an information system characterized by the elements of orality[57], encouraged by visible bytes that classify, typify, and daily reproduce tokens of exotism, which, as if by conveyance, are daily delivered to the countries of origin of this exotism, cultivating a post-modernist taste for the pre-modern, buttressing the politico-culturalist advocacy of right-wing groups and their claims for authenticity, exceptionalism, self-enclosure. This is acted out not only on a global scale, but equally on a local scale, in which diversity of an ethnic and religious nature within western countries is similarly construed.

The global political context of this is not a mystery. It is correlative with the redifinition of relations between what have become to be known as North and South, i.e. of rich and poor, in terms of distanciation and of the confirmation of the failure of text-book developmental projects, and with the collapse of the post Worl War II Keynesean consensus. Correlative with this is a local analogue within western countries of an increasing tendency towards ghettoization buttressed by policies of ethnic confinement and sustained by an ethnic stratification of labour, externally defined by the anti-immigration rhetoric of natural sympathies, a rhetoric with a recent past in the rhetoric of anti-terrorism which had pride of place during the Reagan years.

I have throughout stressed the **objective** complicity between libertarian post-modernism and *tiers-mondisme* in the West, and the delivery in the name of a culture become nature, of peoples of the South to regimes (such as those based upon Islamism) of social retrogression, and of Southern peoples in the North to archaic leaderships, not to speak of the fatalistic naturalization of what we might call Balkanism, exemplified in the conflicts in Bosnia and Rwanda, previously experienced in the Lebanese civil war, and all of which implicate international and local forces in the manufacture of minorities and of ethnic groups. In certain political scenarios, this vision devolves to a bellicose search for enemies now that Communism is no longer so regarded, and not unnaturally, to nightmare visions, sedimented by the persistence of archaism, that conjure up renewed images of the Saracenic threat and the Yellow Menace: hence the call to arms by a hitherto reputable US academic in the face of the "Islamic-Confusian" threat, a threat to Western civilization by other civilizations defined entirely in culturalist terms[58]. I have proposed that the very notions of culturalism and the unreflected theme of cross-cultural conversations should be thoroughly questioned, and I have put forward the view that the politics of culturalist tolerance is by necessity, given the contexts I have taken up, correlative with a discourse on congenital incapacities of Others--incapacity for modernism, for democracy and so forth. If we are capable of understanding the discourses of madness, of the unconscious, of the ancient past, of ethnographic objects, and if we can interpret them consequentially, then surely we can understand "other cultures" without needing to confine them to exotism and, thus constituted, take them for partners in 'conversation'. In order to do this, we need to look at them with the realities of history in view, if we are to go beyond protocols of politely listening and talking at cross-purposes, with due respect for the right of others to be impermeable to the understanding and abhorrent to the sensibility. Conversation should cease to be a form of cross-cultural etiquette, if it is to preserve any of the liberating potential declared in the working paper for this symposium. Otherwise, by turning culturalist, it will leave the setting of terms to the most retrograde and violent forces of livid hatred both in Europe and beyond, and concede to them the claim that they represent all of us. Even authors of pulp fiction are aware that their writings are 'neologic spasms" preceding any concept whatever, slick and hollow "awaiting received meaning"[59]. Intellectuals from the Third World in the West have a particular responsibility there, and they need to eschew the temptation of exoticist posturing, or of the postures of ambiguity, hybridity, and other ways of playing lofty circus. Hybridity, by pretending to be the mix of unmixables, merely confirms the presumption of purity of the two termini it equally claims, post-modernity and pre-modernity, exotism and culturalism. This self-same hybridity, by claiming to be both termini and neither, merely presumes implication in the purity of both. Yet we have seen both to be radically impure, both complicit with each other inextricably; short of the purity of the angels, the only purity we can hope for in this situation of virtuality and of dissimulation, resides in the quality of the critical gaze.

---

1   An earlier version of this intervention was prepared for a conference convened under the title of "Cross-Cultural Conversations". It is also published as chapter 1 in the second edition of the author's *Islams and Modernities*, London, Verso, 1996

2   For instance, Jürgen Habermas, 'Wahrheit und Wahrhaftigkeit', in *Die Zeit*, 8 December, 1995, pp 59-60, and particularly p 60, col 4

3   Ernest Gellner, *Reason and Culture*, Oxford, 1988, pp 14-15. It is noteworthy that this same author abandons his cautionary attitude in his well-known claims concerning what he terms Muslim societies

4   One could cite among the many illustrations of this the statement by the author of what purports to be a history of Muslim societies, that in his book, he will emphasize culture and neglect the economy, as the former, he asserted, was the locus of historical individuation: yet it may be asked why, of all the possible loci, in terms of concept as of temporal and geographical scale, and for the circumscription of an historical individuality, culture is made to overdetemine all the other markers of individuation, and result in an history which is so radically defective when so detached from its structural bearings (I. M. Lapidus, *A History of Islamic Societies*, Cambridge, 1988, p xxiii)

5   On these mattres, one could still most profitably consult Maurice Godelier, *Perspectives in Marxist Anthropology*, tr. Robert Brain, Cambridge, 1977, parts 1, 2, and 4. One index of the sudden rise of culturalism is the fact that a fairly standard book on sociological theory published less than three decades ago has no entry for 'culture' in its indes, and does not include culture as a major theme, which would be unthinkable today, not least because most publishers would not have it (Robert A. Nisbet, *The Sociological Tradition*, London, 1967)

6   Pierre-André Taguieff, *La force du préjugé. Essai sur le racisme et ses doubles,* Paris, 1987, passim

7   The working paper of the symposium for which this paper was prepared

8   Partha Chatterjee, *The Nation and its Fragments. Colonial and Postcolonial Histories* , Princeton, 1993, p. xi
9   Umberto Eco, *Travels in Hyperreality* , tr. W. Weaver, London, 1987, p. 129
10 Marshall Sahlins, *How 'Natives" Think, about Captain Cook, For Example*, Chicago and London, 1995, pp13-14, 180
11 See especially Aijaz Ahmad, *In Theory*, London, 1992, ch 2 and pp 204 ff.
12 Colette Guillaumin, *L'idéologie raciste. Genèse et langage actuelle* , Paris and the Hague, 1972, pp. 2, 13; Taguieff, *La force du préjugé* , pp. 19 ff.
13 For the case of Britain, see Martin Barker, *The New Racism: Conservatives and the Ideology of the Tribe*, London, 1984, pp. 14 ff., 97, & ch. 3 and 4; Frank Reeves, *British Racial Discourse. A Study of British Political Discourse about Race and Race-Related Matters* , Cambridge, 1983, passim
14 See Erich Harth, *Dawn of a Millennium. Beyond Evolution and Culture*, London, 1990, pp. 66 ff.
15 See most pertinently, Pierre Bourdieu, *L'Ontologie politique de Martin Heidegger*, Paris, 1988, and Richard Herzinger, 'Werden wir alle Jünger? Über die Renaissance konservativer Modernekritik und die post-postmoderne Sehnsucht nach der organischen Moderne', in *Kursbuch 122: Die Zukunft der Moderne*, December, 1995, pp 93-118
16 For the vast complexity of the theme in the 19th and 20th centuries, the reader is referred to Lutz Niethammer, *Posthistoire. Has History come to an End?* , tr. Patrick Camiller, London, 1994, where the demotic notions of the end of history theme, exemplified by Francis Fukuyama's *The End of History and the Last Man* (1992) , is aptly described as "a kind of bandwagon operetta" (p. 91, n. 12)
17 On post-modernism and the Gulf war, see Christopher Norris, *Uncritical Theory. Postmodernism, Intellectuals, and the Gulf War* , London , 1992
18 Niethammer, *Posthistoire,* pp. 135 ff.
19 Raymond Williams, *Culture,* London, 1981, p. 205
20 Woodruff D. Smith, *Politics and the Science of Culture in Germany, 1840-1920*, New York, 1991
21 On the notions and metaphors of organism in European thought of the 19th and 20th centuries, the reader is referred to the excellent discussion in Judith E. Schlanger, *Les métaphores de l'organisme* , Paris, 1971
22 For the recent statements of these positions, see Albert Hirschman, *The Rhetoric of Reaction*, Cambridge, Mass., 1991
23 See, among others, D. MacRae, "Populism as an Ideology", in *Populism. Its Meaning and National Characteristics* , ed. E. Gellner and G. Ionescu, London, 1969, esp. pp. 155-8; A. Walicki, *The Controversy over Capitalism,* Oxford, 1969, pp. 3, 35, 64, and ch. 1, passim.; V.I. Lenin, *Complete Works,* Moscow, 1963, vol. 2, pp. 513-7. For the populist character of political islamism, see other chapters in this volume, and Ervand Abrahamian, *Khomeinism*, London, 1993.
24 See particularly Kathleen Wheeler, *Romanticism, Pragmatism, and Deconstruction*, Oxford, 1993. For less enthusiastic accounts, see David Simpson, *Romanticism, Nationalism,*

and the Revolt against Theory, Chicago and London, 1993, and Terry Eagleton, *The Ideology of the Aesthetic*, Oxford, 1990, ch. 5 and 6

25   For instance, Louis Foucher, *La philosophie catholique en France au xixè siècle avant la renaissance thomiste et dans son rapport avec elle, 1880-1880*, Paris, 1955, pp 23-5, 36-8, 258; Robert L. Palmer, *Catholics and Unbelievers in Eighteenth-Century France*, Princeton, 1939, pp 106-112; D. G. Charlton, *Secular Religions in France, 1815-1870*, London, 1963, pp. 200-211. For a more restricted recognition, see Christopher Norris, 'Truth, Science, and the Growth of Knowledge', in *New Left Review*, 210 (1995), pp 105-123. For the same origins for nineteenth and twentieth century Arab Muslim anti-scientism, see Aziz Al-Azmeh, *Al-`Ilmaniyya [Secularism]*, Beirut, 1992, pp 173-5

26   Simpson, *Romanticism*, pp 3-4

27   Edmund Burke, *Reflections on the Revolution in France*, ed. Conor Cruise O'Brien, Harmondswoth, 1969, p 120, and cf. Simpson, *Romanticism*, pp 57-8

28   Johann Gottfried von Herder, *Reflections on the Philosophy of the History of Mankind*, abridged by F.E. Manuel, Chicago and London, 1968, pp 96-7, and *J.G. Herder on Social and Political Culture*, ed. and tr. F.M. Barnard, Cambridge, 1969, pp 272 ff., 291 ff. Cf. R. G. Collingwood, *The Idea of History*, Oxford, 1946, p 92

29   Collingwood, *The Idea of History*, p 182

30   Johannes Fabian, *Time and the Other. How Anthropology makes its Object*, New York, 1983, particularly pp. 15-16, 19

31   For the anatomy of these notions and the ease of transition between racism and culturalism, the reader is referred to Guillaumin, *L'idéologie raciste*, ch. 1, Tzvetan Todorov, *On Human Diversity: Nationalism, Racism, and Exoticism in French Thought*, tr. C. Porter, Cambridge, Mass., 1993, pp. 156-7, 219 ff., and ch. 2 and 3, passim, and Claude Lévi-Strauss, *A View from afar*, tr. J. Neugroschel and P. Hoss, Harmondsworth, 1987, p. 26

32   See Simpson, *Romanticism*, pp. 182-3

33   On the anti-modernism of subaltern nationalisms, illustrated by a particular historical experience (Bengal), see Chatterjee, *The Nation and its Fragments*, p. 75 and ch. 1 & 6, passim

34   See the excellent discussion of the attitudes of Hegel and Marx to Romanticism by Gopal Balakrishnan, 'The National Imagination', in *New Left Review*, 211 (1995), pp 59-61

35   For some important instances of anthropological self-reflection, see James Clifford and George E. Marcus (eds.), *Writing Culture. The Poetics and Politics of Ethnography*, Berkeley and Los Angeles, 1986

36   Witness, for instance, the celebration of epistemological nihilism by Wheeler, *Romanticism*, pp 244-5 and "Conclusion", passim, and Sahlins, *How "Natives" Think*, pp 157 ff., 170, and passim

37   The reader is referred, among others, to the account of Stepan Odouev, *Par les sentiers de Zarathoustra. Influence de la penseé de Nietzsche sur la philosophie bourgeoise allemande*, tr. Catherine Emery, Moscow, 1980

38   See my account of the epistemology of the 'Islamization of knowledge' theme, in 'Al-Lâ`aqlâniyya fi'l-fikr al-`arabî al-hadîth wa'l-mu`âsir' [Irrationalism in Modern Arab Thought], in *Abwâb*, 4 (1995), pp 22-35

39 Odouev, *Par les sentiers de Zarathoustra* , p. 142
40 J. M. Lotman, "On the Metalanguage of a Typological Description of Culture", in *Semiotica* , 14/2 (1975), pp. 97 ff.
41 Abdallah Laroui, "The Arabs and Social Anthropology", in idem., *The Crisis of the Arab Intellectual* , Berkeley and Los Angeles, 1976, pp. 44 ff., Aziz Al-Azmeh, "Islamic Studies and the Western Imagination", in this volume; idem, "Ifsâh al-istishrâq [The Articulation of Orientalism] in idem, *Al-Turâth bay n as-Sultân wat-Târîkh [*"Heritage ":Power and History]*, Beirut and Casablanca , 1990 pp. 61 ff . For consideration of similar attitudes and constructions in a reverse sense, see François Hartog, *Le Miroir d'Hérodote: essai sur la représentation de l'autre,* Paris, 1980, and Aziz Al-Azmeh, "Barbarians in Arab Eyes", in *Past and Present ,* 134 (February, 1992), pp. 3-18
42 The reader is referred to the robust account of I. C. Jarvie, *Rationality and Relativism. In Search of a Philosophy and History of Anthropology ,* London, 1984
43 Roger Keesing, 'The Anthropologist as Orientalist: Exotic Readings of Cultural Texts', unpublished paper read at the 12th International Congress of Anthropological and Ethnological Sciences, Zagreb, 1988, pp 1, 5
44 For what follows, see Aziz Al-Azmeh, "The Discourse of Cultural Authenticity: Islamist Revivalism and Enlightenment Universalism", in this volume
45 Marc Bloch long ago warned against this temptation in his review of Maurice Halbwachs' *Les cadres sociaux de la mémoire*: 'Mémoire collective, tradition, et coutume', in *Revue de Sythèse Historique*, XL (N. S., xiv), 1925, pp 73-83
46 André Green, "Atome de parenté et relations oedipiennes", in *L'Identité. Séminaire interdisciplinaire dirigé par Claude Lévi-Strauss* Paris, 1977, p. 82
47 For instance, Mario Erdheim, *Die Psychoanalyse und das Unbewusste in der Kultur*, Frankfurt, 1988, pp 237 ff., 258 ff.
48 For instance, Rene Girard, *Violence and the Sacred*, tr. P. Gregory, Baltimore and London, 1979
49 Theodor Adorno, *Prisms ,* tr. S. and S. Weber, London, 1967, pp. 152-5
50 For Islamism in the Arab world, Al-Azmeh, "Islamism and the Arabs", in this volume ; for India, Chatterjee, *Nationalism and its Fragments,* ch. 4 & 5 ; for cognate themes, see Eric Hobsbawm and Terence Ranger (eds.), *The Invention of Tradition ,* Cambridge, 1983
51 See the sober reflections of Paul Mercier, 'Anthropologie sociale et culturelle', in *Ethnologie générale*, ed. Jean Poirier, Paris 1968 (*Encyclopédie de la Pléiade*, xxiv), pp907-909, 915, 918-20
52 Roger Keesing, 'Anthropology as Interpretive Quest', in *Current Anthropology*, 28/2(1987), pp 161-3
53 For instance, Ayse Caglar, "The Prison House of Culture in Studies of Turks in Germany', Berlin, 1990 (Freie Universität Berlin, *Sozialanthropologische Arbeitspapiere*, Nr. 31), pp 6-9
54 For instance, the notion of *manna*, discussed by Keesing, 'The Anthropologist as Orientalist', pp 3 ff.
55 See most particularly the sinuous and rigorous considerations of Pascal Boyer, *Tradition as Truth and Communication: A Cognitive Description of Traditional Discourse*, Cambridge,

1990, pp. 2-4, 10, 32-7, 79-86, 118, and cf. Marc Augé, *Le sens des autres*, Paris, 1994, pp 28-9 and passim

56   Benedict Anderson, *Imagined Communities. Reflections of the Origin and Spread of Nationalism* , London, 1983

57   I refer to the catalogue of characteristics treated by Walter Ong, *Orality and Literacy. The Technologizing of the Word* , London and New York, 1982, pp. 37 ff. and passim

58   S. P. Huntington, "A Clash of Civilizations ?', in *Foreign Affairs*, 72 (1993), pp. 22 ff.

59   William Gibson, self-declared author of cyberpunk novels, quoted in Julian Stallabras, 'Empowering Technology. The Exploration of Cyberspace', in *New Left Review*, 211 (1995), p. 5

Don Ihde

Image Technologies and 'Pluriculture'

'Pluriculture' is a term which I wish to introduce here at a juncture between a certain contemporary form of cross culturality and the increase in imaging technologies in communications contexts.

The first, contemporary *image technologies*, although developed in 'first world' countries, now link virtually all countries and cultures. Image technologies are, of course, those technologies which produce 'images' by which we usually mean either *visual* or *audio-visual* presentations, and presentations which need not be verbal, but which in audio-visual forms include the verbal. In the most widespread and popular form, television and cinema are perhaps the most pervasive of the public image technologies. These, at least in communications contexts and in the purveying of cultural dimensions are the most commonly experienced such technologies. Therefore, they can also be the most taken-for-granted and hence often most overlooked with respect to impact and implication.

However, such popular media far from exhaust what is today a virtual explosion of image technologies: (1) In the sciences, image technologies have and are radically transforming the knowledge gathering process. Again, pointing to the most publicized and familiar, distance imaging, such as that used by satellite, astronomical, and space probing sciences are known to all of us. Today, it is possible to purchase high resolution Russian satellite photos which, while taken from several hundreds or even thousands of miles up, reveal details of topography, military installations, or city complexes which are astonishing (US, and even more detailed photography remains unavailable to the public.) One may also see with detail, Callisto, a moon of Jupiter, or, with the use of ' false color' imagery, ranging from infra-red to ultra violet, the seasonal changes of Antarctica via geosatellite surveys. Nor is all imagery distance or macro-visioned. Today we can image even atoms. We can also imitate the heat sensitive perceptual awareness of such animal life as vipers, with heat imagery, or use light enhancing imagery for night vision akin to a cat's or owl's, thus seeing where no "man (or woman) has never seen before."

(2) Medical image technologies are the second most familiar array of imaging devices. We may now examine interiors, without intrusive surgery, through a range of technologies running from sonograms, CAT scans, MRI imagery, and a whole array of enhanced versions of these, to show everything from the sex of a fetus to the micron thin slice of a brain section.

Imaging technologies bring close, or into the range of perceivability, not only surfaces (dear to and restricted to same in classical empiricist epistemology), but interiors, the distant, and the hidden. Everything becomes 'visible' or is made to become visible. I point to this range of imaging technologies, not only to illustrate the explosion of imaging, but to show that in the cultural realm, television and cinema while perhaps now dominant, may be not only added to, but superceded within imaginable contemporary trajectories. I shall later turn to some of these, including the current fascination with projected *virtual reality* and *hyperreality* technologies which today are on the horizon.

The second phenomenon, 'pluriculture,' which is a term I constructed in my TECHNOLOGY AND THE LIFEWORLD in 1990, is a term which describes a unique, late twentieth century form of cross culturality. By 'pluriculture,' I mean a type of cross culturality which is intimately (a) *technologically mediated*, and particularly by imaging technologies, (b) which amplifies the multiplicity of cultures beyond the limits of pre-twentieth century experience, and (c) which, through the very flexibility and pervasiveness of pluriculture, begins to show a distinctive shape in the late twentieth century.

Illustrations of the pluricultural are near at hand: (1) The evening news is one common exemplification. Before us, every evening, and particularly through the now globalized CNN, we *see* imaged what has happened in Bosnia, in Ruwanda, South Africa, perhaps something from India or China, a flood or earthquake in South America, and obviously, various countries in Europe and North America. In short, within the very short span of a fifteen minute broadcast, we glimpse probably more cultures, albeit reduced to fragments, than the most powerful Medieval Potentate ever experienced. (2) And, this multiculturality also pervades, again in a unique way, our own cultural textures. Every major international city is filled with cuisines from exotic lands; every fashion trend borrows from a multiplicity of ethnic styles; and all of this occurs within an ever more internetworked, international context. (3) And, every contemporary culture experiences in some way, changes which face it, and to which there is a range of reactions spanning the reactionary (in the revival of the various religious fundamentalisms) to the radical (particularly in youth cultures which adapt everything from punk to cyberpunk).

All of this is familiar to you. It is part of our contemporary experience, even if not first hand, at least in indirect form via our news media, or science documentaries, or popular magazines. But while I am starting from here, to gain perspective I need to add more depth and distance.

I. *A Brief History of the Cross Cultural*

Were one to arrange cultures on a continuum, at one end one would ideally find a *monoculture*, and at the other end a *pluriculture*. By monoculture, I mean a culture which would have to be relatively either quite isolated, or so rigorously stringent in its cultural form so as to totally resist infusions from any rubbing up against a neighboring culture. There have been near monocultures: for example, although humans arrived in Tasmania, perhaps as long ago as 50,000 years ago, there is a traceable period of roughly 10,000 years during which this culture was isolated from other humans.

One of the fascinating aspects of this monocultural isolation, according to Jared Diamond in "Ten Thousand Years of Solitude," is that this already technologically minimalist people, apparently became even more minimalist in cultural form. They abandoned or lost several technologies which were common to Tasmanians and Southern Australian Aboriginals, for example, they apparently gave up the spear thrower, and along with the tools which enable it, fishing as a major source of protein.

But the monocultural end of the continuum--and we all know this--has shrunk and shrunk in the last two centuries so that today it is extremely doubtful that we shall discover any new such peoples. Indeed, the very discipline of anthropology, which once needed some 'primitive culture' to do its dissertations, today is unemployed in that style of discipline, and has turned to (and transformed) such areas as 'science studies' (exemplified, for example, by Bruno Latour!)

The other end of the continuum is the *pluricultural*, which by contrast must therefore be the most saturated with a multiplicity of cultural forms. This is the contemporary form which I have been preliminarily describing, but again from which I will avert attention for the sake of distance and perspective. But I will note in passing that accompanying cultural maximalism, <u>there seems to be a parallel maximalism of technologies.</u> I shall return to this theme.

Short of maximalist pluriculture, is the taken-for-granted and thus virtually invisible *cross cultural heritage* which marks every so-called 'advanced' culture. My own country, obviously, begins with the multicultural. The indigineous peoples, themselves now known to have been on the American Continent for at least 20,000 years (I am definitively siding with the anthropologists who claim to have broken the previous 11-12,000 year Ice Age arrival theory), had a variety of cultures which included, for example, the Mississippean, with cities of size dating back to 1000 years ago. Were one to compare Copenhagen at the same time--it was first mentioned in 1043 as a fishing village, and only in 1167 was it to have a castle--one can appreciate the strangeness of our older visions. Yet this same time is one of the first historically documented Euro-American exchanges with Leif Ericson getting as far as Vinland in the same century. Then over four centuries later, there would be a more continuous contact, with Columbus, whose quincentennial we have recently observed.

We are going through a rather interesting re-evaluation of our own 'histories' these days, with a proliferation becoming Foucault's multiple *epistemes*. For were we to believe our history texts from my boyhood, one would have thought that we were primarily an English colony. Yet the Spanish colonized, explored, and developed cross cultural contacts in North America not only much more extensively, but fully a century earlier. But, in fact, the dominant minority--all of us are minorities--were *Germanic*, and what few remember from the texts is that German, as the tongue to become the national tongue, *lost by but one vote in the Continental Congress!* New England has a very different history than Florida or California, but the New England version has dominated our 'official history '--until now.

I contend, and in this context, that one of the dominant reasons we are seeing, and cannot help but see--a more multicultural history is because our *present* is so obviously pluricultural. We are no different than the early Renaissance painters who depicted Biblical scenes in the midst of architecture and clothing of the 14th and 15th centuries, in our depictions of a past now become explicitly and virulently multicultural.

Yet, in this new perspective, we have always been cross cultural in our ability to absorb. Ralph Linton, humorously, points out:

There can be no question about the average American's Americanism or his desire to preserve this precious heritage at all costs. Nevertheless, some insidious foreign ideas have already wormed their way into his civilization without his realizing what is going on. Thus dawn find the unsuspecting *patriot garbed in pajamas, a garment of East Indian origin; and lying in a bed built on a pattern which originated in either Persia or Asia Minor. He is muffled to the ears in un-American materials: cotton, first domesticated in India; linen, domesticated in the Near East; wool from an animal native to Asia Minor; or silk whose uses were first discovered by the Chinese. All these substances have been transformed into cloth by methods invented in Southwest Asia. If the weather is cold enough he may even be sleeping under an eiderdown quilt invented in Scandanavia. [Ralph Linton, "One Hundred Percent American," <u>Kinship Terminology and the American Kinship System.</u>]*

The same phenomena could be pointed out in Europe. In 1991, while giving a paper to the German Phenomenological Society on a multicultural theme, Klaus Held gave us a tour of Koln and some of its antiquities. There we saw the adaptation of the Moorish style of the 11th century, with the Moorish arch and the contrasting dark and light stonework columns, we noted that Persian carpets were regularly used in cathedrals, and as far back as Roman times there was a set of Jewish ritual baths to be found alongside the Roman buildings. The cross cultural is not new, but ancient, but we may be becoming more sensitive to its interweaving within our pasts due to its enhanced contemporary presence.

But if multiculturality is part of--even if sometimes forgotten or surpressed--the very warp and woof of 'our' culture, then is *pluriculturality*, a particularly technologically mediated multiculturality, all that different? I shall contend so, but only after we have examined the role of image technologies underway.

However deeply cross cultural strands lie within our histories, there have been more and less exchange within those histories. And there is one interesting connection between *technology and culture* which I want to forefront before turning to image technologies. *Periods of high intercultural exchange often give rise to bursts of technological innovation, or what I term 'technology blooms.'*

This phenomenon has become more and more evident to me in the study of the history of technology--which in Euro-American traditions sometimes is too tightly tied to, and blinded by our prejudices which relate to our pro-science biases. For example, in many engineering circles, there are two virtually standard views about technological innovations: (a) one, that it is primarily under wartime or military necessity that technological innovation arises, and (b) that most innovation comes about, particularly in recent times, in relation to science or theory advance.

That has not always--nor do I think even today--been or is the case. Rather, there is much evidence that cross cultural exchange plays a much larger role in innovation than is usually noted. 'Technology blooms,' I note, can often be located in precisely those junctures where cultures cross.

I further note that one of the reasons for innovative bursts, is to be found in the fact that what we might take as the 'same technology' in two different cultures, is often not the same technology at all. Rather, different cultures *embed* technologies differently, and when the artifact is transferred, both something more than, and less than, is transferred. Let us look at a few suggestive examples:

(1) Lynn White, Jr., perhaps one of the most suggestive mid-twentieth century historians of technology, has long argued that the particular penchant for power in the Latin West led to adaptations or 'transfers' from elsewhere which get used for power purposes in Europe. He notes that the windmill, which as early as the 9th century is being used to pump out the Lowlands, is an adaptation of the Indian prayer wheel which simply turned out prayers to the heavens. Contrarily, the mechanical clock, first invented in China, but abandoned, when re-introduced by the Jesuits in the 16th century, was not used primarily for time keeping at all, but for fashion purposes--part of the reason being that time keeping, whether in the calendar or the clock, in its essence belonged to the Emperor rather than the public. Time keeping was culturally embedded in a different way.

2) Yet, when cultures cross, not only are the different artifacts exchanged, but uses are added or transformed.

An example of this occurs in the Hellenic period, which was one of the richest cross cultural periods in the foundation of European culture. What today we call science, is in fact *technoscience*. It is a science which is embodied in *instruments* and in a kind of *engineering praxis*. That is not what the ancients did--they were much more speculative and deductive. It was the Alexandrians, mixtures of Greeks, Egypt, the Middle East, and other cultural groups, who began to embody science instrumentally. Science as empirical measure begins to occur then, as well as the first development of engineering from post-Aristotlean sources. Hydraulics, measurements of earth/moon and earth/sun distances using simple instrumentation, etc. began to proliferate in Alexandrian, not Athenian science.

I shall not further explore this more generalized technology/culture relation other than to remark that the embeddedness of technologies is always cultural. Now, however, it is time to narrow the focus to *image technologies*.

II. *A Brief History of Imaging*

As I turn to this second brief history, please note that while I use the term 'image' and 'imaging,' I am distinctly uncomfortable with it. For while 'image' has a very long history--in Plato it always plays a secondary or even tertiary role as a copy of a copy--its more recent roots remain tied to Modern, i.e., seventeenth century epistemologies. These epistemologies hold that what we see are 'images' and the image, in turn, belongs to a certain causal account of how one sees. Contrarily, *phenomenologically*, I am more interested in *what* one sees and that is not captured by the term, 'image.' For example, when I train a telescope on the Copernicus crater on the Moon, I see the crater, not an 'image,' albeit, I see the crater *mediated by* the technology of the telescope. The issue becomes more complex when one moves from such bodily-perceptual situations in real time to more distantiated mediations in *depictions* which I prefer since a *depiction* is a mode of presencing. Thus, when I look at an MRI scan, I am looking for some possible abnormality, and while in this case it is more obvious that I am looking at a *presentation* differently presented than in a direct perceptual look into the brain, I am nevertheless object-oriented. In spite of this, I accede to the current use of 'image' and 'imaging' for convenience sake.

In this brief history, I first take some account of imaging as a pre-modern practice of depiction as well. Drawings and paintings, for example, are an ancient as well as modern practice. And, they involve technologies, albeit simple ones: the drawer takes up a stylus, pen, or crayon and applies it to a surface, and similarly, the painter applies pigments through a set of brushes to a canvas or other surface. All of these are technologically constructed depictions or 'images.'

What is of special interest in this context, is that pre-modern depiction, which renders a perceivable (and for purposes here, non-verbal) gestalt, also tells us something about the cross cultural perceptions which occur between the face-to-face visibility of the *other*, and the re-presenting depiction. I shall revert in this history, at first, to some early cross cultural imaging relating to early European contacts with the Americas and of Asians with Europeans.

What I am about to trace, not only summarizes an increasing technologization of imagery--from simple drawings and paintings through photography, cinema, and on into virtual and hyper-reality technologies--but shows an interesting role for 'realism' which will be seen to have certain implications for pluriculturality.

<illustration # 1 >

THE FIRST PICTORIAL VERSION OF COLUMBUS' DISCOVERY OF AMERICA
This woodcut, executed in the year Columbus returned to Spain after his discovery of America, shows the three boats that made up the expedition. After a woodcut in "La lettera dellisole che ha trouato nuouamente il Re dispagan," Florence. 1493

Here, for example, is the very first pictoral representation of Columbus's discovery. Note in the details several correct and incorrect depictions:

* Columbus was supposed to have arrived in Asia, yet the 'Indians' portrayed do not look Oriental--but neither do they look like indigineous Americans.

* Note the long beards on some of the males. This was not the case with the Arawak or Caribs.

* Verbal reports indicate the peoples discovered were naked--here the drawing is partially correct, but modestly does 'Eve-like' clothe the females.

< illustration #2 >

Image Technologies and 'Pluriculture' 109

Here is a depiction of an encounter in Cuba by a somewhat more accomplished artist. Note, again:

* Several new practices are correctly noted--tobacco, one of the new plants and practices is being smoked in the form of a "Cuban cigar." And the practice of starting a fire by using friction is also depicted. Bows, backpacks, and nakedness again seem accurate.

* But physiognomy is inaccurate. These 'Indians' look like typical Renaissance anatomical persons, indistinguishable from Europeans.

Who are the *Others*? Even while what is taken as odd practice is noted, the personal distinctiveness of the other is missed, dissolved in a kind of sameness or generic being of depiction. Nor is this indistictness restricted to the period of the Columbian voyages or to Western eyes:

* I have seen Ice Age cave drawings in which the animals are super by drawn, accurate and realistic, while the hunters remain mere stick figures;

* Or, take the first Japanese depictions of Americans arriving in their harbors during the Perry intrustions:

< illustration #3 >

Commodore Matthew C. Perry as depicted in a Japanese print at the time of his visits to Japan in the 1850's.

Here one can see the Japanese artist doing a counterpart of precisely what we saw from the West. In the depiction of Perry, the clothing is accurate, but the person is now 'Asian' in appearance and does not look either Caucasian or Western. The same applies to this depiction, although skin color is now introduced as a variant.

<illustration #4>

We see, but we do not see.

What kind of failure is this? Is it a failure of how we see? or of our techniques of depiction? Or, is the standard of isomorphic realism itself something which is invented?

Image Technologies: Photography
I now want to leap much closer to the present, to, first, the nineteenth century and the invention of a new *imaging technology*, the photograph. But I cannot make this leap without transition. If I am to take a kind of

isomorphic realism as a variable, then one has to acknowledge that it does not burst upon the world without precedent in photographic technologies. Quite to the contrary, the realistic, or isomorphic depiction of individuals--for example in portraiture--well precedes photography. In a sense realist portraiture is invented in the Renaissance and proceeds apace in a search for realism all the way through the centuries following which include the Dutch painters of the eighteenth century, nineteenth century romantic realism, etc. all the way until the late 1830's when photography begins to be developed. Technology, the photo, does not invent isomorphic realism. But it does transform it.

Portraiture remained an elite process, limited to an aristocracy which could afford an artist who, in turn, could excercise the hours and days needed to accomplish an individual portrait. Painting by hand, through the long apprenticeship of both trained hand and trained eye, was a necessarily highly restrictive technique. It was one which had an interesting parallel in another global technology: writing.

The printing revolution is a revolution which we are all familiar with. Prior to moveable block printing [a technique, by the way, invented about a millenium ago by the Koreans, but separately and much later re-invented by Guttenberg], writing was analogous to the above mentioned tradition of portraiture. And, in another analogue, reading was largely restricted to an elite within the Church and University, those undergoing the long apprenticeships which now every schoolboy and girl undergo in the elementary schools of today. The various elements of the literacy revolution included moving from an esoteric language (Latin) to the vernacular, transforming educational praxis, but, above all entailing a quick and reproducible means of producing the medium needed--easily and quickly available printed materials (books, pamphlets, newspapers, etc.) It was this which the printing press made available, and the same happened just as instantly and revolutionarily with photography. Photography was a revolution in isomorphic realism--but it was simultaneously a revolution in instant dissemination.

The Daguerreotype was invented in 1839 and had such an instant success that (a) there were runs on optical shops for lenses in order to build cameras, (b) articles about and from painters turned hysterical since they now seemed to become obsolete, and (c) a proliferation of photographs thoughout the Western world--photography was an instant, popular cultural success. (We are probably too far from similar effects of the print revolution--I wonder, for example, if the copyists in the scriptoria had a reaction similar to portrait painters?) And, the photographic revolution again revolutionized popular or social vision--I shall note only two American phenomena in this respect.

* Photography revolutionized the imaging of indigineous Americans. Even the paintings of Remington and Catlin became 'photo-realistic' in their depictions of American Indian festivals, villages, etc. But, above all, portraiture of chiefs, individuals, etc. could be and were photographed and thus also popularized.

But now note in passing that with photography there is an *inversion* of the site where the isomorphism shows itself. Still shot portraiture is posed, often in regalia or costume which often <u>is not that of daily practice, but of some special occasion or past nostalgic form.</u> It is the *face* which now shows itself in a distinct individuality and person.

Photography did display itself as a kind of isomorphic realism, reproducible and dissembleable, and easily 'read' or perceived, across both critical and naive audiences. It was a 'mass medium' imaging technology. But from the beginning it was also a 'still' which from the earliest responses carried the metaphor of 'death-like' since it took the subject out of life-time and life-space and fixed he/she/it in a kind of photographic eternity.

The parallel with print maintains itself here: the spoken word belongs to the life-actions of speakers <u>in situ</u> while print materializes in writing what *was* said and the photo makes *still* what had been the motility of bodily life before and after the picture.

And it was with living word that the next inventions moved imaging technologies closer to live processes. In 1876 Bell invented the first telephone which could convey speech, modified and mediated but in real time, and in 1877 Edison invented the first phonograph which while 'fixing' sound in a repeatable form like print, nevertheless reproduced the event-character of speech or music. The same fixing of visual phenomena similarly occured at the turn of the century.

The Moving Image: Cinematography
Motion pictures rapidly followed the still camera, indeed by only fifty years (1839/1889) with the first film a joke, "Fred Ott's Sneeze," followed in six years by a theatrical thriller, "The Arrival of a Train in the Station," which showed a locomotive coming at the audience, stimulating screams and alarms on the part of the viewers and paralleled Edison's peep shows, also cinematographic.

By the 1920's silent movies had already become a Euro-American phenomenon and in 1927-8 came the final synthesis of the audio-visual which now become the paradigm for most of what was to follow in refined imaging technology, the "talkie" or movie with sound track. The visual and the auditory now could attain 'life-like' similitude thereby transcending the 'death-like' still images of the previous technologies. And, as sophisticated as audio-visual imaging has become, with as many effects and through the multiplication of media, the audio-visual still remains the primary standard for imaging in expressive, scientific, and communication domains.

Virtual Reality: the Multisensory
If, first, imaging technologies remained bound to monosensory dimensions--visual imaging and sound reproduction--the *trajectory* towards greater life-like simulation was suggested early. If one could reproduce in most dramatic form in cinerama, or in maxi-theatres with enhanced and surrounding sound equipment, still the full sense of experience could only be suggested. Could one produce a full and deeper sensory range? Three-D effects (with colored glasses followed the stereopticon) and "smellovision", theatres with built in shaking devices to simulate earthquakes, and other sensory devices did begin to appear mid-century. But perhaps the most serious of early 'virtual reality' devices was not in the entertainment, but the military context.

The Link Trainer developed in World War II simulated a much broader range of experience than previous non-flight training devices. Statistics showed that novice fighter pilots usually lost their lives in the first five combat missions--if, somehow, they lived through five missions they were likely to last out the combat service to the end. To give them an edge, the Link Trainer not only showed the simulated targets and landscapes on a screen on a cockpit, but tilted the trainer, provided the sounds, and moved in such a way that not only visual and auditory, but also tactile and kinesthetic experience could be simulated. Here was a kind of 'whole body' mediation and a 'virtual reality' which, like cinema and other earlier imaging technologies, has become so sophisticated that Baudrillard has claimed the Gulf War was pre-fought and that its actualization was a mere extension of the virtual reality battles previously portrayed to tank, airplane, and other vehicle commanders in the virtual reality simulations which now are regularly used in training. This irreal cast, of course, was also not missed by the rest of us as observers, who also saw the reproduction in the 'camrockets' which we vicariously 'flew down' the ventilation shafts of buildings shown on the evening news.

If miliatary applicaitons of virtual reality technologies are the most sophisticated, entertainment variants are now coming on line as well. Video arcades already have the glove and 'face sucker' masks which allow the enthusiast to enter the quasi-worlds of virtual reality wars with aliens and Japanese marketeers have the smae technologies to show prospective home buyers how to 'walk around' their projected kitchen designs.

Hyperreality

There remains one more step in bringing our technologies up to date: *hyperreality*. Hyperreality is enhanced reality, reality better than reality-- or, to put it more directly, a manipulated and constructed reality. In this case we may return to the photgraph in its late twentieth century garb, now become *digitalized photography*.

Technologically, digitalized photography changes the position and role of the camera in the now much more complex process of producing a photograph. Where once might have had a simple photographer who could go out and snap a picture, than have a photolab--now automated--produce the result, now the camera is at best a penultimate step in the process. The result, transferred to a digital computer process, now may be minutely re-worked and re-produced in hyper form and with such sophistication that one cannot tell from the result whether the photo resulting has been tampered with or not.

Some such manipulations are relatively harmless or 'sosmetic,' such as those found commonly in advertising copy. But others potentially hold distortive possibilities--such as 'cooked' pictures for the evening news or even for scientific dishonesty, examples of which are already occuring.

Before we leave this trajectory, which began with simple hand operated technologies of depiction and ascended through the more technologically mediated imagery of first still, then motion animated depictions, into the multisensory and highly constructed hyperreal forms of the present, take note of an interesting apogee in that trajectory.

The earliest depictions seem, to us, *naive*. But naive with respect to the later *apparent realism* of the photograph or cinema verite. Yet, with more and more sophisticated imaging techniques, there is equally a move away from 'realism' towards something approaching technological *fantasizing*. This fantasizing, however, is not naive, it is rather, *hyperreal*. One of the best illustrations of this is the genre of science fiction films with realism-inducing effects such as those in the "Star Wars" trilogy.

III. *Image Technologies and Pluriculture*

It is now time to draw these two histories together. What has technological mediation to do with pluriculture, the phenomenon which I claim is a uniquely contemporary type of cross culturality?

1) That multiple cultural depictions are *technologically mediated* is clear enough. This mediation is a contemporary *mixing device*. And its presence may be found, at least in every industrialized context. High up on Mount Albano, in the tiny village of Bacchereto, Italy, where I had to go to a bar to make international phone calls in 1988, the village youth would hang out while drinking and watching MYV with "French Kiss in America" on the television. Or, at home in our own family's 'media room,' my seven year old son watches a cartoonized version of the "Ninja Turtles" complete with a wise rodent martial arts instructor and meditation guide of Asian cultural descent. The mixing phenomenon, inherent in technological manipulations, also reflects the hyper input possible from the global reach of these technologies. Not only are there more cultures to draw from, but the very overload is such that selectivity itself is a trajectory towards mixture.

2) I have already mentioned the internationalization of cuisines, fashions, to which one could add religions and meditation techniques (Harie Krishna, transcendental meditation, etc.), inter-ethnic physical training (Yoga, Tai Chai, etc.), as well as the very material presence of persons of multiple cultures within any of our urban cultures. The technologically mediated cross culturality, however, is the mediation of the 'sound byte' or *fragment*. The intercultural flood is a flood of *culture fragments*. Mixture yields fragments. But fragments make for collages. Or, to use another metaphor, we have before us the possibility of a cultural pointillism in which the many color dots may yield new depictions.

3) Here the pattern replicates the previously noted pattern of *technology transfers*. One may transfer artifacts, without transferring either the *infrastructure* or the *context* within which the artifact originally developed. This factor lends a certain indeterminacy to the exchange. If the windmill in India serves the religious purpose of sending prayers into the winds, and in Holland it serves the purpose of pumping out wetlands, it is not mere use which has changed, but an entire culturally embedded context. The change in context is one in which infrastructure frequently disappears. This may lead to something like a *surface phenomenon* in which what floats to the top are the various forms, but without the previously underlying cultural justifications for those forms.

4) Moreover, the pattern of rapid culture-fragment exchange, now transferred rapidly and internationally, lends a certain *bricolage* or eclectic texture to the process. In this, pluriculture is distinctly *postmodern*, a form of 'both/and' rather than 'either/or'. For example, one of our recent Ph.D. graduates did part of his work in Wupperthal with Klaus Held. When Held asked him what his religious background was, Tony replied, "I'm both Catholic and Jewish." The startled response was, "You can't be both, which are you?" The retort, "I am both at the same time." To which I add my own son's response, "I'm glad I'm both Christian and Jewish--I get to celebrate <u>all the holidays!</u>" Neither of these persons sees any confict in the 'both/and' of the postmodern. This phenomenon can appear to be decentered. Thus the older 'logics' which could be exclusive (either/or) give way to 'fuzzy' logics which are both/and.

5) But, just as in technology transfer, once again, such mixtures do not simply transfer contexts or infrastructures. Part of the reason that the two young men can be 'both/and' is also because the 'religious' infrastructure and context has itself changed. For in fact, the sets of parents involved, are actually secular rather than religious in an older sense. What is celebrated --"all the holidays'--are cultural artifacts rather than deeply religious ones.

6) What this means is that contemporary pluriculturality as a postmodern phenomenon, is one of multiplicities and multistructurality. But this, too, is a reflection of a kind of multiplicity of imaging. I shall conclude with two 'images,' both present in our contemporary experience:

* One image is the MTV. The contemporary youthful presentation of music televison, combines visual imagery with the song being presented. And while the audio--the song--may be continuous, and even a bit traditional in that it has a tune, refrains, verses, etc., the visuals are almost always dymanically bricoleur in depiction. 'Images' float into and out of the screen, fades and flashbacks are used, there is both continuity and discontinuity, and certainly no simply 'stability.' MTV is an icon for the movement of culture fragments such as are daily present in our pluricultural context.

* The second image, also televisual, is the multi-screen spectrum. A good example, but only one, is that of the television news room. The 'mixer' technician sits in front of a multiplicity of screens. Each screen shows some action, something going on. One is a report from Bosnia, another an automobile pile-up from California, a third shows a Calvin Klein fashion show, a fourth the formation of a new Cabinet in Italy, etc. All of this 'information overload'--but really an 'image overload'--is simultaneously present to the mixer. What the mixer does, however, is to play across the mutiple screens and pick and chose which to show when and it is this choice and pick which then is mediated to your home screen and its singular shifts from Bosnia to California, etc.

The mixer, however, is also an icon. He or she is the 'autobiographical editor' of a pluricultural life. We 'edit ourselves' within and from this plurivocal and plurivisual presence and in the process 'construct' a multi-stable life. This, too, is pluriculture. Some are deeply threatened by this phenomenon--it seems to lack 'depth' or a 'core'--but others celebrate it--it is also variety rich, freer, and cosmopolitan in contrast to parochial or provincial.

The interaction, then, between image technologies and pluriculturality, is an intimate and deep one. Contemporary life is a life which is lived through, in the midst of, and in relation to a kind of maximal technologization, and the image technologies are particularly important as the cultural instruments by which not only culture is mediated, but by which it becomes transformed for better or ill.

The technologies do not determine our fate, but they do make things possible which previously were not possible. Technologies 'incline' rather than determine. And in the cases I have been examining the inclination is towards the making present of the overload of cultures which necessarily appear in the fragmentary forms which become, in turn, the palate from which we draw for the newest creations within what I have called *pluriculture*.

Lars-Henrik Schmidt

Commonness across Cultures

The differences between value systems, which are a major concern of cultural relativism, might be interpreted as a difference between globalists and localists or, referring to the classical discourse on ethics, between Kantians and Aristotelians. In present-day discussions the dilemma seems to present itself as an opposition between liberals and communitarians. The aim of this paper is not to mediate between the two positions or to create a compromise but to take a stand beyond the oppositional framework itself. Thus I want to discuss the possibility of a kind of "commonness" that is neither the general identity of a society nor a common interest shared by a community, one that is neither consensus nor common sense.

Following this line of speculation, this paper stresses the idea of socius (commonness) as distinct from the concept of 'culture' perceived as an entity or a body. Thus 'cross-cultural conversation' is seen not as a dialogue between cultures, but rather as a point of departure for a conjunction against which no one wants to protest. This is, it should be added, a non-pragmatic point of view.

I. *From culture as progress to culture as an offer*
Within the realms of Western civilization there is a tendency to blur or to simply overlook the distinction between transgression and expansion, and this blurring creates a problem regarding the relations between the Western and the non-Western world. In the following I shall offer a brief interpretation of this problem which is also the problem of an ongoing process of universalization and therefore of transformation.

Western thought, when looked upon as *transgression*, seeks to overcome differences by reducing them to difficulties; difficulties to be dealt with and thus, in a way, respected. It is only when one regards Western thought as an endless process of *expansion* that respect for that which is different is lost. The problem in Western philosophy referred to above is, as my thesis goes, *the will to transgress metaphysics in order to achieve an ontology of expansion*. I shall look into the extraction of this somewhat complicated situation and try to elucidate the problem.

First of all, it is necessary to distinguish between Western civilization and Western culture; I don't think the latter exists since a culture has to be limited - be it by a form of identity or within the constraints of a body. Western civilization, however, or Westernalization is an ongoing process.

Mahatma Gandhi was once asked by a Western reporter about his opinion on Western civilization, and his answer was significant: "I think it would be a good idea!", he replied, as the story goes. An astonishing and provocative answer which makes a good point - and yet it was the wrong answer. Western civilization cannot be denied. It has followed its own logic since its origins in view of the fact that it has now become a *technical unification* if not a universalization. The very idea of universalization is now first and foremost a technical one. I believe that Max Weber was right when, in the famous "Preface" to his studies on the sociology of religion, he stated that there was something unique about the rationality of Western civilization.

Drawing on this characterization of Western rationality, we might say that a naïve propagation of 'cross-cultural conversation' is just another way of forwarding a modern Western concept inasmuch as it inherits the idea of "an ongoing process towards universality which is not yet universal" as I would define the modern project according to Habermas.

Along the same lines we find the idea of otherness attached to *what is not yet* Westernalized but which can be reflected in the light of the process towards this specific kind of sameness.

Sameness as opposed to otherness, universality versus contextuality or particularity, absoluteness confronting relativity - and endless rows of similar oppositions - all belong to the same family. In *Götzen-Dämmerung* from 1889, Friedrich Nietzsche brilliantly summarizes Western philosophy in the story about "Wie die 'Wahre Welt' endlich zur Fabel wurde". However, after Nietzsche we have to recognize that his projected 'twilight of idols' has been somewhat postponed, since we keep on producing these oppositions when we try to account for them. In fact, Nietzsche himself could not help doing excatly that. This delicate situation has something to do with Western metaphysics as such, i.e., with the way we speak and think, the way we interpret matters as matter-of-fact, as deeds done, implicating that they are done by someone indeed.

As we face it today, this 'family problem' or genealogy of oppositions presents itself as *globalism versus localism* - the global versus the local perspective. The point is that we cannot get rid of this oppositional or even antagonistic way of rendering the problem - we have to deal with it. Using a pragmatic cliché, one might say that we have to cope with it. We are reduced to reconciliating ourselves to the fact that this problem cannot be transgressed and thereby done away with.

Although we cannot get rid of the problem, we can try to deal with it without subscribing to the antagonistic perspective it creates. In other words, we can go *beyond* the opposition in pointing out the historical solidarity that actually links the oppositions to one another; hence one might follow the local point of view and see how it is globalized in a historical process. Not unlike the way Latin became the language of the entire civilized world, Western metaphysics is heading for the big goal. We have to discuss the relation between the poles (globalism, localism), a discussion which will also be a version of Nietzsche's "Umwertung aller Werte", since the localist point of view is always seen as limited or 'provincial'. The major point being that there is something more sovereign than yourself; an authority which in turn can make you sovereign.

The basic idea in Western thought is the idea of human dependence, of the lack of in-dependence (sameness) and the subsequent striving for this very independence (sameness). The instance which determines our in-dependence has been projected as "otherness" - the otherness of nature, of fellow man, or of yourself. And these three forms of otherness in turn correspond to the three grand traditions of the West, namely Christianity, Humanism, and the Enlightenment. When modern Culturalism talks about "otherness" it is basically a generalization and continuation of the three grand tradition. I shall briefly sketch some characteristics of this Western tradition with respect to the conception of "otherness".

Christianity is the first and foremost of the grand traditions in the West. The main concern of Christian thought is otherness - i.e., that which is not human, the authority through and by which humans become humane; in Christianity this authority is an exterior one, the otherness is something outside man. In this particular tradition the other is considered to be the absolute other; that is to say God or Nature. The exteriority of the other, the absolute difference, is somewhat questioned in the subsequent traditions worth mentioning.

As an heir to, and thus not in a fundamental way opposed to, traditional Christianity, the humanistic tradition in the West transforms the otherness of the other into the otherness of fellow man. Henceforth otherness is something that can be experienced in one's acquaintance with one's neighbor, the point being that one's neighbor could be, and in a certain perspective really is, Christ himself. Otherness is something which is not comprehensible; yet it is located in relation to one's fellow man and not any longer in an exterior, transcendental authority.

By the Age of Enlightenment, the problem of otherness transforms itself once again; otherness becomes something to be experienced in one's own being. One is another to oneself, and Nietzsche, as a latecomer to this tradition, hits the nail on the head: "Wir sind uns unbekannt, wir erkenenden. Wir selbst, uns selbst". In this statement he summarizes the philosophy of the Enlightenment and shows us a new path which we shall follow in due course.

What is significant about this formula is very simple: otherness has become internal to the individual living in the modern age. Otherness is our very "Menschlichkeit", as Immanuel Kant puts it. There is, as Rousseau would have it, an "homme en général" participating in us but which is not identical to us. In theoretical philosophy this authority is considered to be the transcendental subject, but in fact it is the very same authority taking shape in the concept of 'the history of mankind.' Due to this dual position in the philosophy of the Enlightenment, the other must be considered on the one hand as humanity as such - i.e., as a general, transcendental principle - and on the other hand must be seen as a historical principle.

In the age of Culturallism this principle or authority, which was kept unified by Kant and his epoch, is differentiated into two different sets of problems.

On the one hand, otherness as an internal authority is transformed into unconscious structures; these were described by Michel Foucault in *The Order of Things* as linguistic, psychological and kinship structures This way of depicting the internal structures is clearly also another way to inherit the history of the grand traditions outlined above.

On the other hand, the historical dimension of this otherness is transformed into differentiated cultures, thereby doing away with the history of mankind. The internal otherness is projected as an external otherness to be experienced in other cultures. But this projection in turn raises the problem of togetherness. The other is perceived of as the not-yet-realized-posibility-to-become-Western, and to be Western is to possess the possibility of becoming reunited with otherness, whether it is with the otherness of one's internal self or with that of the external self. At this point culture is divided, but in this very division it is also seen as being on the road to gaining a future identity, either as a result of solitary commitment or of interaction with others. The way to uphold the idea of a unified culture can now be identified as one culture trying to become *the* culture. And the strategies at work are integrative.

The traditional Western pattern corresponds to the idea that expansion and transgression are part of one schema, that of progress, and the progressive path thus equals the path of unification or civilization. As progress one hundred years later turns into (or, to be more precise, is made problematiic as) evolution, a completely different pattern emerges: unification is now seen as something bound to happen, not as the result of an effort but out of necessity. And another fifty years later, when evolution becomes imperialism, we are dealing with yet another situation: the Western world is compelled to force unification simply because the others are unwilling to unify. Come the present-day 'world order', Western culture no longer has the need to employ conspicuous force: the demand for unification works in a much more subtle way, since it is now considered 'an offer you can't refuse,' and the Western openness towards the otherness of the other is really the apex of Western self-esteem or self-satisfaction.

The very concept of reason mirrors the relation to the other, the other being the limit to reason itself, i.e., its own limitation. Cultural relativism in all of its different forms is the externalization of the limitations of reason. The universal dimension inherent in relativism is that it respects the individuality of different reasonings. This is the way in which universalism is secured by reason.

Cultural relativism is offered as ideology by progressive and well-meaning, i.e. liberal Western thought when there is little or no doubt about which culture will - for various and perhaps wrong reasons - be preferred.

This is why the idea of 'cross-cultural conversations' cannot rest on the willingness to recognize and respect the otherness of the other. The goal cannot be simply to respect other cultures and to invite them to take part in a dialogue, since this kind of respect is firmly rooted in the idea of cultural relativism, which is itself the apex of Western self-righteousness: the glorification of a local and historical way of thinking. The apparent abandonment of the attempt to universalize turns into a celebration of the very idea of universality in a very tricky manner.

The universal hallmark of cultures is the fact that they are different from one another; what makes them all the same is the fact that they are considered to be cultures. The absolute character of humaneness consists of the singularity of each individual, as we would put it using the language of the only Danish philosopher - Søren Kierkegaard.

Cultures tend to be willing to universalize themselves - or they tend to just do it since they cannot help but to have preferences. And, as a matter of fact, what they prefer is their own preferences, that is to say their specific taste. Whether this taste is articulated as expansion (wanting, in reality, to kill off differences) or as retreat ('respecting' differences to the point of chauvinism), it is nonetheless a preference and as such a will to transgression.

The problem concerning universalism is that a dialogue cannot be symmetrical since it involves what I shall call different experiences and not just different knowledge. True understanding cannot take place if by understanding we think of copying or breaking a code and a message. What can take place, however, is a re-enactment of an offer transmitted, but this is not communication in terms of the theory of communication. It is the asymmetrical element, the strategic element in the tradition from Nietzsche and Foucualt, which provides us with a counterpart to the ethics of discourse proposed by Apel and Habermas. It is possible to make conversations and to do things together without singling out this enterprise as a dialogue or as a conflict.

II: *Conversations should not be reduced to dialogues*
Thus, when we speak of the need for a cross-cultural conversation, we do not think of new dialogue in the sense of an exchange of arguments and ideas. A dialogue means that one respects the other and thus that there *is* another. In a dialogue one can disagree with the other, the point being that the involved parties agree to disagree, and this is what constitutes the condition of a reasonable dialogue. Since, on the other hand, consensus is not the aim of a conversation, the partakers would not have to agree upon the existence of a disagreement for it to take place.

To participate in a dialogue is to take part in an exchange of words between two persons. Of course more than two persons can take part, but in principle a dialogue is a relation of exchange between two parties; and as a way of obtaining the Truth it has its own merits in the history of philosophy. Being a relation of exchange, a dialogue rests on the principle of equivalence and thus respects an equivalence between the two opposing principles or parties. Whereas the principle of equivalence is much needed in the dialogical quest for truth and controlled by truth claims, this is not the case if we turn to the ethical-aesthetical play of a conversation.

In order to distinguish between the two, I should like to define conversation as a certain kind of 'social intercourse' of an informal or even familiar character. In a dialogue talking consists of coherent speech, uttered presumably for the benefit of a listener. It may be purposeful and serious, or insipid and empty. A conversation is - at least to my knowledge - different. It is an interchange of sentiments or ideas between two or more persons, usually upon a subject worthy of attention. Whereas talk can be the endless chatter of one tiresome person, conversation requires that each person contribute his bit. Taking this kind of characterization a bit further, we might say that a chat is a pleasant, familiar talk: it is not senseless, and neither is it serious; whereas a conference is a formalized conversation, taking place by appointment for the discussion of specific subjects. By formalization a conversation may or may not turn into a dialogue, but that is not - and I want to stress this point - the inherent or transcendental purpose of conversation.

Just because it is possible to come to an agreement one cannot say that the purpose of conversation is to agree or to disagree. In order to grasp the kind of conversational (social) interdependence I am aiming at, it might be helpful to turn to one of the founding fathers of sociology, Georg Simmel. He found the main phenomenon binding a society together to be what he analyzed as "Gesellighkeit", which in some respects resembles my idea of a conversation. "Geselligkeit" can just be chatter; it can be seduction, flattery or a joke, and at the same time it can be dead serious. Georg Simmel did not find the pure form of society in "Gesellschaft" (interest), nor in "Gemeinschaft" (purpose), but in "Geselligkeit". Although in my perspective Simmel's purification process by way of abstraction is not the adequate way to handle our present problem, I think that in conceiving of 'Geselligkeit' as a sphere of the 'more-than-just-personal' relations, he offers a guideline to overcoming the logic of exchange systems.

III: *From cultural differences to conflicting value systems*
Basically the idea of exchange is the same as the idea of equivalence. But in the sphere of conversation we do not exchange equivalents.

Cultures can hardly be seen in the same way as individuals, and one cannot analyze the interaction between strategies termed cultural along the same lines as one analyzes communication between two persons. Taking part in a conversation, however, one is more than a person and at the same time less than a person; what we need is an interpretation of this rather complicated simultaneity. If we are able to analyze the interaction between different cultures as an engagement in cross-cultural conversation, we might have a key to grasping the interaction between persons as well. Different strategies clash and are identified in the process of clashing - not beforehand. It might be true of the conflicts between nation-states that they are like generalized personal conflicts, but it is an illusion to think that cultures meet. I am not just contesting the idea of cultures being homogeneous; it is the idea that cultures can be identified within limits or boundaries that I find to be wrong. Or rather, if the concept of culture is identified in this way, then we should be looking for something else. This is why I propose to substitute the concept of culture with another category, namely that of 'commonness' or 'socius' in order to better grasp that kind of 'relatedness' which is neither pure conflict nor true consensus.

It is impossible to be "solely related": one can only be co-related, as the 'social triangle' below is meant to illustrate:

C

A   B

When, for instance, one (A) is relating to another (B), he is also relating to 'other' (C) relations to B. The important thing about 'C' is that we are not dealing with a mediator, only with a 'co-relator' (possible fellow rival) in the unrealized conflictuality or 'rapport' in which we as humans (social beings) relate to one another.

On the one hand, then, there is no immediacy; on the other, this absence is not due to the intervention of a mediator; no one is to blame. Socius is nothing (no-thing) since it always already 'has been', or simply, it is immediacy lost. But then again, this social co-relation is only realized (i.e., simultaneously regarded and brought into existence) as a relationship (fellowship or rivalry) between definite and pre-existing instances. It is in the realization, or naming, of these 'instances' that we tend to forget that they were only co-relations. What we want to expound, then, is the way of relating which is neither mediated nor immediate. Or, in other words, the relation in which the conflictual dimension in social being has not (yet) been realized. This 'not-yet-realized' is enough to be a substitute for the 'disagreeing agreement' which, in the tradition from Kant to Apel and Habermas, forms the prerequisite for human coexistence.

Thus in my perspective of social analysis, human relations are always relations to other relations, realized as relations to definite instances. However, this also means that one's relation to another (or to the Other) is really a relation to a third.

When we are dealing with commonness as a category for grasping the conflictual junction 'inside', for instance, a cultural entity, we do not have to rest on a consensual basis. We do not even need a minimalistic consensus in the form of a disagreeing agreement as it is proposed by Kant in his *Critique of Judgement*, his point being that mere participation in the disagreement over taste gives rise to the fact that taste can in fact be disputed, since the parties involved agree at least to the fact that a case can be made. According to Kant this tiny argument is enough to set our hopes on arguing; reason provides you with sufficient ground for taking a stand. Even when, in his socalled "Fourth Critique", Kant offers the category of "die ungesellige Geselligkeit", it is not enough, since by omitting what would have been 'die gesellige Ungeselligkeit", he only tells half the story.

In a way a prototype of Kant's argument can be found in Plato's "Philebos". If you agree with Socrates on the principles of dialogue, you have always already agreed with his conclusions. This is why the sophist does not want to take part in dialogue, and it is also the reason for wanting to protest against the discourse ethics found in Apel and Habermas. Dialogue is a modern kind of duel which has replaced ability with logic; and it is the civilized way to handle a conflict. Sometimes, however, we do not want to be civilized, since the principle of civilization can been seen as the principle of the supremacy of the other and thus as contrary to one's own principles and interests. We cannot force someone to act civilized since that would be very uncivilized. Once again we face a situation in which we have to interact without being able to determine rules of conduct. Of course laws can be pointed out, but such enforced laws of conduct belong to agreements of one kind or another within the nation-state, so they are not universal; they are the products of power and tradition. If they are to be universalized they will have to be sanctioned in one metaphysical, i.e., universal, instance or another - whether it is in Nature herself or in the nature of man. Along these traditional paths towards universalization one recognizes the ecological movement and the efforts of the advocates of human rights respectively. Nowadays the relationship between human rights (the Law) and ecology (Nature) is one of conflict - which it did not use to be, and this is our actual problem: only the juridical path is left and thus, out of necessity, the resulting globalization will be an enforced one. Ethics has given up striving for globalization and is now working at the local level where virtue and duties are both conceived as self-practices with no need for a higher instance of sanction. Even though the concept of 'self-practices' may be seen as a post-modern phenomenon, it rests on the basis of a pre-modern conception of ethics. Emancipation which includes rights and duties is the modern idea, but in modernity rights and duties have fallen apart, and we are witnessing a juridical globalization along with an ethical-aesthetical individualization.

In my perspective there is no significant difference - that is, a difference producing other differences - between cross-individual conversation and cross-cultural conversation. However, this is not - and I have to stress this point - due to the fact that individuals and cultures are alike. Rather it is because value systems are open and, as a matter of fact, not to be regarded or conceptualized as systems at all. Before venturing further into that discussion, I shall briefly specify the way in which I use the concept of culture.

IV: *Beyond nature and culture*

Before articulation there is no culture, and this is why the popular idea that cultures are constructed is not really an interesting critique of the concept of culture. Of course cultures are constructed: they could not be otherwise. They always have been and they always will be, since they become objects through discourse, and as such they are comparable to individuals or to organisms - i.e., to an order of one kind or another.

But in that case, what is articulated? To understand that we shall have to refer to Rousseau and elaborate on his idea of "la volonté générale". Rousseau did not really succeed in explaining this phenomenon; it has been regarded as the will of all (or the will of the majority) or as a semi-speculative precursor to the concept of spirit as developed by Hegel. In light of the Nietzschean critique of this very concept, we are able to make an alternative interpretation. Rousseau was not able to uphold a distinction between this general will and its form of articulation. That is what I am aiming at with the category of 'commonness' instead of the Kantian version of 'sensus communis'. The point is 'voices heard' but not voices agreeing or shouting

"Yes". What Rousseau could not grasp was the very problem of articulation which he himself introduced. The problem is to understand how the general will is articulated; and now we can see that the general will is not articulated as general will but as something else; from the articulated point of view, however, we have to talk about something that 'has been'. The problem is that Rousseau conceptualizes the general will as something positive, as something that could be realized. Nietzsche showed us the low and mean version of the same phenomenon when talking about decadence and nihilism, but he showed us only its form of realization; what I am looking for is found somewhere in between. In between Roussseau and Nietzsche we would expect to find Kant, but he transformed the very idea into a faculty of judgement, and this is not what we are looking for either.

What we are looking for is the realization of some sort of commonness that takes place in a pleasant conversation - a commonness that cannot be explicated as such but that is characterized by not excluding the conflictual dimension of togetherness; one does not have to agree upon any disagreement in order for this commonness to take place.

V: *Socius as commenness*
In Genesis, Adam and woman are not social beings, just natural ones. God does not function as a third. When the snake enters the scene, the third party is not a real third but just a part af Adam, his penis, which he does not control himself. In sexuality he plays a double role, and his uncontrolled part, his unconscious, plays the role of the third. But when Cain is doomed to meet other people, there are thirds which are not just fellows but also rivals, and with this we have a social organization. We may, accordingly, refer to socius as the link between social conflictuality and conflictual sociality; for this link we have chosen the term commonness. Before there is a rival there is no socius, just one flesh. With socius there is flesh from which we have to abstain. All three 'restrictions' must be at hand, but the abstention from cannibalism has priority since it gives birth to the others: generation is just cultural (or fellowship), and the spread of people is just rivalry if not seen on the background of possible fellowship. And the combination of - or rather the junction between - social conflictuality and conflictual sociality is the new "immediacy", the reflected immediacy, which is the same as the social declination from cannibalism and is neither just the natural command nor the cultural prohibition.

We witness natural or cultural (symbolic) cannibalism all the time, but we do not find social cannibalism since socius equals the very abstention from cannibalism. If social cannibalism takes place, there is no commonness - and vice versa. We are dealing with the extraction of 'the social' and not with the origins of 'the cultural'. One cannot speak of social cannibalism - there exists no anthropophagy, since what one eats is excluded from anthropos. It might be added that the possible new problem we are going to face is autophagy.

So, 'Der Mensch is(s)t nicht was er ist' is my answer to the Kantian question 'Was ist der Mensch?'. Humans do not eat the humanity in themselves or in the other: they simply eat "to-get-her". In other words, man is not one: "He is what he is", which means he is (a) being in a social existence wherein he is not one with himself and his fellows but conflictual with himself and his rivals. And this means that the others are thirds: they are always and already rivals. They could eat what he eats, but in doing so they would have to eat him. They do eat the same food as he does but not the very same or the identical food as he. We are not all but neither are we alltogether. We do not stand all alone by ourselves but are dependent. Only the Lord himself managed to do the trick and say, "I am what I am"; this happened once and never again. So we are reduced to doing other tricks, like my trick with the double s(s), that is, to using more than one signification and thereby producing surplus signification.

The nexus of the social is in the meal. We are both fellows and rivals. We are both of the same and, yet again, different. One does not eat the ones (thirds) one eats with. This is a simple fact of significant consequence. This means that declining from cannibalism is not a sacrifice but an offer, not of but to the other. And in this act of offering, the rival may or may not be transformed into a guest. This is why the meal is simultaneously the most social and the most individual act, as Georg Simmel put it in his time. He did not explore cannibalism though, which is quite significant. He did not think of cannibalism because it is unthinkable. Or, to be more precise, the way we see things one can only think of two forms of cannibalism, namely a cultural (symbolic) cannibalism (eg. the consumption of ancestral strength, wisdom, etc.), or a natural cannibalism in which the consumed body is reduced to its nutritional value. In both forms of cannibalism the consumed body is classified as non-human; that is, as one with whom the consumer cannot be co-related. What is impossible, then, - as a consequence of the way we have defined humaneness (as being co-related) - is social cannibalism.

VI: *No-body protests*

Now, who are these agents assembled in some way by the category of 'commonness'? No one and no-body signifies the same thing, namely we are emphasizing that we are not yet dealing with a 'body' when speaking about socius. They are not some-body and they are not any-body; they do not think of themselves as an imaginary 'we'. They may invite you to participate in this manner, but they are not (at least not yet) identified. Socius is a way of turning the masses into a theoretical object. The masses are not yet collective and they never will be. One could argue that modernity was created to deal with the newcomers, i.e., the masses, but the point is that modernity tried to transform the masses into identifiable collective subjects, into classes, for example. Masses are not-yet-classes, not yet disciplined, and so on and so forth. The theoretical point is that they can never be identified and this is precisely the post-modern condition. We have given up the idea of the masses becoming known collective subjects, and that is the end of the modern project, the project of 'not-yet-but-to-be-in-due-course'.

We are not talking about a compromise here. "Commonness across cultures" does not amount to the idea that we just have to keep on discussing and let the best argument win. On the contrary, one has to agree since there is nothing to agree on. There is no reason to protest either, and as long as no protests are launched things function. The dialogue between cultures is now seen as a social intercourse wherein pleasure must be synchronous.

This does not mean that conflicts are excluded, but there is no universal code and no escaping the asymmetry and the strategic element. What is offered are negotiations, but negotiations are not dialogues. They are not rules of negotiations. Nobody protests, not because they agree, but given the situation this is the best thing to do - in one's own interest. If, in due time, rules are established, we are no longer negotiating. Negotiation is not just another form of warfare and neither is it another way of saying market economy. The point is that one does not have to know what the other thinks in order to negotiate, but one is obliged, in one's own interest, to try to 'understand' the other when negotiating. 'Peace, love and understanding' is the post-modern version of the traditional Christian virtues (faith, hope and charity) and their modernization in the philosophy of Enlightenment (liberty, equality and fraternity). Socius is the willingness to negotiate; that is, to be in a negotiating position, and post-modern or, as I prefer to call it, post-revolutionary conduct is negotiability, which is what we now understand as 'being decent'. To be decent means not to insist on one principle but to be willing to take other possibilities into account. (That is why they are local in principle.) Local conduct willing to repeat itself towards global dimensions without hoping or aspirating for the global perspective. This is why this approach does not need a roundtable (for negotiations) or mediators or professionals or any specific sort of setting. We are talking about the ability to take part in a conversation - and the willingness. We are not interested in rules or laws for proper conversation. That is to say, we are dealing with persons and not just interests.

Unlike a contract, negotiations, like conversations, have to do with a social pact: they only exist as long as the opponents each pursue their own interest by continuing the conversation.

At the market, in the traditional liberal thinking of Adam Smith, war has turned into competition and the market may be generalized. There is, he tells us, a general equivalent which transforms every conversation into a dialogue, which in turn creates an abstract market situation and a price mechanism. We are only in it for the money.

I am not opting for a market of opinions or for "peaceful warfare", since that would be equivalent to dialogue. As I see things, it is from conversations that negotiations may spring and deals may be made. Facing global problems, we thus have to recognize negotiations without a general equivalent. The idea of a world market is impossible. Let us start the negotiations right away, and let us respect the fact that negotiations are provisional and that they are not agreements which can be juridically sanctioned. They are forms of intercourse which we cannot avoid nowadays. The bonds of independence (which was the first form of thinking) have now turned out to be bonds of interdependence which call for a reflection on the possibilities in a conversation. Cross-cultural conversations are not the answer to a problem. They are the laboratory for a decent social intercourse. We know from experience that it is possible to hit that "it" (i.e., commonness), but that is not the same as to suggest that the intellectual market of discourses could be or ought to be a model for negotiations. We cannot ask our opponents to send us some intellectuals whom we can talk to; that is not 'it'. There is no model, but conversations take place nevertheless. Our task is to give them the possibility of taking place.

Søren Christensen

From the Native's Point of View - And Other Paradoxes of Cultural Relativism

Perhaps one of the more significant paradoxes of relativism is that no matter how heated philosophical discussions on the subject tend to get, philosophers generally agree that 'relativism' is a vacuous notion. One party, the 'anti-relativists', claims that it is vacuous because it is incoherent. The other party, the 'anti-anti-relativists', to use a term coined by Clifford Geertz, claims that it is vacuous because it is non-existent. The first party, typically rationalist philosophers, argues that for reasons essentially advanced already by Plato, relativism is untenable. The basic argument is that relativism refutes itself; the thesis that truth is undecidable, must itself be undecidable and so is no thesis at all. Applied to itself, relativism simply evaporates. The second party, on the other hand, argues that relativism is not just indefensible, but rather non-existent, i.e. it is a thesis which is actually defended by no one. This point has been made in the following way by Richard Rorty: »'Relativism' is the view that every belief on a certain topic, or perhaps about any topic, is as good as every other. No one holds this view.« [1] In other words: philosophers constantly discuss relativism, but they do so only in order to affirm the utter vacuity of the very notion of relativism. Some claim that relativism is a view that cannot be held, while others tell us that, as a matter of fact, nobody does.

One possible reason for this paradox - relativism being incessantly discussed even if considered utterly unreal - might be that relativism actually exists, but cannot be formalized into a philosophical thesis without suffering gross distortion. This is true, I think, in particular for cultural relativism, the most important relativism of modern times, and a kind of relativism unknown to Plato's adversary Protagoras or any of his contemporaries. To do justice to cultural relativism, you will have to describe it as a particular *intellectual tradition* rather than as a particular philosophical thesis. As a philosophical thesis it might be refuted; as an intellectual tradition it may be criticized, but not refuted, since intellectual traditions probably never have unambigous philosophical presuppositions. Besides, even if they do, they will tend to be stronger than such philosophical presuppositions.

The claim that cultural relativism is not a philosophical thesis, amounts to the claim that cultural relativism is not the view that all cultures are equally good. In that case it might be refuted simply by using some variant of the Platonic argument. It might be argued for instance, that this statement presupposes exactly the kind of universal idea of goodness that it intends to deny. So, rather than this strange thesis about cultures, cultural relativism should be viewed as the intellectual tradition that has made us believe that there *are* different cultures, that cultural diversity should be understood in terms of a plurality of lifeworlds, each displaying its proper meaning and coherence. In this sense cultural relativism is not a certain benevolent attitude toward cultures, but rather a discursive construct, transforming the disorder of cultural diversity into a well-ordered plurality of collective systems of values, that is, 'cultures'.

To show that this way of reflecting on human diversity is not obvious and that it is in fact uniquely modern, I would like to cite Montaigne, a famous example of cultural relativism, which I shall use, however, in order to show what cultural relativism is not. To put it bluntly, the reason why Montaigne is usually considered a cultural relativist, is that he failed to feel morally offended by cannibalism. According to Montaigne no moral values were more than local oddities. Even if some customs seemed to him more reasonable than others, his basic point of view was that »we have no other ayme of truth and reason, than the example and *Idea* of the opinions and customes of the country we live in.«[2] So no universal moral truths are available. But the reason is not that cultures are different; the reason is that man is a finite being, incapable of rising above his inherent state of ignorance and stupidity. Thus, paradoxically, the enormity of cultural differences only goes to show the monotonous uniformity of human nature. All around the world, men are equally absorbed by petty prejudice. Thus, what our customs are, doesn't matter much; what matters is that everywhere, custom rules. We are all subjected to this opaque and arbitrary power, and in that sense the power of custom does not indicate the presence of any cultural order, but rather the absence of any natural order.

To the extent that to Montaigne, cultural diversity displays no meaning, to the extent it expresses nothing but the all-pervasive power of custom, it makes little sense to call him a cultural relativist. Rather, since to Montaigne custom is above all a limitation of our abiliy to see clearly, his views constitute a sort of cultural *scepticism*. In this sense, cultural relativism is not a scepticism, but rather a way of surmounting scepticism. Cultural relativism is the idea that custom which according to Montaigne was nothing but petty prejudice, abounds with meaning and thus possesses a fundamental existential value. To my knowledge, Herder was the first philosopher to make this point. His first philosophy of history - *Auch eine Philosophie der Geschichte zur Bildung der Menschheit*, written in 1774 - argues that no substantial presuppositions about human nature are needed to make sense of universal history. To show the coherence of human history, you don't have to look for unity over and above diversity, for diversity possesses its own coherence. Historical diversity is neither the kingdom of chance, nor the medium of progress, rather it possesses its own inherent order, to the extent that it divides itself into a well-ordered suite of nations and epochs, each defined by its own unique aspiration. From now on customs are no longer simply examples of the power of arbitrary custom. They have acquired a dimension of depth, they now express a certain intention underlying them. They are all organized in terms of the pursuit of that particular happiness, each people aspires to. »Every nation», says Herder, »has the centre of its happiness in itself, in just the same way as every globe has its centre of gravity in itself.«[3] The stock of customs possessed by each nation has become the expression of a single collective vision which is *unique*, because it belongs to this people alone, and yet *meaningful*, because it ensures the happiness of this particular people. In this way customs have become culture; those local representations that Montaigne ridiculed as petty prejudice, which he cited as evidence of human vanity, have turned into a fundamental condition of human existence. If each people were not absorbed by its own particular prejudice, no human happiness would be possible. »Prejudice is good, for its time«, says Herder. He continues: »It causes *happiness*. It presses together peoples at their centres.«[4] Local prejudice is still evidence to the finitude of man, but it is so in a way which is quite different from the one emphasized by Montaigne. In terms borrowed from Foucault's *The Order of Things*, we might say that finitude has turned from a negative into a positive condition of human existence. It is no longer an inherent flaw in man, showing only the vanity of his apirations. Quite on the contrary, it has become the condition of possibility of all human aspirations. Finitude is no longer the limitation which prevents us from seeing clearly - it is the condition which permits that we see at all. The fact that we cannot see beyond our local values is not a humiliating limitation as scepticism would have it. It is a positive limitation, as it were, for only the limitation of local values is susceptible of giving our life wholeness and direction. From now on, the fact that human beings are finite no longers means that we are subjected to blind prejudice; it means that belonging to a culture is the very condition of human happiness.

Construed in this way, cultural relativism is very unlike the kind of nihilism and scepticism with which it has often been assimilated. Scepticism claims that no universal order of human existence is available. So does cultural cultural relativism. But to scepticism this entails mere contingency, pure absence of meaning, to cultural relativism it entails that all meaning is inherent in diversity itself, in all the local particularities of human communities. In this sense, cultural relativism is an *edifying* discourse rather than a nihilistic one. It surmonts nihilist scepticism, exactly to the extent it tells us that human diversity is not a sort of Babylonian confusion, but rather ordered into a plurality of particular, yet meaningful forms of life.

In this way cultural relativism solves the problem of cultural scepticism. Solving a problem, however, usually causes a lot of new ones. As for the new problems raised by cultural relativism, the issue is above all *hermeneutical*. The paradox of the matter is that in a way meaningful culture is less accessible, less easily graspable than meaningless custom. The reason why this is so, is that unlike the singularity of custom, the whole of culture is not immediately visible. Custom is only the many-coloured, apparently disordered face of culture; what matters is, in Herder's own words, 'the spiritual nature of the nation', that unique vision of the human condition which provides the particular customs with meaning and coherence. This hidden and unique spiritual nature, how can it be described? Herder is aware of the problem and his answer is that, as a matter of fact, it cannot. If every nation is unique, then »really, all comparison is mistaken.« For »who can compare the *different* satisfactions of *different* senses in different *worlds*?«[5] Thus, basically the spiritual nature of the nation is *ineffable*, and it is so because the spiritual nature is always unique whereas language is always general. Thus, the only way of understanding nations turns out te be *empathy*, a non-conceptual, intuitive grasping of spiritual unity.

This solution, however, is of course no solution at all. It tells you neither how to go about, nor where to look. Empathy is a pure imperative, no method at all. Cultural relativism since Herder can be considered one long series of attempts to come up with a better solution to this hermeneutical problem. The answer of the 19. century is, roughly, language. The rise of a new science of linguistics at the beginning of the century is an indispensable condition of this solution. According to Foucault' interpretation in *The Order of Things*, that discursive unity of language which caracterizes the Classical episteme, gives way to an irreducible plurality of national languages, each defined by its proper (and thus unique) grammatical structure. The connection between comparative grammar on the one hand, and cultural relativism on the other is established above all by Wilhelm von Humboldt. His philosophy of language may be viewed as an attempt to introduce language as the spiritual nature of the nation. In Humboldt's view the grammar of any national language is the expression of a particular *Weltansicht*, a particular view of the world, proper to a particular nation. The relation between a language and the people whose aspirations it expresses, is so intimate that Humboldt actually refuses to make the distinction: »If only one was available, the other could be derived completely from it. [...] You cannot imagine the two of them sufficiently identical.«[6] By introducing language as the principle of national unity, Humboldt no longer has to rely entirely on empathy. Now a science naturally proposes itself for the task of understanding nations - namely the new science of linguistics. In making this move, Humboldt has transformed Herder's vague 'circles of happines', and 'spiritual natures' into well-defined linguistic *structures* that can be subjected to scientific examination. The essence of nations has become accessible through meticulous linguistic analysis.

This way of making cultural relativism scientific is basically the strategy taken over by anthropology as it takes over cultural relativism in the beginning of this century. The meeting of anthropology and cultural relativsm doesn't happen until then, I would argue. It does not happen, for instance, in Tylor. Tylor is the father of a certain concept of culture, roughly the idea of culture as 'the whole thing'. This idea is democratic, anti-elitist. Contrary to Matthew Arnold's concept of culture, it includes not just 'the best which has been thought and said', but rather 'everything which has been thought and said'. Still, Tylor is not a cultural relativist, for just like his fellow anthropologists at his time, he is interested in culture, not in cultures. As Ruth Benedict has pointed out, the decisive development in anthropology takes place when anthropologists turn from the study of primitive culture to the study of primitive cultures. And Tylor's famous definition can be found in a book, entitled, precisely, *Primitive Culture*.

It might be tempting, however, to trace the meeting of anthropology and cultural relativism to Franz Boas, since he is the founding father of an anthropological tradition that anthropologists have themselves labelled 'cultural relativism'. But to show how pervasive cultural relativism is - or has been - in anthropology, I would like to cite an equally famous anthropologist, who is, however, not equally associated with cultural relativism, i.e.

Bronislaw Malinowski. In Malinowski's *Argonauts of the Western Pacific* the come-together of relativism and anthropology manifests itself as the claim that anthropology has so far been unscientific. The charge is exactly that previous anthropologists have never gone beneath the surface of mere 'custom'. 'Armchair-anthropologist', as they will be labelled by the new anthropology, have isolated customs from their local contexts and examined them as evidence of the early stages of universal history. This approach is from now on unscientific. Malinowski takes all his pride in the fact that his anthropology is able to do what his predecessors were not able to do, nor, one might add, took any interest in - viz., to expose the local order underlying all the customs of a given group. »Ethnology has introduced law and order into what seemed chaotic and freakish. It has transformed the sensational, wild, and unaccountable world of 'savages' into a number of well ordered communities, governed by law, behaving and thinking according to consistent principles.«[7] Malinowski's account of the task of anthropology is entirely a denigration of what he sees as 19. century curio-hunting, as a fascination by savage disorder, as a fondness of isolated, bizarre exotica. Thanks to Malinowski's new relativist anthropology, 'the savage' gives way to 'cultures', and correspondingly, the bizarre and disordered of savage existence gives way to »a picture of the natives subjected to a strict code of behaviour and good manners, to which in comparison life at the Court of Versailles or Escurial, was free and easy.«[8] Thus, as for anthropology the disorder of savage existence has been replaced by the order of culture, and as for relativism grammar has been replaced by social structure as the framework through which the spiritual unity of nations can be made accessible. The kaleidoscopic variety of customs is ordered in terms of what Malinowski calls a »permanent and fixed structure« that has its proper »anatomy«.

This structure can be analyzed in terms of function. But the distinction between function and meaning is not exclusive. Although the early stages of 20.- century Anglo-Saxon anthropology are defined by two schools of which one - which is also British - emphasizes function (and consequently the concept of 'society') whereas the other - which is also American - emphasizes meaning (and consequently the concept of 'culture'), anthropological relativism is based on an emphasis of both notions - 'function' and 'meaning', and not on the exclusive emphasis on meaning which was the weakness of Herder's relativism.

This difference is clear in Malinowski, as is the fact that he remains the inheritor of Herder's intuition. In his view human communities are integrated wholes, organizing biological, social and metaphysical needs in very different, but equally consistent ways. This basic relativist conception has a functionalist, as well a hermeneutical dimension. It tells us that cultures are both *banal* and *unique*. Primitive communities are governed by an anonymous social code and since their behaviour is rule-governed they can be apprehended scientifically - in terms of those 'tables of kinship terms, genealogies, maps, plans and diagrams' in which Malinowski takes such pride. This approach is never sufficient, however, social structure as such remains empty, purely mechanical. It can take you some of the way, but in the end what matters is hermeneutics, the grasping of the the uniqueness of each culture, the particular kind of happiness it aspires to. »In each culture«, says Malinowski, »the values are slightly different; people aspire after different aims, follow different impulses, yearn after a different form of happiness.«[9] Thus, no matter how much empathy has been reduced by the expostion of scientifically accountable systems of rules, one last empathic leap is needed to grasp what really matters, the spirtual nature of the nation, or as Malinowski chooses to express it, »the native's outlook on things, his *Weltanschauung*, the breath of life and reality which he breathes and by which he lives.«[10]

There is a lot of continuity in this story - the continuity of an intellectual tradition. But there is not the identity of a philosophical thesis. However, cultural relativism often has been made into a philosophical thesis, and not only by its opponents. I guess the most eloquent example is the kind of cultural relativism which Humboldt invented and which Sapir and particularly Whorf carried into this century. Humboldt proned a sort of cultural relativism which was not available to Herder, not just because it was based on a science of linguistics posterior to Herder, but also because Humboldt took a certain Kantian approach to the whole problem, a linguistic turn of Kantianism, as it were. In Humboldt's view language was a *Weltansicht*, a view of the world in the very particular - Kantian - sense that language structures experience, and in this sense shapes phenomenal experience. Humboldtian language does not, however, shape experience in the same way as Kantian intelligence. In this context the crucial point is that human beings have one kind of intelligence but many kinds of languages. Thus, the decisive difference between Kant and Humboldt is that whereas in Kant's view there was one cognitive structure for all human beings, in Humboldt's view there are in principle as many cognitive structures as there are languages.

In Humboldt's work this point was still modified by his belief in the universality of logic. In this century it has been rephrased more unambiguously by Benjamin Lee Whorf who claimed - in his more radical moods, at least - that the idea that language determines thought is an incorrect generalization of the fact that each native language determines thought. Whorf even said that languages with markedly different grammars could not be 'calibrated' to each other and so seemed to suggest that utterances made by Hopi indians, for instance, could not be translated into English.

Probably neither Humboldt nor Whorf ever really meant anything like this. Still, among philosophers this has been the dominant conception of cultural relativism, and it has of course been refuted over and over again. In doing so, most philosophers have been employing some version of the argument of selfreferential inconsistency which I mentioned in the beginning of my paper. It has been argued that the idea of an intranslatable language is incoherent, simply because translatability is a criterion of languagehood; and in a similar vein, it has been argued that if alien languages were as alien as Whorf pretended, he could not even have highlighted those differences.

Still, correct as these criticisms may be in relation to certain imprudent remarks by Whorf, they don't really get to the heart of cultural relativism. The best illustration of this is the anthropological version of cultural relativism. In a non-pejorative sense, it constitutes a banalization of cultural relativism. It speaks neither of ineffable spiritual natures, as Herder did, or of hidden cognitive processes, as Whorf did. Relativist anthropology is a distinguishedly *tempered* kind of cultural relativism: its proponents have always firmly believed in what they call 'the spiritual unity of mankind'. They have rarely cultivated a sense of dramatic otherness, but have rather, as my Malinowski quotations earlier were supposed to show, presented alien cultures as alternative normalities, living off their exotic banalities, just as we are living off our familiar banalities. Thus, disposed as they are towards humanism, relativist anthropologists have practically never pretended that different cultures cannot understand each other, and therefore they cannot be reached by any philosophical arguments about the incoherence of relativism.

This does not mean that anthropology should be acquitted of any complicity in the problems of cultural relativism, it just means that cultural relativism should be criticized along different lines. What Whorf has in common with other forms of cutual relativism is not some excentric philosophical claims, but the idea that the social life of a people constitutes a unified whole. That is the idea expressed by his metaphysics of language. If reality is filtered through language in the way Whorf pretends, then the social reality of a people is both *unique*, since its reality is shaped by its particular language, and *uniform*, since all aspects of its reality is shaped by the same linguistic system. This is an intuition which he shares with the rest of cultural relativism, and this intuition is responsible for his philosophical predicament - not the other way round. In short, the problem of intranslatable languages is caused not by certain erroneous philosophical views, but rather by the very idea that the social life of human communities constitutes unified forms of life governed by coherent systems of values. In this view cultures are self-enclosed entities, bodies of meaning between which communication must be established. The point is that as long as you think this way you will have to wonder how to get out of your own culture and how to get into other ones; as long as you believe in the uniqueness and unity of cultures, you will always be faced with the problem of getting inside, of building bridgeheads, of figuring out whether the aliens have rational beliefs or rather utterly different cognitive systems.

To the extent the decisive problem of cultural relativism is its obsession with wholeness, the most incisive criticism of the idea of untranslatable languages has in my view come from Peter Winch. In a recent article called 'Language, Belief and Relativism' he argues, not that the idea of untranslatable languages is selfrefuting, but rather that the entire discussion about it is misguided. His point is that it is based on a chronic confusion of two different ways in which we talk about 'languages' and the relations between them. In one case we talk about 'natural languages' - say, English and Hopi. In the other case we talk about different types of discourse - i.e. 'the scientific language', 'the religious language', etc. Referring to the magic of the Azande - his recurrent example- Winch expresses the point in the following way: »When we are considering the 'translatability' of the Zande language into English, these ways of distinguishing 'different languages' overlap. There would be little difficulty, over a wide area, in agreeing that certain expressions in the one language 'mean the same' (roughly) as certain expressions in the other. But in other areas, to demand a translation from the Zande into English would be like asking for a translation of something mathematical into something non-mathematical.«[11] Winch is making several points here. One is that the Whorfian mystification of language, the mythology of mother tongues has been made plausible by the fact that when you are trying to make sense of the behaviour of an alien people, you are learning a new language and new types of cultural discourse at the same time. His second point is simple and familiar to any anthropologist: not all parts of a culture are equally difficult to understand. But the conclusion he draws is less trivial: that we should not talk about problems of interpretation in terms of languages in the first, Whorfian, sense - as whole ways of life - but rather in the second sense, as unfamiliar discursive practices that are not necessarily the expression of any unified vision of life.

The same point has been made by Ian Hacking who has claimed that the famous problem of establishing 'bridgeheads' inside an alien culture is the least of problems. According to Hacking there exists a significant stock of 'intercultural banalities' (like watching out for snakes) that makes intercultural communication relatively easy. The problem lies elsewhere, in the existence of what he calls 'styles of reasoning'[12], particular discursive practices that may be unique to a certain community, like the Zande magic, but unlike mathematics, nowadays common to a lot of communities. In Hacking's view the banalities and the styles of reasoning of a particular community do not constitute a unity, as little as the different styles of reasoning of a community constitute a unity. There is what he calls 'a looseness of fit' between the different areas. This is not to say that styles of reasoning are utterly independent on each other and on the day-to-day banalities of a community's life. These areas influence each other in different ways, but they do not add up to a coherent whole. Thus, what Hacking says about science is also true about culture: he firmly believes in its disunity. In an essay on Donald Davidson he has expressed this as a point about language and has done so in the following way: »Let us conclude, not [as Davidson has done] that 'there is no such thing as a language' that we bring to interaction with others. Say rather that there is no such thing as the one total language that we bring. We bring numerous only loosely connected languages from the loosely connected communities, that we inhabit.«[13]

One possible way of rephrasing Hacking's point would be that we should have a *contextualist* rather than a *holist* approach to culture. We should not go back to the atomism of 'custom'. We should stick to the view that you can only make sense of a cultural practice by looking at the context in which it exists, but we should not expect it to form a coherent whole with this context. Rather, we should expect some parts of this context to be irrelevant, and other parts of it to conflict with it and contradict it in various ways. Thus, we should stress the disunity of culture, the fact that culture is as much a field of conflict as the kind of existential guidance with which it has often been identified. This would be a point about culture, not about the relation between cultures. In this sense conflict and cultural confusion would be a dimension of culture itself, not an offense caused by the meeting with different cultures. Applying Lyotard's point about language to culture, we might say that the fundamental reason for cultural conflict is not, that cultures are different, but rather that culture is heterogenous - that even at its most local level it is made up of different and partly contradictory perspectives. No matter how thoroughly you split up a modern nation state into ethnic subdivisions, you will never end up with something homogenous and pure. The same applies to culture: there is no bounded whole at any level.

The consequence of such a perspective would be a blurring of the distinction between the intracultural and the intercultural levels. All cultures display a certain degree of disunity, they all experience conflicts between cultural practices and thus live with a certain level of incommensurability. The incommensurability we experience with alien cultures is not in principle any different from this. We try to make sense of unfamiliar types of discourse. The problem is the same even if more difficult because the contexts are generally less familiar to us.

This point can be used as a criticism of a certain subjectivism pervasive in cultural relativism. The traditional anthropological ideal of grasping 'the native's point of view' remains a subjectivism, a collective subjectivism to put it oxymoronically. But if you take Hacking's distinction between intercultural banalities and styles of reasoning the problem is no longer about persons. That which can differ and be hard to understand are certain ways of thinking and acting, not the 'mentality' of persons, for this mentality are - for better or worse and taking into account the intercultural banalities - the same as ours.

The advantage offered by this view is a dedramatization of the problem of intercultural communication. One significant paradox of the last few years is that everywhere people are writing books saying more or less the things I have been saying - that we should not believe much in the relativist concept of culture. And at the same time this concept is being taken more seriously than it has been for a long time, by various peoples around the world, but also by political scientists who have given up a political vocabulary that doesn't work any more and therfore propose to explain global conflicts as a spiritual battle between cultures. In the face of this new culturalism there may be no better strategy than to go on dismantling intercultural problems rather than trying to overcome them. The greatest problem of intercultural communication may still be an excessive seriousness about culture, the idea of culture as a unified spiritual treasure whose integrity, whose fragile wholeness must above all be protected and fought for. Maybe we could learn something from Montaigne's irony which was supressed by the solemn discourse of cultural relativism - a certain lightmindedness about cultural differences. The relativist concept of culture is the idea of an *a priori* obstacle to conversation with strangers, and that is the problem about it. Building a bridge is less of a merit when you have made the gap yourself. No such obstacles should be admitted prior to conversation. To the extent obstacles are presupposed, they are expected, and such fulfillment of expectations is exactly the opposite of the *happening* that differentiates a conversation from all the ordinary forms of communication. This is not to say that there will be no cross-cultural obstacles. But they should not be the foundations of communication; they should be the peripeties of conversation.

---

1   R. Rorty, 'Pragmatism, Relativism, and Irrationalism', in *Consequences of Pragmatism*, University of Minnesota Press, Minneapolis 1982, p. 166.
2   Montaigne, 'Of the Cannibals', in *Essays* Vol. I, J.M. Dent, London 1980, p. 219.
3   J.G. Herder, *Auch eine Philosophie der Geschichte zur Bildung der Menschheit*, Suhrkamp, Frankfurt am Main 1967, p. 44f.
4   Ibid., p. 45f.
5   Ibid., p. 44.
6   W. v. Humboldt, 'Ueber die Verschiedenheit des menschlichen Sprachbaues', *Gesammelte Schriften* VII, p. 42f.
7   B. Malinowski, *Argonauts of the Western Pacific*, Routledge and Kegan Paul, London 1978 (1922), p. 10.
8   Ibid.
9   Ibid., s. 25.
10 Ibid., s. 517.
11 P. Winch, 'Language, Belief and Relativism', in *Trying to Make Sense*, Basil Blackwell, Oxford/New York 1987, s. 198.
12 See I. Hacking, 'Styles of Scientific Reasoning', in J. Rachman/C. West (Eds.), *Post-Analytic Philosophy*, Columbia University Press, New York 1985.
13 I. Hacking, 'The Parody of Conversation', in E. LePore (Ed.), *Truth and Interpretation. Perspectives on the Philosophy of Donald Davidson*, Basil Blackwell, Oxford/Cambridge 1986, p. 458.

Thomas M. Seebohm

Literary Tradition, Intercultural Transfer and Cross-Cultural Conversations

Introduction
The first two parts of this paper introduce a series of theses I have explained in greater detail in other essays[1]. These theses are the premises for the other theses developed in the third part of the paper. The first part develops some basic characteristics of "archaic" non-literary and literary cultures and the very limited possibilities of intercultural contacts for such cultures. The second part investigates different stages in the development of literary cultures and the correlated possibilities, even necessities, of entering intercultural transfer in cultural contacts. We will distinguish between cultural contacts: violent and non-violent destruction of other cultures, violent and non-violent acculturation, intercultural transfer including unconscious transfer i. e. transfer without recognizing the other culture as other in itself and conscious transfer, and finally cross- cultural conversations. The third part of the paper raises the question of the framework for such conversations in highly developed literary cultures, their presuppositions and their limits. It is necessary to ask this question because an cross-cultural conversations presuppose a long prehistory of other forms of cultural contacts. Cross-cultural conversations are not only threatened by the regressive power of drives leading back again to archaic patterns of behavior. Ethnical purges, racism and fundamentalism, other forms of xenophobia belong to the realm of archaic cultural attitudes lingering in the background of modern cultural consciousness. Cross-cultural conversations are plagued in addition by paradoxes and antagonisms on the highest levels of self-conscious reflections. One present expression of such antagonisms is the antagonism between the school in hermeneutics that preaches a return to the "unity of interpretation and application" under the umbrella of a tradition providing the source for the advent of truth in hermeneutics and the emphasis on the need of fragmentation and a somehow masochistic self-hate of western "ethnocentrism"[2]. Finally for this purpose it is also necessary to criticize the concept of culture that defines culture as "organic

whole" and a unity in itself. "Culture" in this paper will be defined as "tradition via fixed life expressions". Further conclusions will be drawn in the third part of the paper[3].

Part I. *Cultural contacts among "archaic societies"*

1. A culture is not possible without tradition. Traditions presuppose fixed life expressions of the culture governing the behavior of a string of generations, their laws, values and truths. Life expressions are not fixed if they lack the capability being given as the identically the same in the future, like the spoken word or a dance or a song. They can be memorized, but changes of memories remain hidden for the process of memorizing and remembering. Fixed life expressions are buildings, tools, cultivated fields but also written speech[4]. To preserve tradition is essential for the survival of a society living in this culture. Traditions govern production, trade, family structures, principles of right and wrong, and the rules for the legitimate use of violence in the society originally laid down in the law systems provided within the framework of religious systems.

2. The intrinsic power of tradition serving the survival of a culture, among other factors, depends on the degree of complexity of expressive power, integration and durability of its fixed life expressions. In most cases of known cultures, literary or not, spoken language is the main tool among the life expressions serving communication within a culture. Spoken language is not fixed and that means communication is restricted to the realm of face to face relations, including some social relations close to face to face relations, e.g. in a calling distance. The power of written language is that written language - alphabetic or not - is capable of creating fixed life expressions in a sign matter that can be identified as the same again in different places and times and by different persons. It is also required that it can be linked with the life expressions of oral discourse, i.e. oral discourse can be transformed into written discourse and the art of reading is the ability to transform written discourse back into some, not necessarily the same, spoken language. Chinese writing e. g. is not alphabetic and can be read in different languages. Only with the aid of written language it is possible to "send" messages beyond face to face relations into times and spaces at a far distance: commands, ordinances, laws in the first place. Laws and ordinances - including laws and ordinances in the framework of religious texts or texts referring to religious cults - are fixed life expressions in a culture laying

down the rules of to be and not to be, of well being and misery of the individuals living in a culture according to the positive and negative sanctions set up for certain deeds or properties, e.g. the property of being male or female. Larger empires surviving for long periods of time presuppose written language and they presuppose a certain division of power between those who use the sword and those who administer the tradition, i. e. the priests.

3. Written discourse is a powerful instrument, but it is given on the background of other fixed life expressions. This fact is often forgotten in "philosophical hermeneutics" and similar types of lingualism. A literary tradition is possible only in a living tradition within a pregiven system of other fixed life expressions of a culture: cultivated fields, animals kept for certain use, buildings, tents, tools, temples, gathering places, villages, weapons. It is the main function of oral discourse within a culture to refer to fixed life expressions of this sort and discourse refers to other objects outside and to individual members of the cultural society almost exclusively to the degree in which they are related to such objects. Written discourse in the beginning is bound to the same context of referents. It cannot be separated from its foundations "in the life world" and the other fixed life-expressions of this lifeworld.

4. We can, therefore, distinguish between two types of archaic cultures: Cultures without and with written discourse. The tendency to call the first group "primitive" in highly complex literary traditions is an expression of the power of archaic behavior in such cultures. Even for famous Greek philosophers the "barbarians" were "by nature" possible slaves, Greeks, of course, were not. We will come back to intercultural contacts between archaic cultures in the next point. "Primitive cultures" are by no means primitive. Their system of fixed and not fixed life expressions can be highly complex. I will call them non-literal[5]. As mentioned: written discourse is a powerful tool. Since this tool is missing in non-literal cultures they are extremely vulnerable. Higher developed forms of non-literary cultures do not last long. A natural catastrophe lasting for two or three generations is able to destroy complex networks of communication in oral discourse and memorizing - the only tool of bridging time distances in non literary cultures. The phenomena belonging to this specific type of vulnerability are perplexing. I cannot deal with them in this paper, but we have to consider their fate in cultural contacts with archaic literary cultures and literary cultures in general.

5. Cultural contacts between cultures with a literary tradition and those without it are deadly encounters for the latter. They will be destroyed, their population will be enslaved or hopelessly contaminated. Their only chance is to develop a literary tradition for their own language. Even cultures that to a very high degree developed the ability to integrate foreign cultures with literary traditions, like Rome in late classical antiquity, have rules according to which they judge cultures to be human or not. The emperor Claudius the Stutterer, though one of the most educated "humanists" of his time, decreed that the head hunting and men sacrificing culture of the Druids was inhuman and did whatever he could to destroy the celtic culture. The Christians did the mop up operations. Even the contact with cultures with an interest in ethnology and an interest in preserving primitive cultures will, in the long run, destroy the non literary cultures, though not necessarily their people. The first step in the destruction of non-literary cultures is to provide them with tools, fixed life expressions, referring to another cultural context. The last step is to teach them to write and to read and the attempt to "fix" their tradition in written discourse. The fixation itself destroys the most essential features of a non-literal archaic culture. This is the most favorable scenario one can think of and it becomes possible only after the long development of literary cultures to be considered in the second part of this paper.

6. The character and the structures of cultural contacts between archaic literary cultures and non-literary cultures but also between archaic literary cultures are determined by the internal function of the production of texts within an archaic literary tradition. This function is not an aspect of literary tradition itself. It belongs to tradition via fixed life expressions as the essential feature of culture in general. The function is to guarantee the integrative power of the dominating structures of action and evaluation within a culture and that means as well to be a measuring rod of what is "right" and "wrong" in the broadest sense. Given that original function it is very much the question whether the term "structure" can be used for intercultural contacts between archaic cultures. It can be used only if it is understood that a structure revealing primarily antagonistic relations can be called a structure. In the beginning literary tradition serves no other purpose but preserving the unity of the culture over larger distances of space and time. To be able to do that is vital. It is a matter of life and death for a society. In cultures living under the rule of what Charles Sanders Peirce called "the method of authority" all doubts in "what has been written"

and disobedience receive exemplar punishment[6]. I call such cultures "archaic literary cultures". To be hostile to changes within the own tradition implies a potential hostility to other cultures. The hostility is potential as long as there is no immediate cultural contact with the exception of occasional trade if trade does not involve the import of behavioral patterns harmful for the patterns of behavior within the culture. The hostility is actualized in immediate cultural contacts. A brief survey of the possible "structures" of such encounters is necessary. It is also necessary to mention that such structures of archaic behavior can still govern the relations between further developed literary cultures.

The simple case is the case in which the powers of two cultures are balanced. The consequence will be a violent struggle interrupted by instable peaceful periods. Complex cases, sometimes producing active intercultural encounters, are the cases in which one culture wins the victory. Set aside the complete destruction of the other culture we have enslavement in some cases allowing the survival of a spoken language and some remnants of habits characteristic for slaves. The best possibility is the survival of the now powerless culture as a subculture with a literary tradition of its own. What happens is that the two cultures, though existing together economically, provide defenses, shields, separating themselves in providing a ghetto for the weaker culture, inventing separating laws for strict endogamy, in addition rules for nourishment, regulations for admitted and not admitted encounters. Under such circumstances there potential is left for riots of the members of the underprivileged culture on the one hand and pogroms exercised by the members of the dominating power on the other hand. But there are also possibilities of cultural contacts within such a society belonging already to the possibilities of further development of the literary culture leading to the final destruction of archaic literary cultures from within.

7. One final point has to be mentioned in this part. Non literary archaic cultures can win a short lived triumph over literary cultures, in the most cases literary cultures that moved beyond the archaic stage of their development. The presuppositions of such a triumph are: high mobility, highly developed new war techniques connected with mobility, a strict command - obedience structure with a certain degree of sophistication, again closely connected with conquering military activities. Given that and other supporting factors the "fall of Rome" is a phenomenon to be observed again and again in ancient history. But precisely at this point the power of literary

culture emerges again. The conqueror wants the riches. The production of riches requires the production means. The production means as a necessary condition imply the art of writing. Written language is more powerful than spoken language. Consequence: The conqueror will loose its own culture with the exception of some insignificant traces and the conqueror will even even loose its own spoken language. The "Bulgars" are called "Bulgars", but their language is slavic, the vast majority of the population is slavic and the language of the Bulgars is extinct as well as the language of the teutonic tribes conquering those parts of the Roman empire now belonging to France, Italy and Spain. Conclusion: non-literary cultures perish in cultural contacts with literary cultures or they are capable to transform themselves into new literary cultures.

In general: the ability of entering cultural transfer in archaic literary cultures is very limited. If it happens it has to happen below the level of a conscious encounter. Influences can only sneak in without being noticed as such. To be able to recognize such encounters - and such encounters are far from being "intercultural conversations" - needs first a further development taking place within literary cultures.

Part II. *Stages of the development of literary culture*

First Cycle
Stages of such developments and stages of the development of non-violent cultural contacts are in strict correlation. A rather schematic picture of the different phases possible in such a development will be given in the following paragraphs. The available underlying material is restricted to the study of the western literary tradition. Therefore I have to admit that I am only able to document and illustrate the structures mentioned with considerations restricted to the European tradition. I can make some guesses about similar or different features in other traditions but I would not be able to document them in a scholarly fashion. Comparative studies are necessary, but they can be prepared only in future "cross cultural conversations". I assume, however, that it is possible to develop some abstract general theses with the aid of my restricted material.

1. The first step beyond an archaic literary culture is a further division of labor. We can observe the emergence of different literary genres. Myths,

reports of godlike heros and godlike emperors included, religious and social laws, philosophical-theological reflections are presented in archaic literary cultures without separating specific literary genres. Crafts, trade, reports about facts are not yet represented in the literary culture. The first stage of the development of a literary culture exhibits a separation of the "professions" of priests and theologians, philosophers and their schools, lawyers and lawgivers organized in different institutions and producing different literary genres. In addition new genres emerge, first the "narratives", the histories, *historiai*, i. e. reports of facts of all kinds. Such facts may be collected in a "history of animals", in histories about certain events - a kind of journalism and by no means history in our sense, and finally reports of travellers following the travel routes of trade and war, often involved in both[7]. Such reports are the first documents of conscious cultural contacts. "Conscious" in a literary tradition of a culture just means: documented as such in texts and specific genres of texts. Two new genres emerge later. Between histories, i. e. collection of facts, philosophical reflections, interest in the crafts as providers of "mechanical tricks" a new type of literature emerges: scientific literature. Neither the genre nor the concept of science has been well defined for a long time - set aside some special disciplines like geometry or astronomy. A further secondary genre is poetry. It has its origin in a certain degeneration of theological literature. Myth and poetry, prophets and poets in the beginning are not distinguished. The heritage of the prophets/ poets later is administrated by priests and the main concern of priests is to organize this wealth for the sake of a stabilization of society and culture and to determine the right and the wrong, the true and the false understanding of the sacred texts. In a long development finally leading to the *l'art pour l'art* principle the human *fonction fabulatrice* creates its own medium, poetry, because it has lost its place in mythological contexts administered by priests and theologians. I mention an additional thesis. The indicator of the "freedom" and the emancipatory character of poetry is the freedom in which cultural contacts can be accepted in poetry as an independent literary genre. The minstrels of the medieval knights reveal an arabic influence. The freeing of poetry in the beginning of the renaissance precedes the development of the fully developed humanism.

2. The distribution of "labor" generates tensions. Philosophers and their institutions claim to have an independent and immediate access to truth. They challenge the mythological but also the legal tradition and its claims. The arguments of philosophers at this stage are not "scientific". They are

moral. What is challenged is the legitimacy of the rules of behavior laid down in an archaic literary culture. The gods, as described by the myths, display a blasphemous, immoral picture of divinity. The laws legitimized by tradition create unjust states. Plato started it, the Stoics draw the final conclusion in classical antiquity. Such an approach opposing tradition by "reason" - whatever that means in different cultural contexts, it implies the claim that human thinking has an immediate access to eternal truth. It is the first attempt in which tradition as such becomes dubious and even false. Eternal truths are truths accessible to all mankind. Seen from the outside such eternal truths are by no means universal but closely connected with the presuppositions of their own literary culture. Given the belief in reason and its ability to judge the past development of the own tradition, the same reason can be used to judge other cultures and their beliefs and such judgments very often lead to a positive evaluation of other cultures. The wisdom of the Egyptians, the Persian virtue, the virtue of the Teutonic tribes, but later on for instance Turkish justice or Chinese wisdom are judged with sympathy, but this sympathy is a sympathy grounded in a type of reason that has emerged within a literary culture and, seen from a later point of view, it implies serious misconceptions of foreign cultures.

Philosophical reflections, with many different admixtures, later including also motives taken from *historiai* and scientific-technological literature, but also by adoption of mythical elements, oppose each other in further development. Their claim to have access to eternal truth becomes dubious within the culture. Criticism of the "falsehood" of the tradition is turned against the development, the tradition of philosophy itself, and, with growing inconsistencies inside the tradition, has the tendency to threaten the unity of the literary culture as such.

The law, originally immediately connected with religion in this context, receives an independent status and an independent literary tradition. Influenced to a certain degree by philosophical motives, but tied back to very pragmatic viewpoints of a partially secularized state, it develops its own systems. Society gains certain advantages. Under this formal umbrella of power it is able to "rule" different cultures. They are, essentially, treated as different subcultures. An empire unified by naked military power, trade interests, and legal principles not bound to the specific religions and literary traditions of the different people living in the empire provides the most favorable medium of intercultural transfer at this stage of development. The reaction of members of different traditions is by no means positive in many cases. It is noticed with disgust that the old rules of conduct of the own tradition loose their power. At this stage of the development of literary traditions one has a situation in which one cultural tradition created a powerful and energetic society capable of subjugating many other cultures and tolerating them as subcultures. The survival of such an empire can be secured if the leading cultural tradition is able to develop a legal and administrative system to a high degree independent from the religious tradition, a secularized law system, in part backed by certain philosophically justified principles. Rome was capable to achieve that, Athens was not.

3. The original social function of literary tradition was to integrate society and to guarantee its durability. It was an instrument for the most urgent needs of an archaic culture. If, however, a culture develops a more and more complex system of different genres and a memory of many different texts and isolated textual traditions the life energy of literary tradition turns itself against the original interest of the archaic society. This is not an intentional process. It happens in a similar fashion in which economical changes happen in a society. The process of desintigration already in its beginning but then very influential in the end creates two types of reaction.

a. The need of society to preserve its tradition and to understand it, first of all to understand it as an integrated unity, creates a new literary profession already in the first cycle of development of literary traditions: the philologist, mostly in personal union with the rhetorician on the one hand and the pedagogue, the schoolmaster, on the other. A growing literary tradition is first of all in need of an "art of grammar", a collection of methodical viewpoints of the discipline of interpreting texts developing different viewpoints for the interpretation of texts - in short: what was called "hermeneutics" later. The knowledge of the figures of literary and spoken speech and the function of such speeches for different groups of addressees at different occasions is on the one hand a specific area of specialization in philology and on the other hand the tool of those who want to apply the universal wisdom of the culture available with the aid of philology to the needs of the society in specific situation, i. e. those who practice the art of rhetorics. A person who masters both arts, philology and rhetorics, i. e. the art of interpretation and application, has the highest wisdom within the culture. Such a person is a *vir bonus* and a "humanist". His art is superior to all other arts, including the art of the philosopher who might be right in having access to universal truth, but does not know how to apply it. It is the art in which the own, just available tradition is understood as the universal unity of truth, of true humanity, of the true, the good and the beautiful[8].

The most challenging task for the philologists is the apparent contradiction between partial literary traditions within the literary tradition. The most urgent contradiction is the contradiction between the layer of the mythical archaic literary tradition and the more recent levels of the literary traditions. A certain remedy is the invention of allegorical interpretation as a new tool of the philologist. Allegorical interpretation has the task to bridge the tensions and gaps between the old archaic literary culture and the literary products, first of all of philosophical, then poetical, modern legal and then even "scientific" literature. It has to be shown that the truths of the later developments of literary tradition are already the essential truths of the old mythological literature hidden in the allegorical disguise if the general thesis that the system of erudition of one's own culture - understood as the erudition of humanity as such - is a reliable well rounded unity for the future of the literary culture.

Humanism is fragile. It has the character of mending again and again a network of pipes leaking everywhere and finally solving serious problems in just not looking at them. Humanism is in a similar situation if it confronts different cultures and cultural transfer under the umbrella of partially secularized legal institutions. On the one hand it embraces other cultures as other testimonies of the universal truth, goodness and beauty of mankind and, on the other hand, is limited to the scope of its own literary tradition. It is not aware of the fact that the fragmentation of its own tradition which it tries to overcome is the very source of its limited capability to appreciate foreign cultures within the limits of the own tradition. It has, on the other hand, rigid limits in its capability to appreciate other cultural traditions. At some point cultural differences, are seen as the difference of the human and the inhuman.

b. The mending of the humanists, in the long run, is not convincing. The apparent inconsistencies in the literary tradition are overwhelming and steadily multiplying. The counterpart of the philologist and humanist is the sceptic, teaching against this proclaimed "unity of interpretation and application of the true tradition" absolute, unbridgeable fragmentation, a fragmentation in which no position can prove its mettle against others because there are good immanent reasons for each of them but also good immanent reasons within each position against all others. There is no universal truth, the search for truth is in itself an illusion. The opposition of humanism and scepticism completes the desintegration and fragmentation of the unity literary tradition by means of which it was capable to serve the needs of the archaic society.

The Second Cycle
1. The archaic urge for a unified literary tradition is a powerful force in the background of a desintegrated literary tradition. It can be satisfied only by a new myth, a new religion. But this religion has lost its innocence. In order to become the dominating power within society it has to declare as false everything in the old tradition, thus strictly distinguishing between a true and a false tradition. The growing scepticism within the old literary tradition is one of its most powerful allies. It can use its arguments to convince society that the old tradition is indeed false throughout, rotten and incapable to satisfy the needs of men - now men in general! The hostility towards other cultures, practiced in innocence in archaic literary traditions, turns against other literary traditions as such. They are not considered simply as foreign. They are considered as the products of rotten and pervert adult human beings ready to be condemned. The social consequences are tremendous. The first task is the pitiless material destruction of the old tradition. The transition to an archaic literary culture of second order is accompanied by a universal purge, a universal cultural revolution. But this motive is now also a powerful instrument for defending the integrity of the new literary tradition. Those who deviate are the creators of a false tradition, rotten and condemned. They can and must be eliminated for the sake of the salvation of the "true" believers in the eminent texts of the new religion. The eminent texts <u>and their interpretation</u> by the followers of the true tradition are the touch stone for the distinction between the one "true" and the many "false" traditions of unbelievers and heretics. Both are lumped together. This attitude, of course, now also dominates cultural contacts and creates crusades - especially against other second order archaic literary cultures. The main point of difference between archaic literary cultures of the first and second order has to be emphasized again. Second order archaic cultures presuppose in themselves the knowledge, the consciousness, that literary culture as such is not the warrant of truth. It is now recognized that literary traditions can be intrinsically false and that it is only the own literary culture which is the warrant of truth and that this truth is revealed to it in its eminent texts separating truth and falsehood.

2. Archaic cultures of the second level cannot escape the laws of development of literary traditions. In themselves after some centuries they have the need to bridge tensions in their own tradition with the aid of refined allegorical techniques. There is also the need to prove the <u>concordance</u> of the own tradition against "seeming" contradictions. The original motivation of the philologists is now satisfied with refined tools of interpretive and logical devices. We have "scholasticism" replacing philology[9]. The task of scholasticism is extremely difficult. Cultural contacts and cultural transfer cannot be avoided in literary genres separated from the archaic core. They can also be instrumental for a reinforcement of the remnants of the old literary tradition. Thus it is necessary to establish a concordance between an assumed "natural revelation" for human reason common to mankind as a whole - again seen in the framework of the own literary tradition - and the truths of the revealed truth of the eminent texts and their official interpretation. Tensions occur again, fragmentation occurs again. The main problem is now to determine the borders between a natural reason in concordance with the true tradition and "perverted forms" of natural reason and the fragmenting struggle is a struggle about the determination of such borderlines. The chaos is complete at the very moment in which the older tradition comes to the surface again and gains power in a "renaissance". It is complete because it restores old-fashioned humanism in the place of "natural reason" and leads to a partial justification of literary traditions condemned as false in the beginning

2. Again, the urge for having a pure and true tradition is unbroken. There are now new means for the satisfaction of the urge. Archaic literary traditions of the second order are dominated by eminent texts, separating true and false tradition. Their interpretation now has its own long and complicated tradition full of tensions and fragmentations. The urge to return to the old simplicity can be satisfied in a new move. It can now turn against the older tradition of interpreting eminent texts separating true and false tradition with the claim that this tradition of interpreting them is "false". The result is a reformation. But such a reformation is a turn in which the very core of the literary tradition responsible for the integration of the society is understood as false. It is no more the falsehood of a simple literary tradition. A tradition of interpreting eminent true texts is declared to be false. This discovery creates a new type of radical falsehood, the falsehood of a tradition of understanding the roots of a tradition[10]. The consequences are long and

cruel religious wars within a culture. Hostility has turned inside. The praxis of reformers, of protestants, to declare the traditions of interpreting eminent texts as false can lead to splits within the protestants or reformers themselves. This tendency comes to an end only if the reformers succeed and gain control over the further development of literary tradition in alliances with political powers.

3. The step taken by reformers in a complex literary culture with roots in a secondary archaic culture has a significant effect. Within literary tradition it creates the possibility of a new attitude towards literary traditions, i. e. in the long run not only its own but also other literary traditions. Such consequences were by no means intended by the reformers. The further development shows that such consequences are counterproductive for their original goals. Their intention is only to start a renewal of the secondary archaic literary tradition "from the beginning". The new turn in understanding literary tradition and its premises has several aspects that must be carefully distinguished.

a. Secondary archaic traditions refer back to a group of eminent texts as the touch stone of the distinction of the true from the many false traditions. The suspicion that a false interpretation of the eminent texts has happened in the past was sufficient for the emergence of the further suspicion that a new tradition of the interpretation of the "sources" of a tradition created also a false tradition. There was no specific methodical criterion for proving that an interpretation as an interpretation is false. There was only one and only one criterion for the truth of an interpretation: the unity and harmonious "concordant" development of the tradition of the interpretation of the eminent texts. One of the consequences of the reformers' unreflective attack was that their rejection of a concordant tradition of interpretation of eminent texts was indeed also an attack against the distinction of the true and the many false traditions. A solution for this problem had to be found.

b. The assumption that a "concordant" tradition of the interpretation of eminent texts can be false seemed to be an absurdity for its defenders. The Catholic defenders at the time of the counsel of Trent collected many sophisticated and in their situation very convincing arguments proving the impossibility of separating tradition and interpretation, interpretation and application. A considerable effort had to be made on the side of the protestants to cope with such arguments that have by no means lost their charm today, though they now occur in different literary contexts in the so called "philosophical hermeneutics". An older variant was mentioned above: the unity of philology and rhetorics in classical antiquity and its revival in the Renaissance.

c. The basic problem is: who is able to imagine an interpretation of texts written in a far temporal distance so to speak "through empty space" without being mediated by tradition. It is simply not possible to know that such texts exist without a mediating unbroken tradition. The protestants used the possible difference between the knowledge of the existence of texts, the simple encounter with them as texts written in a certain past, and the problem of different interpretations of the text at different times in the past. The interpretation the text received by contemporary addressees of the texts will be the best among them, because they knew the language perfectly well and also knew about the many circumstantial facts the texts refer to[11]. In addition: this understanding of the text is not corrupted by errors occurring later in the tradition. The task is, therefore, to reconstruct the understanding of the contemporary addressees of the eminent texts of revelation. The understanding of the contemporary addressee can be reconstructed with the aid of the art of grammar provided by the humanists of the Renaissance who renewed this art that had been developed in classical antiquity. The protestant theologians used this art only as a methodical tool to understand their eminent texts and not to gain the "universal wisdom" of the ancient philologist.

The third cycle

Reformers using this tool are by no means aware of the serious consequences. For their own tradition created with this new turn they still claim the unity of truth, tradition, true interpretation and the possibility to distinguish between the true and the many false traditions with the aid of eminent texts. The consequences lead to the complete destruction of this framework. This happens in the third cycle of the development of literary tradition. The third cycle creates also the possible recognition of other cultures as other in their own right. This cycle, therefore, belongs already to the third part of my paper. The price to be paid for the new development is a radicalized fragmentation of literary culture in itself. The steps of the development of the third cycle are highly complex. I have to restrict myself to some very abstract and basic features.

a. It has been mentioned that some literary genres and cultural activities of second order, e. g. concerning technology in the broadest sense, science, trade, and economics, but also poetry and the fine arts have from the very beginning a certain freedom in their development. Precisely for that reason they "travel" easily from one culture to the other in intercultural transfer. Such literary genres are able to free themselves completely from the control of the tradition at the very moment, in which the role of tradition as the warrant of truths becomes doubtful. Especially in science tradition becomes quickly the target of critique. Tradition as such is considered as an obstacle for the approach to truth. Only independent research guided by the latest steps of progress discovers truth.

b. A real crisis emerges, however, for philosophy, law and religion. *Prima facie* it seems to be possible for philosophy to leave the neighborhood of theology and the law and to enter a symbiosis with science. Such a symbiosis seen from the main viewpoint of the topic of this essay, is not without problems. From the very beginning the claim of philosophy was to have an immediate access to eternal truth, an unchangeable human reason, and to be able to derive the guidelines for human conduct from such eternal principles. In its alliance with science philosophy can claim as well that traditions can be judged from the viewpoint of a "scientific" philosophy. The knowledge about other cultures via cultural transfer increased by the new means of science and technology is judged according to the same principles. But the intercultural transfer of philosophical principles and scientific research is different. Technological possibilities developed with the aid of science and later on the practice of scientific research can be adopted by other cultures without immediately interfering with the immanent claims of their own literary tradition. Philosophical principles belong to the web of the value system of a literary tradition, their conceptions of "eternal truths" included. Especially practical and ethical principles of philosophy, i. e. a philosophy raising the not justifiable claim to be a science, a pure rational enlightenment, will not immediately be included in cultural transfer - cultural transfer in violent acculturation excluded of course.

c. The real change in the attitude towards other cultures has other presuppositions. It has its roots in the further development of the principle that a text has to be understood in the context of the contemporary addressee, The principle was later called the "first canon of hermeneutics". As a pure methodical principle it demands that a text has to be understood in its own context and not in the context of the interpreter. Already the first formula confronts the interpreter with a new situation. In order to understand the understanding of the contemporary addressee the interpreter has to interpret texts belonging to literary traditions explicitly condemned in the tradition of the interpretation of the eminent texts as belonging to a "false" tradition. The texts, belonging to the false traditions must be understood in their own context. But "understanding" them cannot mean to agree with them, i. e. to recognize them as testimonies of a truth bearing tradition that has to be applied. Agreement and understanding (*Verständnis* and *Einverständnis*), interpretation and application must be separated. This is by no means an "unnatural" attitude in dialogical discourse. It happens very often that a person or two persons decide that even a serious disagreement can be neglected for the sake of the solution of practical problems necessary for the survival of both sides. The task of the correct understanding of a text becomes separable from the question of its truth. No practical problems are connected with this attitude as long as the text and the contexts in question belong to realms in a large temporal and spatial distance.

d. It is only a "quantitative" not a "qualitative" step if the interpretation of the whole context of a culture is the aim of a methodical understanding instead of the understanding of a text and its context. This can be done in a more or less romantic attitude, trying to grasp the "spirit" of the culture as a whole. It was done in the end of the nineteenth century with much more methodical rigor. Given that the "effective connectedness", the *Wirkungszusammenhang*[12] in the development of a culture and with it cultural contact and cultural transfer and the development of literary culture as such is of interest.

e. With the last step of the development for the first time we have the possibility of a recognition of a foreign culture as foreign in itself, in its otherness. This recognition is a recognition in understanding, by no means in agreement and application. The recognition in the beginning is still bound to the limits of the own cultural tradition, in this case, however, a cultural tradition with a fully developed "historical consciousness". The historical consciousness does not, as such, reach the level of "cross cultural conversations" necessarily including, like all dialogues, also cross cultural conflicts. The foreign cultures of historical consciousness are cultures of the past, cultures understood as representing "false literary traditions" for a long time or discovered in the course of the pursuit of the method penetrating context after context. It is also possible to evade cross cultural conversations and conflicts if the historical research restricts itself to periods of foreign cultures in their past - at least before the 19th century. Finally it is easy to do research in so-called "primitive" or almost "primitive" cultures. They will not be able to challenge the own culture. Nevertheless, the very possibility of recognizing another culture as another in its own right presupposes at least for one culture the whole course of the development of the literary culture characterized in this paper.

Part III: *Consequences*
Some conclusions following from the preceding descriptions must be considered before saying something about the nature and the possibilities of "intercultural conversations". The first group of conclusions are conclusions following from the general definition of "culture" in the introduction of this essay. Some further conclusions follow from the observations made in part I and II.

The term "culture" was used to denote contexts of literary traditions. It was understood that a literary tradition includes and is determined by other fixed life expressions. Change is a basic cultural category and refers first of all to changes in the structure of literary traditions. Cultural change creates different contexts in a literary tradition having very few features in common. Furthermore cultures understood as literary traditions can partially or completely merge with each other and a culture can split into different cultures or in a main stream culture with one or more subcultures. The unity of a culture is the unity of a tradition and the unity of a tradition is constituted by references, quotations. The creation of new fixed life expressions in the present includes always explicit or implicit references to fixed life expressions created in the past. The references are by no means in all cases a positive application of the tradition and a merging with the tradition. We find reference qua pure positive application only in the beginning in archaic cultures and in phases of culture exhibiting no significant capability of change and without significant intercultural transfer. The presupposition for change and the emergence of something new in a culture is a negation and rejection of parts of the own past tradition. One can speak of the "unity" of a culture in two radically different senses. The first is the formal concept of the unity constituted by references. It is obvious that this type of unity has space enough for positive cultural contact, intercultural transfer and even cross-cultural conversations in developed literary traditions. The second sense is the sense in which a literary tradition understands its unity versus other such unities <u>in a given phase of its development</u>. This sense or better "feeling" of the unity is material, i. e., it is bound to specific contents. It is a selection of certain contents of the past of the culture, understood as essentials of the own tradition and connected with the decision to preserve this heritage in the future and to defend it against change and influences from outside. This self-understanding and this desire, as explained, is overwhelming in archaic cultures in which the art of writing is used exclusively for this purpose. The "feeling" of unity has partially always the character of an illusion created by the desire for a simple and reliable life style. The art of writing is able to preserve the past for the future, but the ability to preserve is also the presupposition of the critical rejection of contents of the tradition. The degree in which this takes place is the degree of cultural change and change always creates the fragmentation of the literary tradition, of the culture. It should be obvious that already this general conception of culture is radically opposed first to the romantic concept of culture as an organic whole closed in itself and secondly opposed to a concept of tradition emphasizing first of all a steady positive application and merging with the texts produced in that past of the tradition in projections of truth[13].

Some general remarks about cultural contact and intercultural transfer are also necessary. They imply closer considerations about the development of fragmentation and the different types of fragmentation in a culture: the development of fragmentation and conscious intercultural transfer are correlates in the development of literary traditions. How cultural contacts and cultural transfer happen in societies with non-literal traditions is in its essential aspects a difficult question that must be bracketed. The easy part is intercultural technological transfer. Archaeology is able to find interesting results in this respect. It is, however, very difficult to say something about the development of ideas and value systems in such societies. History working with written sources can have a rather limited picture of cultural contacts between societies with non-literary and literary traditions: the sources are all written from the viewpoint of the literary tradition. The result is always the same. Such contacts are deadly for the non-literary tradition. They perish by violence and/or contamination.

Archaic literary traditions represent a class of cultures only if the cultures come to an end before significant change cane take place in their development. The term "archaic" is, therefore, primarily used to denote the earliest and in itself not stable phase in the development of literary traditions. The hostile rejection of change in the tradition is the correlate to the negative attitude towards other cultures in archaic cultures. Cultural contact between archaic societies leads to intercultural transfer, but this transfer first of all is the result of violent acculturation. Technological transfer happens in archaic cultures. It happens because of economic and military needs to the extent in which such a change is understood as irrelevant for the contents of the literary tradition. It can be understood - and misunderstood! - this way because technology is in the early phases of its development not a central topic of archaic literary traditions. Technological transfer can nevertheless sooner or later trigger changes in the literary tradition itself.

Conscious and non violent intercultural transfer happens in more developed literary tradition in strict correlation with the development of the fragmentation of the culture in itself. A brief review of the most relevant steps in the development of fragmentation is, therefore, necessary. The first step is the fragmentation into different and more or less independent literary genres. One of the possible genres is literature dealing with technological questions and with it the genre of scientific literature. Of greatest significance is the development of a genre in which universal cosmological questions as well as questions of the human conduct are treated with the claim that the human mind, the human reason, has in immediate access to truth. Fragmentation is conscious fragmentation with the occurrence of this genre because the archaic literary tradition can now be itself criticized and understood in part as "false in the light of reason". This possibility is a basic presupposition for a new approach to other cultures. They and their traditions are no longer considered in the archaic attitude. They can be evaluated and this evaluation can lead to the judgments that there are valuable and reasonable elements in foreign literary traditions. The evaluation is, of course, determined by the "principles of reason" developed in the literary tradition in which specific opinions about principles of reason emerged.

The presupposition for a universal non-violent intercultural transfer is the development of a secularized legal literary tradition in connection with the raise of an empire. There are empires without secularized systems of the law and the administration of power. Whether the different cultures represented by different literary traditions in such empires live together in peace depends on the person of an enlightened ruler, like in the case of Akhbar the Great, and will soon find an end after his death.

The development of secondary archaic literary traditions creates a new situation. Their main features are: (1) The psychic energy behind their emergence is the desire to overcome fragmentation and to find a new system offering a unified world view and simple and strict rules for human conduct. This is the first sense in which they are archaic. (2) The addressee of such texts and of the tradition of their interpretation in positive application is not a specific isolated society but mankind in general. This marks the difference between primary and secondary archaic literary traditions. The eminent texts and later also the process of their interpretation serve as a demarcation criterion between the true and the many false literary traditions. False traditions are the old literary tradition but first of all other secondary literary traditions. The attitude towards other literary traditions is archaic in a radicalized sense. They are unacceptable not because they alien to "our" tradition, but because they are false, rotten and all humans following such traditions will be punished by God. (3) Secondary archaic literary traditions cannot remove the difference of literary genres in a developed literary tradition, but they will try to control them. Their main interest will be to control the law system and to shape it according to their principles. The doctrine that they have the right to control state power can in addition be essential for such secondary archaic literary traditions. The unity of power, law and religion as the leading factor of archaic societies is restored.

The second and the third cycle in part II was a sketch of the development of a secondary archaic literary tradition into renewed fragmentation and the emergence of the possibility to develop a new attitude towards foreign cultures and their literary traditions in the human sciences. Only the final outcome has to be reconsidered. One remark is necessary about the first steps in the development of the human sciences. The idea of cultures as organic wholes, closed in themselves, though governing the beginnings of philological-historical research in the nineteenth century, is not essential for philological-historical research as such. The shortcomings of this idea, at best applicable to comparatively archaic literary traditions, can be discovered with the aid of the method itself. The inner independence of other cultures and their development, documented in fixed life expressions and first of all in their in themselves fragmented literary traditions in the past and the present is recognized by the principle that they have to be understood in their own terms. But this principle implies as well that they have to be considered and explored from an objectifying distance. Philological understanding does not imply agreement. It "reconstructs" cultural contexts given in a temporal and/or geographical distance. Research is "value free" which means, it puts in brackets all feelings and thoughts of the interpreter about agreement and disagreement. To be "value-free"is essential for "historical positivism". Such a positivism does not imply the acceptance of the method of the natural sciences in the human sciences. It is positivism because the main goal of the method is to create an objectifying distance. It can be said that the historical-philological method is the type of reasoning and the attitude permitting the most tolerant and understanding approach to foreign cultural contexts developed in the history of literary traditions. It may serve as a tool in cross-cultural conversations but the objectifying attitude involved creates a counterproductive distance for cross-cultural conversations.

The problem of the "unity" of a culture with a developed literary tradition, i. e. a literary tradition with developed fragmentation requires a final reconsideration. The formal unity is a unity of reference. The most easy path to reference is, of course, a common linguistic medium, a "nation". But language cannot be the criterion of the unity of a developed literary tradition. The state and the law system has its unity, but it is not the unity of a culture. Different, even opposed literary traditions can live together in one state, even in the special case of an identity of the unity of a state and a common language, the ideal of nationalism. Religion, beyond the stage of the development of primary and secondary archaic societies is not a criterion of unity either. In a developed literary tradition in most cases we find several religious communities with their own literary traditions. We find in addition several independent traditions of literary genres and within a literary genre further splits and affinities and coalitions connecting different literary genres. The unity is a unity of a multidimensional context and such contexts merge in different dimensions with other contexts. They are open for new and for unlimited intercultural transfer. Cultural contexts merge, influence each other and change. The "individuality" of a context can be determined only in a given "slice" in time and space. There will be a different "individuality" in another slice, even if the slices overlap. Slices are arbitrary. They might be justifiable for research projects interested in specific features of a context remaining comparatively stable in a slice and changing quickly in its fringes.

The problem of "cross-cultural conversations" in addition requires some further considerations of the meaning of the word "conversation" and related terms like "dialogue"[14]. The most general requirement is, that the utterance of a speaker can receive an answer form one or more partners in the dialogue and that every utterance in the following exchange is itself at least partially an answer. There must be a productive <u>present</u> activity of all participants in the dialogue. This implies that the participants share a common phase in intersubjective time. In most cases there is an oral exchange, but there is also the possibility of a dialogue using texts, fixed life expressions: the written exchange of messages. Seen this way it cannot be said that the exchange between an interpreter and a text of an author who does not share the "present" can have the character of a dialogue. A text is an utterance as a fixed life expression that happened in the past and a text is not able to expand itself by giving answers to the utterance of the interpreter. It can be said, that the interpreter can find answers for her/his questions in the further study of the text, but the activity in this case is only on the side of the interpreter. The author(s) of the text do not produce new texts with new answers[15].

Dialogues have different structures. It is essential for concrete dialogues that the partners can switch easily from one structure to another. But a dialogue can be completely dominated by one structure. Several types of structures can be distinguished. This is necessary to determine the specific expectations connected with "cross-cultural conversations". There is a group of structures in which "convincing the partner(s) about x" is of main concern. They could be called rhetorical disputes. "Rhetorics" here is understood in the old classical sense. Such dialogues can have the character of speeches only interrupted by possible questions if they are dominated by one speaker. The extreme case is "preaching". They have also the character of a dispute, a medieval *disputatio*, i. e. a dialogue in which each side tries to "win the argument". Sometimes this can be done without an interest in the "truth" of the defended thesis. Other types of dialogues are interpretive. Their procedure requires that the partners begin and continue with expressions and explanations of their feelings and thoughts. The interest can be directed towards a simple understanding of the other, the goal can also be to find possible realms of agreement and disagreement. Finally there are creative dialogues with the goal of reaching agreement and truth via compromising changes in the positions and attitudes of the partners of die dialogue and inventing new projections. They can be called "diplomatic". Diplomatic dialogues may include agreement about disagreement and the attempt of finding ways to tolerate each other in fields of disagreement to the extent in which conflicts can be avoided. This list is by no means complete, but it is sufficient for a stipulated definition of "conversation". A conversation is a dialogue using all the possibilities mentioned. The purpose is to reach the highest degree of communication, understanding, and, where necessary, agreement. Disputes may occur, but they have only the purpose of clarification. The leading purpose must be mutual understanding and, in some cases, the attempt to reach agreements if possible and to create pragmatic solutions for conflicts in case of disagreement.

The subject matter of a dialogue has influence on its formal structure. There are some fields in which disputation and argument will be an essential part of the argument and in which procedures for compromising are most essential. These are on the one hand dialogues about laws and principles of lawgiving binding all partners involved. On the other hand we have dialogues entered with the goal to develop a contract. Topics from science and technology have the goal to achieve results acceptable for all who share the same methodical procedures. This is also true in the human sciences to the extent in which common methodical procedures are used. Finally we have the conversations in which the main interest of the partners is to exchange their feelings and opinions for the sake of mutual understanding. The partners of such conversations can be without any interest in changing the opinions and beliefs, but an interest in convincing the other and/or defending the own opinion can occur in different degrees.

Cross-cultural dialogue and conversations will in general follow the rules of such patterns with some modification: (1) Cross-cultural dialogues cannot occur in the field of science and/or technology. The methodical boundaries for reaching acceptable results are rigid in this field. Disputes about the method, if there are any, are strictly bound to the principle of success. Disputes about the question whether specific technologies and specific scientific investigations are acceptable or not involve always some principles of evaluation outside of science and technology.

(2) Cross-cultural diplomatic dialogues and negotiations are as old and even older than archaic societies. Such negotiation do not deserve the name "cross-cultural". The main concern of each party is its interests and one of the main interests is always to preserve ones own patterns of behavior. Cultural technological transfer as well as diplomatic contracts can have unforeseen consequences for the development of cultural traditions, but such changes are neutral with respect to possible cross cultural conversations.

3) Dialogues, conversations, with an interest in the exchange of opinions and feelings with the goal of a better mutual understanding are the ideal candidates for cross-cultural dialogues. The main technical difficulties for such dialogues are linguistic barriers between different cultural contexts. The philological-historical method in the human sciences, known and practiced with insignificant variations in all developed literary traditions today, is the best tool for the solution of this problem. The method is also a remedy against the temptation to evaluate and perhaps attack other opinions with arguments because the method demands the suspension of evaluations, hasty agreements or rejections. The disadvantage is, of course, that such cross-cultural conversations will be restricted to scholarship. They happened before the development of the human sciences in the last two centuries, but they were always restricted either to circles of scholars or to certain persons, like Marco Polo, who had the chance to collect experiences in other cultures. However, the chance of such knowledge to have significant influence in their social contexts is slim.

(4) A special type of cross-cultural conversations reaching beyond the task of mutual understanding is possible in the field of the law and the administration of power. Such tasks occur with the desire to develop international laws regulating the behavior of states - not cultures! - but also principles of human rights of persons living in other states. A law is an obligation for all parties involved and that means that an agreement between all involved parties must be possible. Cross-cultural conversations in this field have a specific character. It is necessary to determine fields of agreement and points of disagreement. Knowledge about fields of disagreement is a presupposition of finding solutions. The scholarly cross-cultural conversations mentioned in (3) can be a helpful source of information, but they are not able to find binding solutions in such cases. A technical presupposition for success is the degree in which the parties involved are able to recognize a secularized concept of law. This means, however, that agreements in this field have of serious consequences for certain literary traditions and can, therefore, create considerable resistance.

It is a well known opinion that intercultural technological transfer leads to serious changes in societies and is, therefore, a strong factor for the development of a world culture in which the differentiation of cultural contexts vanishes. But there are also serious doubts that precisely this development can be a a factor working for the further development of cross cultural conversations. A stronger thesis is that intercultural technological transfer is in its essence a process of acculturation in which the western culture destructs all other cultures. Some remarks about this problem from the viewpoint of the theses developed in this essay are possible.

Three distinctions are necessary. We have to distinguish between technological transfer of the technology of the media and technological transfer in the field of production means[16]. Furthermore we have to distinguish between technological transfer with and without a significant transfer of scientific literature necessary for the development of technologies with a higher degree of complexity.

Technological intercultural transfer without scientific literature in the background never happened with a conscious intention to change cultural contexts and the contents and values of a literary tradition. Cultural changes triggered by new technologies remain unnoticed and, if noticed in the end, are only in very few cases the reason for a simple rejection of certain technologies. The economical consequences are too serious. There will be, however, efforts to assimilate the consequences and the outcome can be very different in different cultural contexts. The differences between cultural contexts do not vanish under the influence of this kind of intercultural technological transfer.

Technological transfer accompanied by the transfer of scientific literature has different consequences. The emergence of scientific literature in a literary tradition presupposes a high degree of its fragmentation. The rational critical approach to its own literary tradition is characteristic for the development of scientific literature. In addition it can associate itself easily with the literary genres in which tradition in general is is criticized from the viewpoint of "reason" in the sense mentioned in the first part. However it is possible to minimize such consequences in cultural contexts in which the religious literary tradition is still the dominating part of the literary tradition. In its essence scientific literature is, in its essence, intercultural. But this means, as indicated above, that the transfer of scientific literature does not have the character of a cross cultural conversation and, set aside the human sciences, cannot be used as a tool in cross cultural conversations.

The transfer of media technologies is a special case. The emergence of literary tradition is itself a revolution in media technology. Its development is influenced by new developments of media technology, e. g., already the art of printing. Modern media technologies, necessary first of all for the development of a world wide economy, therefore, have a serious revolutionary influence in the development of the traditions of different cultural contexts.

One of their side effects is that messages about foreign cultural contexts and their development are available for the general public, including pictorial messages. The outcome in the meantime is well known but it must be said that it is more or less chaotic. It is as chaotic as the outcome of new technologies of transportation for migration. Both have positive side effects but both are also destructive. They destroy the structures of cultural contexts without replacing them by other livable structures and can trigger the development of xenophobic attitudes. The negative as well as the positive outcome should be studied carefully and criticized in cross cultural conversations with the aid of the human sciences.

In all cultural contexts strong forces are working against the development of cross cultural conversations. They belong in part to the sphere of naked group interests. There are material interests in repression of other cultures and subcultures and again and again they create the ghetto problem of underprivileged cultures known since the beginning of the development. They lead necessarily to violent eruptions mostly beginning with riots, then continuing in guerrilla-warfare and possibly ending in open battle. Such conflicts can be mended if the groups involved can be convinced that they do not fight for the eternal values of their tradition but actually about economical quarrels. This is not easy but it is possible. The main point is to convince them that they are in general not so serious about their own eternal values if they consider their material welfare excluding, first of all, the necessity of killing and being killed.

The chances for fruitful cross-cultural conversations presuppose fragmented literary traditions. Attitudes turning themselves against fragmentation will also be opposed against cultural transfer and cross cultural conversations. The attitudes always have the same psychological roots and they have, I use psychoanalytic jargon, the character of a regression with destructive consequences. It is a regression back into archaic attitudes creating new forms of secondary archaic literary traditions and cultural contexts. The driving force behind them is the yearning for simplicity with strict uniform rules for human behavior. The life in a fragmented cultural context is difficult. It requires a high degree of sophistication and education for the mastery of different and varying contexts. It requires also the ability to handle inconsistencies and disagreement without developing hostile attitudes against otherness. The regression can occur in different ways. The most simple brand is religious fundamentalism. It is a straight forward regression to a secondary archaic literary tradition with all of its implications. The other brand presupposes the creation of new ideologies, secularized religions. This brand dominated the violent eruption of wars in the twentieth century. They are, for the time being, not the real threat. What survived are more or less radical types of fundamentalism. They occur actually and potentially in all old religious traditions and have the same consequences. In addition both kinds have the tendency to develop a strong version of national and/or cultural chauvinism[17]. We first observe a hostile and violent reaction against all elements in the own fragmented literary tradition incompatible with the new, simplified and unified world view. A second consequence is a hostile attitude against those groups of the population who do not fit in the new unified context. The extreme case is genocide. Finally there is a hostile attitude towards foreign cultural contexts. It leads to open aggression if there is a chance for success, but also, if that seems to be useful for the internal purposes of the regime. Cross cultural conversations are impossible in societies dominated by such a regression. The attempt to begin a cross cultural conversation with members of such a society is extremely difficult. The main task for research done with the goal to develop cross cultural conversations is, therefore, to investigate the roots and the nature of such developments and to prepare appropriate reactions.

1   "Deconstruction" in the Framework of Traditional Methodical Hermeneutics, in: *The Journal od the British Society for Phenomenology*, Vol. XVII, No. 3, 1986, 275 - 288. Falsehood as the Prime Mover of Hermeneutics, in: *The Journal of Speculative Philosophy*, Vol. VI, No. 1, 1992, 1 - 24.
2   The two main protagonists of the opposed viewpoints are Hans Georg Gadamer and Jaques Derrida.
3   The third part is an extended version of the third part of the paper presented at the conference. I tried to say something in addition about topics in other contributions of the conference from the viewpoints developed in part I and II.
4   The term "fixed life expressions", *Fixierte Lebensäusserungen*, is taken from Wilhelm Dilthey, *Der Aufbau der geschichtlichen Welt in den Geisteswissenschaften, Gesammelte Schriften (GS.)* 1914 ff, Vol, VII, cf. 226 ff.
5   Derrida's "arche-writing" in the framework of methodical hermeneutics could be understood as a metaphor denoting fixed life expressions in general. What has to be dropped is the speculative impact of his position.
6   *The Fixation of Belief*, Collected Papers 5.358 - 387.
7   Cf. the material in Gerald A. Press, *The Development of the Idea of History in Classical Antiquity*, McGill - Queens University Press, Kingston and Montreal, 1982.
8   Cf. the material in Heinrich Kuch, *"Philologus"*, Untersuchung eines Wortes von den ersten *Anfängen* seiner Tradition bis zur ersten *überlieferten lexikalischen Festlegung*, DAdW, Sektion Altertumswissenschaften, Berlin, 1965.
9   The first *quaestio* of the *Summa Theologiae* of Thomas of Aquinas deals with the problem of the interpretation of the Scriptures. The first four methodical principles of Abaelard's *Sic et Non* are also principles of interpretation.

10   Cf. Wilhelm Dilthey, *Die Entstehung der Hermeneutik*, GS V, 321 ff.
11   Cf. Dilthey, l.c. The inaugurator of the new canon was Flacius.
12   Cf. Dilthey, *Der Aufbau*, GS VII, 229 and in other passages.
13   Cf. the contribution of Aziz Al-Azmeh in this volume: "Against Culturalism". I agree with his criticism but I prefer "context", understood in the sense of methodical hermeneutics, instead of "mass" in connections like "culture as a historical mass". I admit nevertheless that this term, understood as a metaphor from physics, has the advantage of connoting "energy" and "force" understood here as social energy, social force.
14   The contribution of Lars-Henrik Schmidt "Commonness among cultures" part II, is a serious approach to the problem. My terminology and its taxonomy is different. It is different because methodical hermeneutics excludes the speculative elements implied in the references of his essay.
15   A detailed account can be found in my: The Significance of the Phenomenology of Written Discourse, in: *Interpersonal Communications*, ed. J.J. Pilotta, Center for Advanced Research in Phenomenology and University Press of America, Washington D.C., 1982, 141 - 159.
16   Cf. the contribution of Don Ihde: "Image Technologies and "Pluriculture"" in this volume for interesting considerations of the problem of non-literal media in the earlier tradition of cultural development.
17   Cf. The critique of S. P. Huntington in the contribution of Anindita Balslev "Cross Cultural Conversations: its Scope and Aspiration". Not different cultural contexts but regressive attitudes in them trigger possible conflicts. The precautions recommended by Balslev are, unfortunately, powerless in the virulent stages of the disease.

Christopher Norris

Postmodernizing Science: Against some Dogmas of the New Relativism

What is the status of scientific truth-claims? Can they purport to hold good for all time across vastly differing contexts of language, culture, and society? That is to say: is science in the business of providing valid explanations of physical objects and events whose nature remains constant despite such deep-laid shifts of cultural perspective? Or is it not rather the case - as currently argued by relativists, pragmatists, and 'strong' sociologists of knowledge - that those contexts provide the only means of understanding why science has taken such diverse forms (and come up with such a range of competing 'truths') throughout its history to date? (See for instance Barnes 1985; Bloor 1976; Fuller 1989; Woolgar 1988.)

These questions are of interest not only to philosophers and historians of science but also, increasingly, to cultural and critical theorists influenced by the widespread 'linguistic turn' across various disciplines of thought. (Fish 1989; Rorty 1989; Docherty [ed.] 1993) They are often linked with the issue of ontological relativity, that is, the argument - deriving principally from W.V. Quine's famous essay 'Two Dogmas of Empiricism' - that there exist as many ways of describing or explaining some given phenomenon as there exist ontological schemes or systems for redistributing predicates over the entire range of sentences held true at any particular time. (Quine 1953) On this holistic account there is no means of drawing a firm, categorical line between synthetic and analytic propositions, or matters of factual (contingent) truth which might always be subject to revision in the light of further evidence, and on the other hand those so-called logical 'laws of thought' whose truth is assumed to be a matter of *a priori* necessity and hence - by definition - valid for all possible contexts of enquiry. (See Fodor and Lepore 1991) And with the collapse of this distinction, so Quine argues, we must also relinquish the idea that philosophy of science might yet come up with an adequate method for linking observation-sentences to theories (or vice versa) through a clear-cut set of logical procedures. For in a holist perspective those sentences can possess meaning - that is to say, be assigned determinate truth-values - only as a function of their role within the entire existing 'fabric' or 'web' of beliefs', or the entire set of truth-claims ('empirical' and 'logical' alike) that currently happen to command widespread assent. Which is really to say that there are no such determinate truth-values since theories are always at some point 'underdetermined' by the best evidence to hand, while that evidence is always 'theory-laden' - or committed to some prior ontological scheme - right down to the level of its basic data as given in first-hand observation-sentences. Thus for Quine it follows that one must apply a principle of strict ontological parity as between (for instance) Homer's gods, centaurs, numbers, set-theoretical classes, and brick houses on Elm Street. Any preference in the matter - and Quine admits readily that he has a whole range of such preferences - must in the end come down to one's particular choice of ontological scheme. (For further discussion see Harding 1976.)

There are many other sources of this relativist trend in contemporary philosophy of science. They include Thomas Kuhn's highly influential account of the way that science alternates between periods of 'normal' and 'revolutionary' activity, the former characterized by broad agreement on what counts as a proper (constructive and disciplined) approach to certain well-defined problems, the latter by a sense of impending crisis - and an absence of agreement on even the most basic principles - which heralds the transition to a new epoch. (Kuhn 1970; also Hacking [ed.] 1981) Here as with Quine it is taken for granted that all the components of a given scientific 'paradigm' - from observation-sentences to high-level theories - are intelligible only in terms of the prevailing consensus, or according to the overall framework of beliefs that provides its own (strictly immanent) criteria of truth, progress, theoretical consistency, evidential warrant and so forth. But it then becomes difficult - if not impossible - to explain how we could ever gain insight into scientific world-views other than our own, or again, how historians of science could ever claim to understand the reasons (i.e., the scientific grounds) for some decisive paradigm-shift, as distinct from the various short-term cultural, social or historical factors that may have played some part in bringing them about. Hence Quine's recourse to the idea of 'radical translation' as a means of (purportedly) bridging this otherwise insuparable gulf between different observation-languages or ontological schemes. Hence also the difficulties that Kuhn confronted in his 1969 Postscript to *The Structure of Scientific Revolutions* when responding to his critics on the issue of relativism and its self-disabling consequences. For it is far from clear that these difficulties are in any way resolved by his Quinean (radical-empiricist) line in the face of such strong counter-arguments. (On this topic see Laudan 1990; Hollis and Lukes 1989.)

The problem is yet more acute with those kinds of ultra-relativist position adopted by proponents of the present-day 'linguistic turn' in its full-fledged (postmodern) guise. Thus it is sometimes claimed - as for instance by Richard Rorty - that our best model for interpreting the process of scientific paradigm-change is what happens when poets and novelists come up with striking new 'metaphors we can live by', or again, when strong-revisionist literary critics interpret such metaphors after their own fashion. (Rorty 1980) Then again there are those - Paul Feyerabend chief among them - who espouse an anarchistic philosophy of science which rejects all appeals to truth, logic, reason, consistency, experimental proof, etc. (Feyerabend 1975, 1992) On this view the idea of scientific 'progress' is nothing more than a piece of bogus mythology, one that takes hold through our myopically equating 'truth' with what currently counts as such according to this or that (self-authorized) 'expert' community. Much better, Feyerabend thinks, to have done with this misplaced reverence for science and in stead take account of the various factors - social, political, psychological, careerist and so forth - which have always played a decisive role in the history of scientific thought. For we can then see how mixed were the motives (and often how random or opportunist the methods) which gave rise to some so-called 'discovery' or 'advance' that is nowadays treated as a text-book example of its kind. And this will bring two great benefits, as Feyerabend sees it. First, it will help to demythologize science - to remove some of its false prestige - and thereby open it up to criticism from other (i.e., non-'expert' but socially and ethically more responsive) quarters. Second, it will encourage scientists to become more adventurous in framing risky conjectures or in pursuing novel and hererodox lines of thought.

There are various explanations that might be adduced for the current appeal of such ideas. One is the widely-held view that philosophy of science can no longer have recourse to any version of the logical positivist (or logical empiricist) distinction between truths-of- observation on the one hand and self-evident (tautologous) truths of reason on the other. (Quine 1953; Harding 1976) There are similar problems - so it is argued - with the appeal to nomological-deductive (or covering-law) theories, those that would seek to account for observational data by bringing them under some higher-level (metalinguistic) order of logical entailment-relations. (See Newton-Smith 1981; Salmom 1989.) For here again the way is open for sceptics like Quine to argue that any such distinction will always be drawn according to some preferred ontological scheme, some language- or culture-specific set of descriptive or explanatory priorities. One alternative that has enjoyed wide favour, not least among practising scientists, is Karl Popper's hypothetico-deductive account whereby the measure of a theory's claim to genuine scientific status is not so much its truth as established by the best current methods of experimental testing but its openness to falsfication by those same methods. (Popper 1934) This account has the signal advantage of explaining how a great many scientific theories that once enjoyed widespread credence should eventually have turned out mistaken, or - as with Newton's conceptions of absolute space and time - 'true' only relative to a certain restricted spatio-temporal domain. It thus meets the criticism of those, like Feyerabend, who would exploit such evidence to the point of denying that notions of truth have any role to play in the history and philosophy of science.

But there are difficulties with Popper's position, among them its reliance on under-specified criteria of what should count as a decisive falsification (or as grounds for rejecting some candidate hypothesis) in any given case. In other words, the methodology of 'conjecture and refutation' - as Popper describes it - amounts to just a minor inverted variation on the positivist or logical-empiricist theme. Moreover, so his critics maintain, Popper has made illicit use of this dubious methodoloy in order to attack what he sees as the pseudo-scientific pretensions of Marxism and other such 'historicist' trends in the sociological, interpretive, or humanistic disciplines. (Popper 1957) For if there is one type of argument that always draws fire from the present-day cultural relativists it is the idea that science should enjoy any privileged truth- telling status, any method or set of validity-conditions that would place it apart from those other (on its own terms) less rigorous or rationally accountable modes of knowledge. Such is the distinction standardly drawn between the 'context of discovery' for scientific truth-claims and the 'context of justification' wherein those claims are subject to testing by the best available criteria of experimental warrant, theoretical consistency, causal-explanatory yield, and so forth. (Reichenbach 1938) But this distinction is rejected by those who maintain - whether on grounds of 'ontological relativity' or in pursuit of the so-called 'strong programme' in sociology of knowledge - that truth is just a product of localized beliefs whose origin should be sought in their cultural context or in the socio-biographical history (the professional interests, careerist motives, childhood experiences, religious convictions etc.) of the scientists who held them. (Barnes 1985; Bloor 1976; Fuller 1988)

The poet Auden nicely epitomized this genre in its vulgar form: 'A penny life will give you all the facts'. More sophisticated - but no less sophistical - variants would include Feyerabend's well-known claim that in the case of Galileo *versus* Cardinal Bellarmine and the Church authorities it wasn't so much an issue of truth - i.e., of the heliocentric as against the geocentric hypotheses - but simply a question of who had the better argument on rhetorical, social, or political grounds. (Feyerabend 1975) Thus if Bellarmine sought to promote the interests of communal stability and peace, while Galileo can be shown to have fudged certain details (observational data) in order to preserve his theory, then the Church comes off rather better on balance and - so Feyerabend advises - should even now stick to its doctrinal position and not lean over to accommodate the present-day scientific orthodoxy. Other versions of this argument (if rarely pushed to such a provocative extreme) are often to be found in the current literature on history and sociology of science. What they all have in common is the nominalist persuasion that 'truth' is just a term honorifically attached to those items of belief that have managed to prevail - by whatever strategic or rhetorical means - in this contest for the high ground of scientific 'knowledge' and 'progress'. Other sources include the 'social construction of reality' thesis (taken up in philosophy of science by writers like Barry Barnes and David Bloor); the sceptical 'archaeology' of knowledge essayed across a wide range of disciplines by Michel Foucault (1973); and the argument of postmodernist thinkers such as Jean-Francois Lyotard that science is just one amongst a range of incommensurable language-games (cognitive, ethical, historical, political etc.) and no longer exerts any privileged claim in respect of knowledge or truth. (Lyotard 1988)

We have seen already how such scepticism extends to philosophies of science that invoke some form of deductive warrant from covering-law theories or hypotheses framed with a view to experimental proof or refutation. But the same sorts of objection have also been brought against inductivist arguments, i.e. those that take the opposite route, seeking to derive generalized descriptive or explanatory accounts from observed regularities in this or that physical domain. David Hume was of course the first to remark upon the problems that arise in offering any adequate (i.e. more than 'commonsense' or probabilistic) defence of inductive procedures. (Hume 1975 [1777]) As he saw it, our ideas of causality came down to just a matter of regular succession, contiguity, and 'constant conjunction', or our indurate belief that if one event normally follows another in the order of phenomenal experience then this must be due to some intrinsic causal nexus or relationship between them. This fallacy ('post hoc, propter hoc') was for Hume the product of a manifest non-sequitur, albeit one so deeply embedded in our everyday as well as scientific habits of thought as to leave little hope of effective reform. More recently the 'puzzle of induction' has been re-stated in various elaborate and ingenious guises, some of them due to the philosopher Nelson Goodman. (Goodman 1983) Even where not thus intended they have all served to reinforce the widespread trend toward sceptical or relativist philosophies of science which assimilate 'truth' to the shifting currency of in-place consensus belief.

However these arguments have not gone unopposed, as indeed one might expect given their strongly counter-intuitive character and our natural disposition - as Hume recognized - to attribute something more to scientific truth-claims than mere lazy-mindedness or force of habit. (See especially Mackie 1974) The challenge has come from various quarters, among them the Critical Realist school of thought whose chief proponent is Roy Bhaskar, himself much influenced by the work of Rom Harré. (Bhaskar 1986, 1993; Harré 1972, 1986; also Collier 1994) Central to their case is a 'stratified' conception of reality, knowledge and human interests where distinctions may be drawn between, on the one hand, a realm of 'intransitive' objects, processes and events - i.e. those that must be taken to exist independently of human conceptualization - and on the other hand a 'transitive' realm of knowledge-constitutive interests which are properly subject to critical assessment in terms of their ethical and socio-political character. To conflate these realms - so Bhaskar argues - is the cardinal error of relativist philosophies and one that leads to disabling consequences in both spheres of enquiry. Thus it relativizes 'truth' (in the natural and human sciences alike) to whatever form of discourse - or *de facto* regime of instituted power/knowledge - happens to prevail in some given discipline at some given time. And it also undermines any critical questioning of scientific projects, investigations or research-programmes that would argue in terms of their ethical implications or their consequences for human individual and collective well-being. Such criticism can have no purpose - no grounds or justification - if it fails to take adequate (realistic) account of what science can or might achieve on the basis of present knowledge and research.

So Bhaskar has a twofold reason for maintaining his 'transitive'/'intransitive' distinction. It is necessary, first, as a condition of possibility for science and also (*a fortiori*) for the history and philosophy of science. That is to say, these projects would be simply unintelligible in the absence of a presupposed object-domain which is *not* just a construct out of our various (e.g. linguistic, discursive, historical, or cultural) schemes. Where the relativists err is in confusing *ontological* with *epistemological* issues. Thus they take the sheer variety of truth-claims advanced (and very often subsequently abandoned) down through the history of scientific thought as evidence that no truth is to be had, and that nothing could justify such claims aside from their own 'internalist' perspective on issues of truth, realism, progress, adequate explanation etc. And so indeed it must appear if, as in Wittgenstein's resonant but not very helpful phrase, 'the limits of my language [for which read "discourse", "paradigm", "conceptual scheme" or whatever] are the limits of my world'. (Wittgenstein 1953) But this conclusion holds only on the mistaken premise - as Bhaskar sees it - that *ontology* (questions like 'what things exist?' 'what are their real attributes, structures, generative mechanisms, causal dispositions, etc.?') is synonymous with *epistemology* ('how does such knowledge come about?', 'according to what criteria?', 'within what limits of human cognitive grasp or knowledge-constitutive interest?'). Whence his second main point against the relativists: that by confusing these questions they deprive criticism of any effective purchase on the way that science has actually developed to date and the extent to which - within practical limits - its potential may be harnessed for the communal good.

These objectives both find expression in the title of Bhaksar's best-known book *Scientific Realism and Human Emancipation* (1986). Here he argues that relativist (or anti-realist) doctrines may well start out with the laudable aim of opposing that narrowly positivist conception of science which excludes any concern with ethical issues by reducing truth to a matter of purely instrumental (or means-end) rationality. But their proposed alternative is not much better, amounting as it does to a species of cognitive scepticism devoid of critical content and lacking any basis for informed evaluative judgment. Thus it simply reproduces all the well-worn puzzles - like Hume's problem of induction - which result from a reified conception of the physical object-domain joined to a passive spectator-theory of knowledge. Bhaskar is not alone among recent philosophers of science in arguing the case for a return to causal-explanatory modes of understanding. Wesley Salmon offers numerous convincing examples of advances that have come about through the achievement of a deeper, more adequate grasp of precisely such underlying causal mechanisms. (Salmon 1984, 1989) These advances would include (for instance) the capacity to define and measure heat in terms of the mean kinetic energy of molecules;

the understanding of electrical conductivity in terms of the passage of free electrons; or the characterization of the colour 'blue' as that which pertains to wavelengths within a given frequency-range (as distinct, say, from Plato's idea that blue objects were perceived as such on account of their participating in the Form or the Essence of blueness).

Thus the case for causal realism, in Nicholas Rescher's words, is that 'every objective property of a real thing has consequences of a dispositional order', even if - as he readily concedes - they 'cannot be surveyed *in toto*'. (Rescher 1987, p. 116) For this latter is in fact not so much a concession as a further strong argument for the realist case. That is, our chief evidence for the mind-independent status of real-world objects is precisely their possession of attributes, properties, causal dispositions etc. which may always turn out to be *not* what we expect according to our present state of knowledge. In which case, as Rescher shrewdly points out, the relativist 'argument from error' (i.e. that scientists have often been wrong in the past so could just as well be wrong all the time) is one that fails to stand up. It is not so much an argument against scientific realism as an argument against 'the ontological finality of science as we have it'. (Rescher 1987, p. 61) Thus Caesar didn't know - could not have known - that the metal of his sword contained tungsten carbide and that this was an explanatory factor in its fitness for the purpose intended. Moreover we can now give additional reasons (molecular and sub-atomic) for the fact that certain metals or metallic compounds possess certain well-tried physical qualities.

Nor are such claims in any way confounded by the high probability - indeed near-certainty - that future science will come up with yet further, more detailed or depth-ontological explanations. For this doesn't alter the knowledge we have that our current explanation is better (more adequate) than anything available to Caesar. (See especially Muntz 1985; Hillel-Ruben, 1990; Lipton, 1993; Smith 1981). That is to say, we have rational warrant for supposing that the objects, theories and causal postulates involved in our own best constructions are closer to the truth than what Caesar (or the scientific experts of his time) might have counted an adequate hypothesis. And this despite the always open possibility that certain gaps or shortcomings in our present state of knowledge might yet be revealed by some further advance - some improvement in the means of observation or the powers of theoretical synthesis - which rendered that knowledge either obsolete or henceforth restricted in its range of application. The most obvious example is that of Newtonian physics in the wake of relativity-theory, where classical conceptions of gravity or of absolute space and time continue to play an explanatory role, albeit under certain limiting conditions or in certain specified regions of enquiry.

Such instances are often adduced in support of the standard relativist claim, i.e. that there exist as many ways of construing the phenomena as there exist scientific theories, paradigms, ontologies, conceptual schemes and so forth. But this argument misses the point in two crucial respects. First, it fails to note that Einstein's General Theory of Relativity itself has recourse to an absolute value - the speed of light - which then serves as an invariant measure for assigning all loci in the space-time continuum. Thus it is wrong - little more than a play on words - to confuse 'relativity' in this well-defined sense with the kinds of all-out ontological or epistemic relativism which Einstein strenuously sought to avoid. And second, such arguments ignore the extent to which past theories are often not so much discredited *en bloc* as conserved and refined through the ongoing process of scientific elaboration and critique. (Muntz 1985; also Laudan 1977))

Sometimes this occurs when previously well-established items of knowledge are shown to possess only a partial truth or a power of explanation that is no longer adequate for present purposes. Such would be the case with (for instance) those advances in the fields of particle physics or molecular biology which built upon the work of earlier physicists, chemists and biologists, but which reconfigured the object- domain by opening up new regions of depth-ontological enquiry. At other times this process may operate (so to speak) in reverse, starting out with some relatively abstract conjecture regarding the existence of as-yet unobservable entities, and then seeking to verify its claims through experiment or further research. Thus, as Newton-Smith notes, the term 'electron' was at first a 'predicate . . . introduced [by Roentgen] with the intention of picking out a kind of constituent of matter, namely that responsible for the cathode-ray phenomenon'. (Newton-Smith 1981, p. 173) Thereafter it not only 'entered the vocabulary' of theoretical physics - as a Kuhnian relativist might choose to phrase it - but also attained the status of a necessary postulate and then (with Rutherford's pioneering work) that of an entity whose passage could tracked and whose causal- explanatory role placed its existence beyond reasonable doubt. And the same is true of a range of other items - such as molecules, genes, DNA proteins, and viruses - which have likewise exhibited a power to explain what previously lacked any adequate account. This is the chief virtue of a realist approach, according to Rescher: that it pays due regard to the prior claims of a 'non-phenomenal order from which the phenomena themselves emerge through causal processes'.

(Rescher 1987, p. 51) For otherwise - lacking such grounds - we should have absolutely no reason to think that electrons (or molecules, genes, viruses, etc.) exerted any greater claim upon our credence than phlogiston, magnetic effluxes, or the lumineferous ether.

At this point the relativist will answer - most likely with reference to Kuhn - that those grounds are indeed lacking since there is no guarantee of the meaning-invariance of terms from one theory to the next. For if it is the case (as Kuhn thinks, following Quine) that all terms are 'theory- laden', object-languages and observation-statements included, and moreover that theories are radically 'underdetermined' by the evidence, then it follows that scientists perceive different objects under different theoretical descriptions. (Kuhn 1970: Quine 1953) Thus - for instance - the ancient atomists were in no sense talking about the 'same' entities as those later physicists (from Dalton to the present) who have themselves come up with such a diverse range of models, metaphors, 'elementary' particles, etc., as to render their theories strictly 'incommensurable'. And again, to take one of Kuhn's best-known examples: Priestley and Lavoisier each laid claim to have discovered the chemical process involved in combustion, although the latter based his account - correctly as we now think - on the existence of a hitherto unknown element named 'oxygen', while the former adhered to the phlogiston-theory and produced experimental results which fully confirmed it. Thus where Lavoisier detected the existence of oxygen Priestley talked about 'dephlogistated air', along with a whole set of congruent hypotheses and reasonings on the evidence that amounted to a counterpart theory with similar explanatory scope. Kuhn offers many such examples, among them the difference of views between Aristotle and Galileo regarding what we now - after Galileo - perceive as the gravity-induced motion of a pendulum, but what Aristotle 'saw' as matter seeking out its rightful (cosmological) place in the order of the elements.

This is all taken by Kuhn's relativist followers (and arguably by Kuhn himself) to justify a stance of thoroughgoing cognitive scepticism vis-a- vis the issue of scientific truth and progress. But there are obvious problems with any strong version of the incommensurability-thesis. One is the straightforward logical point that we could be in no position to mount such a claim unless we were able to recognize the differences between two rival theories, or possessed at least some minimal ground of comparison on which they could be said to diverge. After all, as Andrew Collier remarks, 'nobody bothers to say that astrology is incompatible with monetarism or generative grammar with acupuncture'. (Collier 1994, p. 91) And there is also the fact -

well-attested by numerous examples from the history of science - that knowledge accrues around certain topics <u>across</u> <u>and</u> <u>despite</u> the widest differences of theoretical framework, ontological scheme, investigative paradigm or whatever. Thus it does make sense to think of modern (post-Dalton) atomic and particle physics as belonging to a line of descent from the ancient atomists, even though the latter may be said to have inhabited a different 'conceptual universe', and to have advanced their ideas on a purely speculative basis, devoid of genuine scientific warrant. What enables us to draw this distinction is precisely our knowledge of the growth of knowledge, our ability to grasp those salient respects in which the current understanding of atomic or subatomic structures differs from - and has indeed advanced far beyond - the ancient atomists' conceptions. (For further discussion see Lakatos and Musgrave [eds.] 1970; Russell 1948; Zimon 1978.)

Thus the Quinean/Kuhnian thesis of radical meaning-variance gives rise to some awkard, not to say nonsensical conclusions. It would require us to believe not only that the Greek atomists were talking about something completely different, but also that later physicists - such as Dalton, Rutherford, Einstein and Bohr - were themselves working on such disparate assumptions as to rule out any meaningful comparison between them. One might perhaps be tempted to adopt this outlook in other, more extravagant cases, like Anaximander's idea of the earth as 'a slab-like object suspended in equilibrium at the centre of the cosmos'. (I take this example from Rescher.) But even here it can reasonably be argued that we have grounds for thinking Anaximander wrong - and subsequent thinkers right - with respect to a given planetary body (the earth) whose structure, properties and place in the universe are now much better understood. And the same would apply to a great deal of early science, including Aristotle's theory of matter as composed of a mixture, in various proportions, of the four 'elements' (earth, air, fire and water), along with the 'humours' supposedly produced by their manifold possible combinations. The trouble with such a theory is not that the evidence fails to bear it out but, on the contrary, that it is perfectly compatible with any kind of 'evidence' that might turn up. In Popper's terms it is so vaguely framed as to lack the falsification criteria - or the grounds for its own subsequent disproof - which mark the difference betwen science and pseudo-science.

But there is a stronger argument that avoids the above-noted problems with Popper's account. This is the causal-realist theory according to which scientific explanations have to do chiefly with the properties of things themselves - with their structures, effects, 'transfactually efficacious' powers (Bhaskar), etc - rather than the various propositions or logics of enquiry that purport to account for them. Thus, in Bhaskar's words: 'if there is a *real reason*, located in the nature of the stuff, such as its molecular or atomic structure, than water *must* tend to boil when it is heated'. (Bhaskar 1994, p. 35) It is worth noting that this proposed shift from a descriptive-analytic to a causal-explanatory approach is one that finds a parallel in recent philosophy of language, notably Saul Kripke's influential work *Naming and Neccesity*. (Kripke 1981) In both cases it entails the argument that certain words - those denominating 'natural kinds' - possess reference by virtue of their capacity to pick out certain corresponding objects, substances, or real-world entities. These words ('proper names' in Kripke's non-standard usage of that term) are defined as such through a chain of transmission which at each stage relates them back to their referent, itself 'baptized' in a first (inaugural) act of naming and thereafter subject to various modifications or refinements in the light of newly-acquired scientific knowledge. Kripke's chief aim in all this is to avoid the kinds of problem that arise with descriptivist theories (like those advanced by Frege and Russell) which make truth-values a function of reference and reference - in turn - a function of those meanings (or senses) that attach to a given term. For it is then a short step to Quinean and other such forms of wholesale ontological relativism, arrived at by rejecting any clear-cut distinction between analytic (logically necessary) and synthetic (empirical or factual) propositions. For Kripke, conversely, there is an order of a posteriori necessary truths which have to do with the way things stand in reality and with our knowledge of them as expressed in the form of propositions about natural-kind terms.

Bhaskar again provides some pertinent examples from the scientific field. Thus: 'if there is something, such as the possession of the same atomic or electronic configuration, which graphite, black carbon and diamonds share, then chemists are rationally justified in classing them together - the reason is that structure'. (Bhaskar 1993, p. 35) He also makes the point rather neatly with regard to the standard text-book instance of a deductive syllogism: 'All men are mortal. Socrates is a man. Therefore, Socrates is mortal.' On Bhaskar's causal-realist account this becomes: 'in virtue of his genetic constitution, if Socrates is a man, he must die'. (p. 35) That is, we have grounds - experiential as well as scientific - for asserting the order of necessity here quite apart from the syllogistic structure that identifies a well-formed deductive inference. And the same would apply to propositions about other natural-kind terms, as for instance (to repeat) that *water* tends to boil when heated, that electrical *conductors* are characterized by the passage of free electrons when a current is applied, or that the *blueness* of an object consists in its reflecting light in the region of wavelength 4400A. These are all cases of what Kripke would call *a posteriori* necessity. Their names denote precisely those sorts of occurrent phenomena - structures, qualities, causal dispositions etc. - which on the one hand require our having found out about them, through experience or scientific investigation, while on the other hand belonging to their intrinsic (necessary) character as *just* that kind of phenomeonon. And, as Bhaskar would claim, it is just this kind of knowledge that enables us to make sense of science, along with the history and philosophy of science.

Of course there are always counter-examples which the sceptic can adduce by way of contending that science deals only with hypothetical entities or with constructs out of this or that preferred ontology, conceptual scheme, etc. Such doubts attach most often to objects (or quasi- objects) at the leading edge of current speculative thought, as with the various postulated items - from electrons to mesons and quarks - that have figured in the history of modern particle physics. There is also the question as to how far science may create (rather than 'discover') such putative realia through its own, ever more resourceful techniques for manipulating the materials at its disposal. Examples might be drawn from the field of recombinant DNA technology, from the new range of particles observed [or produced] with the advent of high-energy accelerator programmes, or from the filling-out of Mendelev's periodic table with elements previously unknown in nature. (See Rouse 1986) Even so it is the case - as Ian Hacking remarks in his book *Representing and Intervening* - that such proteins, particles or elements are possessed of both structural and causal-explanatory attributes which define their role within an ongoing project of scientific research. Thus some new particle may well start out as a purely speculative construct, an hypothesis required in order to balance the equations or to fill the gap in an otherwise attractive and powerful unifying theory. But its existence will remain matter for conjecture until that hypothesis can be proven, perhaps through the arrival of an electron-micrsocope with higher powers of resolution, or an accelerator capable of achieving the required velocity. In which case, as Hacking more succinctly concludes, 'if you can bounce electrons off it, it is real'. (Hacking 1983)

Such arguments would of course carry little weight with cultural or literary theorists for whom realism of any variety is an option scarcely to be thought of. In these quarters it has become an article of faith - whether derived from Saussure, Foucault, Rorty, or Lyotard - that 'truth' is a wholly linguistic or discursive construct, and 'science' just the name that attaches to one (currently prestigious) language-game or discourse. Hence their inordinate fondness for loose analogies with those branches of 'postmodern' science that may be thought to exhibit (in Lyotard's parlance) a sublime disregard for ideas and values like truth, rationality, or progress. This new kind of science, 'by concerning itself with such things as undecidables, the limits of precise control, conflicts characterized by incomplete information, "<u>fracta</u>", catastrophes, and pragmatic paradoxes, is theorizing its own evolution as discontinuous, catastrophic, nonrectifiable, and paradoxical'. (Lyotard 1984, p. 112) And again: since 'the reserve of knowledge - language's reserve of possible utterances - is inexhaustible', therefore it is no longer a question of truth (of that which pertains to the cognitive or constative phrase-regimes), but rather a question of the sheer 'performativity', the power of suasive utterance, that enables scientists to pick up research-grants, plug into information- networks, and so forth. In so far as this 'increases the ability to produce proof', so likewise it 'increases the ability to be right'. Thus Lyotard comes out pretty much in agreement with Feyerabend. On his account the best (indeed the only) criterion for scientific 'progress' is that which seeks to multiply discursive differentials, to judge (so far as possible) 'without criteria', and thereby do away with all those authoritarian constraints imposed by notions of scientific 'truth' and 'method'.

With Foucault one can see yet more clearly what results from an ultra-nominalist stance coupled to a deep suspicion of science and all its works. In *The Order of Things* this approach takes the form of an 'archaeological' questing-back into the various discourses, 'epistemes' or structures of linguistic representation that have characterized the natural and the human sciences alike. (Foucault 1973) Their history is marked - so Foucault contends - by a series of ruptures, or 'epistemological breaks', which make it strictly impossible to compare them in point of scientific truth, accuracy, scope, or explanatory power. The only meaningful comparisons to be drawn are those that operate (in Saussurian terms) on a structural- synchronic axis, that is to say, between the various disciplines that constitute the field of accredited knowledge at any given time. Foucault's chief interest is in those ambivalent regions of enquiry - midway between the physical and the human sciences - where issues of truth are most deeply bound up with questions of an ideological, interpretive, or hermeneutic nature. Thus he tends to avoid the 'hard' disciplines of (e.g.) physics or chemistry in favour of those - like philology, economics, and biology - that can plausibly be treated as interpretative constructs out of this or that dominant (period-specific) 'discourse'. (See Gutting 1989) So it is that Foucault's self-professed 'archaeology of the human sciences' can also lay claim to a generalized validity for branches of knowledge outside and beyond what would normally fall within that sphere.

The most famous passage from *The Order of Things* is also the passage that most vividly displays Foucault's extreme anti-realist, conventionalist or nominalist viewpoint. It is taken from one of Borges' riddling parabolic fictions, and purports to reproduce a Chinese enclopaedia entry wherein 'animals' are classified as follows: '(a) belonging to the Emperor, (b) embalmed, (c) tame, (d) sucking pigs, (e) sirens, (f) fabulous, (g) stray dogs, (h) included in the present classification, (i) frenzied, (j) innumerable, (k) drawn with a very fine camelhair brush, (l) *et cetera*, (m) having just broken the water pitcher, (n) that from a long way off look like flies'. (Foucault 1973, p. 7) Foucault treats this as an object-lesson in the fact of ontological relativity, an index of the culture-bound, parochial character of even our our most deep-laid concepts and categories. Thus '[i]n the wonderment of this taxonomy, the thing we apprehend in one great leap, the thing that, by means of the fable, is demonstrated as the exotic charm of another system of thought, is the limitation of our own, the stark impossibility of thinking *that*'.

Three responses would seem to be in order here. First: the *possibility* of thinking such exotic thoughts is demonstrated clearly enough by the existence of Borges' fable, of Foucault's commentary on it, and of our (i.e. the readers') capacity to perceive it as just such an instance of wild or zany categorization. But second: we do so on the understanding that this is, after all, a piece of fabulous contrivance, a fiction invented by Borges (and cited by Foucault) with the purpose of offering an 'exotic' slant on our naturalized habits of thought and perception. In which case (third): it is an error - a confusion everywhere manifest in *The Order of Things* - to argue from the mere possibility of thinking such starkly 'impossible' thoughts (whatever this might mean) to the idea that all our concepts, categories, ontological commitments and so forth are likewise fictive constructions out of one such 'arbitrary' discourse or another. But this is exactly the premise that underwrites Foucault's entire project, from his early structuralist-inspired 'archaeology' of knowledge to the Nietzschean-genealogical approach that characterized his post-1970 works. It is perhaps best seen as a *reductio ad absurdum* of that anti-realist line of argument which begins by locating truth in propositions about things, rather than in the things themselves, and which ends up - as with Quine, Kuhn, Rorty, Lyotard et al - by holistically relativizing 'truth' to whatever sorts of language-game happen to enjoy that title. In other words it presses right through with that rejection of de re in favour of de dicto necessity which then turns out to undermine the very grounds of science as a truth-seeking enterprise. This irony indeed finds pointed expression in the title of Foucault's book. For on his account there cannot exist any 'things' - any extra-discursive objects, entities, kinds or categories of thing - whose various 'orderings' by language or discourse would render his thesis intelligible.

It is worth noting that there may be a common source for some of these issues that have recently emerged in both French and Anglo-American philosophy of science. It is to be found in the work of Pierre Duhem (1861-1916), a thinker whom Quine has acknowledged as a major influence, and whose name is standardly coupled with his own in discussions of the Duhem-Quine thesis with regard to ontological relativity. (Duhem 1954; Harding 1976) Duhem, it is worth recalling, was a physicist who specialized in thermodynamics, as well as a philosopher-historian of science and a practising Catholic. Hence his belief that science was not in the business of providing ultimate explanations, but should rather confine itself to a conventionalist account of those truths that held good with respect to some given (ontology-relative) conceptual scheme. In this way he could keep science from encroaching upon matters of religious faith. In France there is a clearly-marked line of descent which runs from Duhem, via Gaston Bachelard, to that structuralist 'revolution' across various disciplines which achieved its high point in the 1960s and '70s. Structural linguistics was at this time seen as converging with that movement in philosophy of science, represented most notably by Bachelard, which likewise sought to define the conditions under which a discipline could properly assert some claim to theoretical validity. (See Gutting 1989; Lecourt 1975) But this is now treated as a byegone episode in the history of thought, a distant prelude to the dawning awareness that science - like philosophy - is just one 'discourse' among others, a language-game with its own favoured idioms and metaphors, but without any privilege in point of epistemological rigour or truth. And since these include (as in Wittgenstein) the 'language-game' of religious belief it may not be fanciful to trace the line back to Duhem's attempt at a negotiated truce between science and Catholic doctrine. (Incidentally this might also cast a revealing light on Feyerabend's treatment of the issue between Galileo and Cardinal Bellarmine.)

If Bachelard is remembered nowadays it is chiefly for works like *The Psychoanalysis of Fire*, his essays in reflection on those modes of metaphoric or creative reverie that stand, so to speak, at the opposite pole from the scientific language of concept and rational inference. (Bachelard 1964, 1971) What is thereby forgotten - one might say repressed - is the fact that these writings were themselves a part of his epistemolgical project, his attempt to distinguish more clearly between the two realms of thought. It is a plain misreading of Bachelard's work to extract from it the modish doctrine that 'all truth-claims are fictions', 'all concepts just sublimated metaphors', or '"science" merely the name we attach to some currently prestigious language-game'. On the contrary: Bachelard's aim was to prevent such promiscuous levelling of the difference - the more than contingent, linguistic or localized (culture-specific) difference - between scientific epistemologies on the one hand and poetic- metaphorical 'reverie' on the other. Thus what Bachelard meant by his term 'epistemological break' was a decisive rupture with pre-scientific modes of thought, one that marked the crucial stage of advance to an adequate conceptualization of some given domain. (Bachelard 1968, 1984) It retains this significance - if more problematically - in Louis ALTHUSSER's structural-Marxist account of the science/ideology distinction. (See especially Althusser 1990.) But with Foucault the idea of an 'epistemological break' has been relativized to the point where it means nothing more than a random shift in the prevailing (discursively produced) 'order of things'.

That Saussure should nowadays be routinely coopted by adepts of this ultra-relativist view is, to say the least, something of an irony given his methodological concerns and his desire to set linguistics on the path toward a genuine (structural-synchronic) science of language. (Saussure 1974) Such was indeed the main source of its appeal for that earlier generation of theorists who saw in it - as likewise in Bachelard's work - a means of articulating the difference between metaphor and concept, ideology and science, natural (everyday) language on the one hand and theoretical discourse on the other. But in both cases, Saussure and Bachelard, these claims were lost from view with the postmodern turn toward an out-and-out conventionalist theory of science, knowledge and representation which treated such ideas as merely a species of 'metalinguistic' delusion. Thus Bachelard was read - or standardly invoked - as arguing that all scientific concepts could in the end be traced back to their subliminal source in some privileged metaphor or image-cluster. (See Derrida 1982 for a cogently argued critique of this reading.) And Saussure's theoretical commitments counted for nothing in comparison with the prospects that were opened up by treating all theories (his own presumably among them) as 'constructed in' or 'relative to' some localized signifying practice. For it could then be maintained - without fear of contradiction on reasoned philosophical grounds - that literary critics were among the the vanguard party in a coming 'revolution' of the instituted order of discourse, an event whose signs they were able to read through their knowledge that 'reality' was merely the figment of a naturalized (though in fact merely 'arbitrary') relation between signifier and signified. (Mowitt 1992)

The problems with this doctrine are those that have bedevilled every version of the relativist argument from Protagoras down. That is to say, if we redefine 'true' as 'true relative to L' (where L is taken to denote some language, paradigm, conceptual scheme, 'interpretive community' or whatever) then there is no way of counting *any* belief false just so long as it can claim - or could once claim - some measure of communal assent. (Putnam 1983) From which it follows *ex hypothese* that all beliefs are true by their own cultural lights, or according to their own immanent criteria as manifest in this or that linguistically mediated 'form of life'. Every single truth-claim that was ever entertained by a community of like-minded knowers must count as valid when referred to the language-game, vocabulary, or belief-system then in place. Thus for instance it was once *true* - not just an artefact of limited knowledge or erroneous 'commonsense' perception - that the fixed planets were seven in number; that the Sun rotated about the Earth; that the process of combustion involved the release of a colourless, odourless, intangible substance called phlogiston, rather than the uptake of oxygen; and that no fixed-wing aircraft could possibly get off the ground since the necessary lift could be generated only by a bird- like flapping motion, or perhaps - as Leonardo was first to suggest - a rotary-blade arrangement of the helicopter type. In each case and numerous others besides - one could multiply examples at leisure - the belief in question is no less true, or no more demonstrably false, than those other beliefs that are nowadays widely (even universally) taken for matters of scientific fact. What counts is their suasive efficacy as measured by the current norms of 'science' as a going enterprise, a rhetorical activity where truth is defined in performative (not constative) terms, and where any distinction between concept and metaphor turns out to be merely - like the word 'concept' itself, not to mention the concept of 'metaphor' - a species of repressed or sublimated metaphor. From which it follows, supposedly, that all truth-talk - whether in the natural or the more theory-prone human sciences - comes down to a choice of the right sort of metaphor (or the optimum rhetorical strategy) for conjuring assent from others engaged in the same communal enterprise.

Scientists (and at least some philosophers of science) have understandably considered this an implausible account of how advances come about through the joint application of theory and empirical research. Hence - as I have argued - the recent emergence of anti-conventionalist or causal-realist approaches which offer a far better understanding of our knowledge of the growth of knowledge. After all, there would seem rather little to be said for a philosophy of science that effectively leaves itself nothing to explain by reducing 'science' to just another species of preferential language-game, rhetoric, discourse, conceptual scheme or whatever. The current revival of realist ontologies (along with the return to 'natural-kind' theories of reference) betokens a break with this whole - as it now appears - misdirected line of thought. In a longer purview it simply takes up the position attributed to Aristotle by his commentator Themistius: namely, the principle that 'that which exists does not conform to various opinions, but rather the correct opinions conform to that which exists'.

References

Althusser, Louis (1990): *'Philosophy and the Spontaneous Philosophy of the Scientists' and other essays*, trans. Gregory Elliott. London: Verso.

Bachelard, Gaston (1964): *The Psychoanalysis of Fire*, trans. A.C.M. Ross. Boston: Beacon Press.

Bachelard, Gaston (1968): *The Philosophy of No: a philosophy of the new scientific mind*. New York: Orion Press.

Bachelard, Gaston (1971): *The Poetics of Reverie*, trans. Daniel Russell. Boston: Beacon Press.

Bachelard, Gaston (1984): *The New Scientific Spirit*. Boston Beacon Press.

Barnes, Barry (1985): *About Science*. Oxford: Blackwell.

Bhaskar, Roy (1986): *Scientific Realism and Human Emancipation*. London: Verso.

Bhaskar, Roy (1993): *Dialectic: the pulse of freedom*. London: Verso.

Bloor, David (1976): *Knowledge and Social Imagery*. London: Routledge & Kegan Paul.

Braithwaite, Richard B. (1953): *Scientific Explanation*. Cambridge: Cambridge University Press.

Brannigan, Austin (1981): *The Social Basis of Scientific Discoveries*. Cambridge: Cambridge University Press.

Collier, Peter (1994): *Critical Realism: an introduction to Roy Bhaskar's philosophy*. London: Verso.

Derrida, Jacques (1982): 'White Mythology: metaphor in the text of philosophy', in *Margins of Philosophy*, trans. Alan Bass, pp. 207-71. Chicago: University of Chicago Press.

Docherty, Tom ed. (1993): *Postmodernism: a reader*. Hemel Hempstead: Harvester-Wheatsheaf.

Duhem, Pierre (1954): 'The Physics of a Believer', in *The Aims and Structure of Physical Theory*, trans. Philip Wiener. Princeton, NJ: Princeton University Press.

Feyerabend, Paul (1975): *Against Method*. London: New Left Books.

Feyerabend, Paul (1992): *Farewell to Reason*. London: Verso.

Fodor, Jerry and Lepore, Ernest (1991): *Holism: a shopper's guide*. Oxford: Basil Blackwell.

Foucault, Michel (1973): *The Order of Things: an archaeology of the human sciences*. London: Tavistock.

Fuller, Steve (1980): *Social Epistemology*. Bloomington: Indiana University Press.

Fuller, Steve (1989): *Philosophy of Science and its Discontents*. Boulder, Colorado: Westview Press.

Goodman, Nelson (1983): *Fact, Fiction and Forecast*, 4th edn. Indianapolis: Bobbs-Merrill.

Gutting, Gary (1989): *Michel Foucault's Archaeology of Scientific Reason*. Cambridge: Cambridge University Press.

Hacking, Ian ed. (1981): *Scientific Revolutions*. London: Oxford University Press.

Hacking, Ian (1983): *Representing and Intervening*. Cambridge: Cambridge University Press.

Harding, Sandra G. (1976): *Can Theories Be Refuted? essays on the Duhem-Quine thesis*. Dordrecht: D. Reidel.

Harré, Rom (1972): *The Philosophies of Sciences*. London: Oxford University Press.

Harré, Rom (1983): *Great Scientific Experiments*. London: Oxford University Press.

Harré, Rom (1986): *Varieties of Realism: a rationale for the social sciences*. Oxford: Basil Blackwell.

Hempel, Carl G. (1965): *Aspects of Scientific Explanation*. London: Macmillan.

Hollis, Martin and Lukes, Steven, eds. (1982): *Rationality and Relativism*. Cambridge, Mass.: MIT Press.

Kripke, Saul (1980): *Naming and Necessity*. Oxford: Blackwell.

Kuhn, Thomas (1970): *The Structure of Scientific Revolutions*, 2nd ed. Chicago: University of Chicago Press.

Lakatos, Imre and Musgrave, Alan eds. (1970): *Criticism and the Growth of Knowledge*. Cambridge: Cambridge University Press.

Laudan, Larry (1977): *Progress and its Problems*. Berkeley & Los Angeles: University of California Press.

Laudan, Larry (1990): *Science and Relativism: some key controversies in the philosophy of science*. Chicago: University of Chicago Press.

Lecourt, Dominique (1975): *Marxism and Epistemology: Bachelard, Canguilhem and Foucault*. London: New Left Books.

Lepin, J., ed. (1984): *Scientific Realism*. Berkeley & Los Angeles: University of California Press.

Lipton, Peter (1993): *Inference to the Best Explanation*. London: Routledge.

Lyotard, Jean-Francois (1984): *The Postmodern Condition: a report on knowledge*, trans. Geoff Bennington and Brian Massumi. Minneapolis: University of Minnesota Press.

Lyotard, Jean-Francois (1988): *The Differend: phrases in dispute*, trans. Georges van den Abbeele. Manchester: Manchester University Press.

Mackie, J.L. (1974): *The Cement of the Universe: a study of causation*. Oxford: Clarendon Press.

Margolis, Joseph (1991): *The Truth About Relativism*. Oxford: Basil Blackwell.

Mowitt, John (1993): *Text: the genealogy of an antidisciplibary object*. Durham, NC: Duke University Press.

Muntz, Peter (1985): *Our Knowledge of the Growth of Knowledge*. London: Routledge & Kegan Paul.

Newton-Smith, W.H. (1981): *The Rationality of Science*. London: Routledge & Kegan Paul.

Papineau, David (1978): *For Science in the Social Sciences*. London: Macmillan.

Popper, Karl (1934; 2nd ed., 1959): *The Logic of Scientific Discovery*. New York: Harper & Row.

Popper, Karl (1957): *The Poverty of Historicism*. New York: Harper & Row.

Putnam, Hilary (1983): *Realism and Reason*. Cambridge: Cambridge University Press.

Quine, W.V.O. (1953): *From a Logical Point of View*. New York: Harper & Row.

Reichenbach, Hans (1938): *Experience and Prediction*. Chicago: University of Chicago Press.

Rescher, Nicholas (1987): *Scientific Realism: a critical reappraisal*. Dordrecht: D. Reidel.

Rorty, Richard (1980): *Philosophy and the Mirror of Nature*. Princeton, NJ: Princeton University Press.

Rorty, Richard (1989): *Contingency, Irony, and Solidarity*. Cambridge: Cambridge University Press.

Rouse, Joseph (1987): *Knowledge and Power: toward a political philosophy of science*. Ithaca, NY: Cornell University Press.

Ruben, David-Hillel (1982): *Explaining Explanation*. London: Routledge.

Russell, Bertrand (1948): *Human Knowledge: its scope and limits*. New York: Simon & Schuster.

Salmon, Wesley C. (1984): *Scientific Explanation and the Causal Structure of the World*. Princeton, NJ: Princeton University Press.

Salmon, Wesley C. (1989): *Four Decades of Scientific Explanation*. Minneapolis: University of Minnesota Press.

Smith, Peter J. (1981): *Realism and the Progress of Science*. Cambridge: Cambridge University Press.

Woolgar, Steve (1988): *Science: the very idea*. London: Tavistock.

Zimon, John Michael (1978): *Reliable Knowledge: an exploration of the grounds for belief in science*. Cambridge: Cambridge University Press.

Carol L. Bernstein
Interpretive Play:
Masks, Bicycles and Heliotropes

During a visit to Japan June 1994, several people asked my spouse and me whether we planned to write a book on the country. After a visit of three weeks, at least half of which we would spend as interpreters of Western literature and philosophy, to write a book on Japan! After all, we heard, Barthes had written *The Empire of Signs* on the basis of a stay of ten days. The question, apparently so direct, was both ironic and provocative - and it was the irony that struck home first. At the most obvious level, the question evoked the presumption of trying to interpret any culture on the basis of first impressions, gathered over a brief period of time. If we were to entertain the idea, a scant knowledge of Japanese would form an additional handicap: we would have to rely upon other cultural cues, coupled with non-linguistic responses by and large, to produce that interpretation. That situation, however, would lead to still another problematic level: Because we didn't know Japanese, we were accompanied almost constantly by friends, interpreters and scholars. Any book on Japan would incur the risk of mediation or, even worse, contamination: the scene of writing would be produced by mingled perspectives, thereby blurring if not begging the question of interpretation. Such a process would involve not so much the fusion of horizons as the engulfment, however innocent, of one horizon by another. Consequently, our experience might turn out to be "safe" and non-controversial, an intellectual travelogue at best.

Suppose, however, the question really meant, "Will you make *us* the *objects* of your inquiry?" Such self-directed irony has nearly global consequences, for it reinstates the very issue of otherness that was beginning to fade from the prior train of thought. Mediation, after all, often diminishes otherness: now, it seems, our hosts were inquiring about the possibility of - and the barriers to - intercultural interpretation.

What, then, did the question mean? A polite gesture, at the level of sophisticated chit-chat, to foreign scholars? Ironic doubts about the adequacy of such a project - or perhaps a veiled warning, tinged with xenophobia? An indirect question - by people who were eager (or anxious) to learn how Japan appears to outsiders? The sheer enjoyment, alternatively, of being on display? Was my interpretation of the question, finally, limited to Western categories of thought?

The query was also, however, provocative. If irony performs the self-reflexive function of making one aware of the ambiguities in any interpretive stance, aware of the cultural baggage that constantly accompanies one, necessity may very well force one to take leaps. Our experience in Japan brought this home to us because, largely deprived of direct conventional linguistic cues, we turned to images and artifacts as ways of making sense (literally) of the interplay of "same" and "other" that is likely to inform an untutored Westerner's experience in the East. Gardens, pottery, Kabuki theater: these images, objects and spectacles became data for interpretation. If the textual critic's theoretical blindness supplies the occasion for insight, as Paul de Man claims, then linguistic blindness, imposing its own limitations upon perception, might also offer paths to insight. Imperfections of theory, necessary perceptual constraints: more than we know, these empower cultural logic.

Masking the Scene of Interpretation
The interpretation of images, after all, frequently comes to the foreground in the absence of other transparent cultural cues. Such a process focuses upon concrete objects that are accessible, one assumes, to neutral, transcultural interpretive strategies, Levi-Strauss's readings of Caduveo face-paintings, his critical narrative of their decipherment, offer one such model, following a trajectory from his initial mystification through a set of structural paradigms, before returning to the specific role of these paintings in Caduveo culture.[1] He begins with the assumption that a people's customs or styles result from systems, so that their originality is never absolute: a group chooses from a combination of possible styles. If only one knew them all, such motifs would form a kind of "periodic table" of stylistic elements, determining the image as much as specific cultural tensions.

Levi-Strauss begins his account of the Caduveo Indians by comparing them to the designs on a pack of cards - and to the representation of cards in Lewis Carroll's *Alice in Wonderland*. He ends by suggesting that Caduveo art represents a Golden Age that the Indians may have dreamed of, but never experienced. In between, he surveys the contradictions in the designs, their uncertain meaning, their multileveled dualism. Their art is so extraordinary that it must be explained by "features native to the Indians" (173): internal factors whose interpretation transcends any sources in European Renaissance art (173). The cultural baggage Levi-Strauss brings to this chapter is itself complex: the theoretical insistence upon a structural system governing the visual aesthetic, the accompanying assumptions concerning stylistic combinations and social contradictions, the universal story of the passage from nature to culture, or from a state of mindlessness to a state of civilization or civilized awareness, the recognition that artistic play, like dreams, has both a social function and a social meaning. Even the allusion to the myth of the Golden Age is ambiguous, insofar as it assumes for the Caduveo both a universalism and a desire for what one never had, an idyllic existence far removed from the mindlessness of "real" nature or the tensions of "real" civilization: a desire that one identifies through a series of sophisticated theoretical mediations whose trajectory may be far removed from Caduveo minds. (In this respect, a structural hermeneutics has affinities with Benjamin's metaphor of the tangent in translation, involving the detour of language in moving from the plane of assertion to the plane of interpretation.[2]) The allusion to *Alice in Wonderland*, however, constituting a telling reference to European satire, to its flattening effect ("'You're nothing but a pack of cards!'"), complicates the perspective with the suggestion of a patronizing air. Should one indict Levi-Strauss for Eurocentrism? Derrida's observation that ethnology employs the very Eurocentrism it denounces emerges from his reading of Levi-Strauss.[3] Yet the allusion comes at the beginning of the chapter, whose unfolding one may read as an effort to invest the face masks with the conceptual dimensionality denied to them in the "first impression" shaped by Lewis Carroll. No matter how immanent the structures, they must still be joined with cultural particularities.

We have not as yet taken into account the generic requirements implicit in an autobiographical narrative such as *Tristes Tropiques*: the dynamic of interpretation embeds the initial encounter with the mystifying image within a combination of personal reflections and ethnological assumptions. Whatever the perspective or angle of vision, the very metaphor returns us to the bias that inheres even in a structuralist approach: the meeting of the universal with the concrete migrates into the interplay of interpreter and object of interpretation, as if they were engaged in some allegorical scheme. Yet neutrality's fictiveness need not constitute a cause for alarm: it is the move beyond formalism, the recognition of interpretive interventions and the uses to which one puts them that counts.

Any image, therefore, and especially one that has been appropriated into a text, is apt to bear the double burden of representing the culture from which it comes and either resisting or acceding to the interpretations that arrive at its threshold. If the very process of interpretation itself invites scrutiny, and if the metaphors we use - including neutrality and resistance, dimensionality and direction - imply politics and judgment, if the very secondariness of images raises old philosophic suspicions about the efficacy of representation: what trust can we place in the interpretive process? Let us turn to some representative images, variously construed: African sculpture, Balinese theater, Brazilian face-paintings, Japanese Bunraku puppets, and Western philosophical metaphor. Whether object, performance, or text, each image dramatizes the burden of otherness, the problematic of interpretation and the ambiguous positions of its interpreters. Each has occasioned some discussion, if not outright debate, about its meanings and cultural provocations.

Easy Rider
Some of the most charged debates and contested sites of intercultural interpretation appear in museum exhibits and in texts produced by the museums. Unlike Walter Benjamin, who found himself disappearing into his collection of books,[4] collectors of objects, especially "primitive" objects, are often appropriative. The logic of positioning an object as the source for Western art requires that it be subsumed in the later production. Anthony Appiah opens his discussion of "The Postcolonial and the Postmodern" with observations on a 1987 exhibit mounted by the Center for African Art in New York.[5] In this exhibit, entitled *Perspectives: Angles on African Art* - whose title I have anticipated above - ten "cocurators" were each invited to select ten objects from over a hundred photographs of African art. Appiah points to the criteria, questionable on several counts, used to select the art: A Baule artist, whose aesthetic standards are assumed to be limited to those of his own people, is given only an assortment of Baule objects to choose from; David Rockefeller associates "considerations of finance, of aesthetics, and of decor": "The best pieces. . . .have a way of becoming more valuable. . . . I like African art as objects I find would be appealing to use in a home or an office" (138). David Rockefeller, Appiah observes, treats African art as a commodity; nevertheless, he is placed in some sense at the "*center*" of choice, in contrast to the positioning of the Baule artist, Lela Kouakou, at some cultural margin. At best, *his* words or choices become central only

insofar as they are subsumed by the process of commodification. In Appiah's account, any interpretive activity on the part of these oddly associated cocurators is largely tacit: David Rockefeller adopts a framework of Western standards of commerce and decor, eliding inner meaning. It is the surface that counts; a cultural hermeneutics would be irrelevant. Lela Kouakou turns out to be, as Appiah notes, a composite voice (made up of several artists) whose intracultural choices are constructions that cannot be attributed to a single individual. These two perspectives mark limits to the exhibit in which interpretation defines the context rather than the object. The outsider elides otherness into Western decor, and the insider's voice is elided into a Western construction. Appiah foregrounds the ironies of judging by one's own standards: the curator's desire to avoid the biased standards of the Baule sculptor is contradicted by the patent self-interest of a Rockefeller or, as we will see, Baldwin's "judging by his own standards." The irony in this curatorial self-contradiction is remarkable. Even if the text of this catalogue pushes interpretation to its parodic antithesis, however, it should be possible to think of alternative interpretations that are legitimate. Part of the project of situating otherness, after all, requires that it be recovered from any extremes to which it may have been relegated.

Appiah's identification of the questionable perspectives that governed the exhibit clears an interpretive space into which there rides the *Yoruba Man with a Bicycle*, a twentieth century work. Even in relation to this piece of sculpture, the comments clash. The catalog description identifies it this way: "The influence of the Western world is revealed in the clothes and bicycle of this neo-traditional Yoruba sculpture which probably represents a merchant en route to market" (*IMFH*, 140). Nevertheless, this work eludes the Primitivism that characterizes so many of the exhibit's choices, as Appiah notes. James Baldwin, co-curator for this piece, describes it in a way that is observant, casual, and speculative:This is something. This has got to be contemporary. He's really going to town. It's very jaunty, very authoritative. His errand might prove to be impossible. He is challenging something - or something has challenged him. He's grounded in immediate reality by the bicycle.... He's apparently a very proud and silent man. He's dressed sort of polyglot. Nothing looks like it fits him too well. (139)Baldwin, too, has his own "grid," one determined by earlier experiences with the Schomberg collection of African-American art in Harlem.

His imaginative openness, however, allows Appiah to return to the piece after a long, central exploration of postcolonialism and postmodernity in African culture; he uses the *Yoruba Man on a Bicycle* as an image to introduce certain tenets concerning otherness. He assigns it a set of intentions, virtually personifying it; the sculpture represents an African, rather than a Euro-American, perspective on modernity. The artist is not identified, although the purpose of the art is: it was produced, as neo-traditional works are, for the West. The ideology that motivates its production is modernist: in some universal, timeless mode, it represents "Africa": it is designed for a museum culture, rather than "consumption" in the home. Its otherness, therefore, is manufactured for others all too willing to maintain it at the same time that they appropriate it into the Western museum as a source of Western art, etc. Nevertheless, that otherness of this sculpture, Appiah suggests, is far less monolithic than one might think. From a postmodern perspective, the Yoruba man is a polyglot, not too carefully dressed, indifferent to who invented the bicycle - and more concerned about its functionality ("it will take us further than our feet will take us") and its absorption into African life. The modernist universal symbolism of the Yoruba piece thus metamorphoses into its local, practical, postmodernist "meaning." The bicycle need not stand for an "Otherness-machine"[6]; it can just as easily signify the give-and-take, the easy interchange of Africa and the West, African indifference to portentous Western symbolism.

Thus constituted, the *Yoruba Man on a Bicycle* cannot escape Appiah's own call for polyphony and openness. Even if this sculpture has been produced, both industrially and aesthetically, by Western technology and a Western museum/commodity culture, it turns on its origins and demonstrates an alternative set of significations. This bicycle rides on a two-way street. One further comment: The modernist interpretation, by dint of its very universalism, is a bit flattening, much like the pack of cards; it certainly doesn't require a deep hermeneutic strategy. The postmodernist interpretation avoids a complicated hermeneutics by its antithetical turn to literalness and practicality. The Yoruba man's "less-anxious creativity" challenges theoretical postmodernism by relying upon "the changing everyday practices of African cultural life" (157). Appiah's reading doesn't argue against interpretation, however. Rather, it calls for a dialogical interpretation in which cultural icons assume the power to speak and advise. Just as postmodern African texts represent a variety of voices, the Yoruba man becomes the site on which many contesting voices can meet. What Bakhtin claims for textual voicing, the Yoruba man opens up for visual art: the power to embody contest and contradiction. The sole voice of the interpreter, positioned against an object, is only too likely to freeze its object

Interpretive Play: Masks, Bicycles and Heliotropes

in a position of otherness. Appiah's "it is too early to tell" refuses that constrictive authority.

A Package Deal

In contrast to Appiah's suspicions about an otherness driven by a modernist museum culture, Barthes's reading of Japan in *The Empire of Signs* seems to revel in the dual possibility that opacity produces cultural insight, and that otherness reverberates as cultural critique. It is opacity, however, that seems to inform the "first impression." Barthes reads Tokyo as a city with an empty center:

The entire city turns around a site both forbidden and indifferent, a residence concealed beneath foliage, protected by moats, inhabited by an emperor who is never seen, which is to say, literary, by no one knows who . . . One of the two most powerful cities of modernity is thereby built around an opaque ring of walls, streams, roofs and trees whose own center is no more than an evaporated notion, subsisting here, not in order to irradiate power, but to give to the entire urban movement the support of its central emptiness, forcing the traffic to make a perpetual detour."[7]

This structure is replicated at various levels: At the level of empire, the emperor is no more than an "empty subject," an invisible figure. At the urban level, there is, practically speaking, no city center. At the level of objects, Japanese packaging is elaborate, often multi-layered, surrounding a thing which is often no more than insignificant. Such formal repetition conveys a problematic significantly different from the one we found in the African exhibit. In that, we posited a hidden meaning, subject to both identification and misidentification, as well as marginalization. Here, Barthes posits an "empire" without interiors, centers, or conventional subjects. The exterior really does seem to be all there is. On what grounds, then, does Barthes write a book about Japan in which interpretive arrangements are clearly at work?

Barthes observes that the spiritually empty neighborhood center, the railway station, or the subjectless urban center of Tokyo, the Imperial Palace, forms an architectural challenge to Western notions of truth: in Western metaphysics, "every center is the site of truth, the center of our cities is always *full*: a marked site, it is here that the values of civilization are gathered and condensed" (30). Churches "condense" spirituality, offices "gather" power. But not in Tokyo. From an interpretive point of view, therefore, it seems that *The Empire of Signs* might have been called "The Empire

Speaks Back." To be sure, spoken language is insignificant in Barthes' account of Japan, and indeed, it plays only a "trivial" role in the Bunraku puppet drama, to which we now turn. Although voice runs through the "gamut of emotions," it ultimately signifies only its own excess in relation to the other aspects of the spectacle, in effect turning itself inside out. Voice, too, functions as a kind of wrapper, flattened to a single meaning by its very intensities. Voice is marginalized by gesture in Bunraku, on the level of the dolls and on the level of the manipulators, who sit in full view of the audience. Bunraku thus subsumes three kinds of "writing" - what is voiced, the silent gestures of the puppets and the silent actions of the manipulators - that together produce a powerful spectacle. The discontinuities of these "writings" result in a kind of "alienation" effect that is extremely powerful. What is limited to the actors in Western theaters here results from the combination of distinct codes and signs.

Where Appiah reads the "opaque" Yoruba man as an open cipher, Barthes reads opaque Japanese cultural productions as a series of highly organized structures whose inner meaning has been written out of court. Its external meaning is portentous - not only for "the country I am calling Japan" (79) but for the West. Bunraku problematizes a series of Western antinomies: animate versus inanimate, body versus soul, body-as-fetish versus lovable natural body, agent and actor, cause and effect; it even questions the separation between stage and spectators. In addition, it turns to illusions of totality and origins. Bunraku puppets, therefore, signify as forms without enacting any particular drama: in effect, Barthes delineates a composite "writing" whose otherness deconstructs cherished Western antinomies. If Barthes retreats from identifying the "real" empirical Japan as the object of study - his metaphors of line, packaging, writing, maps, gesture all bespeak a semiotics removed from "the real thing" - then he ends up in a role similar to that of the puppet manipulator. His interpretive grid bespeaks a systematic project inviting Westerners to self-scrutiny by way of a package deal. Visitors to Japan will recognize the accuracy of the images; nevertheless, they may wonder whether Barthes' interpretive grid replicates the same circuit of detours and returns he discovered in Tokyo. The antinomy that remains - that between East and West - becomes necessary to prevent all signs from collapsing into mere circulation around empty subjects on both sides.

Japan offers its own answer to the problem in one of its most important Shinto shrines, Ise; the central structures are closed to the general public, who can catch no more than glimpses of them through a surrounding fence.

Interpretive Play: Masks, Bicycles and Heliotropes   205

No one (unless, perhaps, a priest) can see what is inside; it is the opaque outside, rather than the inside, that must be interpreted as a kind of architectural religious wrapping.[8] The shrine is torn down and rebuilt every twenty years; the fragments are dispersed among other Shinto shrines. Is this an allegory? It dismantles antinomies but retains a meaning, if a mysterious and not easily definable one. Built upon silence and exclusion, change and dispersal, Ise is a magnet to pilgrims. If antinomies do indeed collapse within it, then it cannot be read as either signifier or signified; but neither can it be read as the sign of their absence. "Emptiness" is too facile a term for what is closed to spectators but open to speculation.

Appiah warns against the facile global symbolism in "African Art" or "Primitivism," both terms excluding individual nuance as well as any indigenous African perspective, and offers in return the uses of the empirical, the man on the bicycle negotiating cultures with ease but not superficial facility. In his way, Barthes elides empirical Japan into what is, variously, a country of the mind or a system of writing. As a result, Japan emerges as a country of forms that challenges Western categories of thought, including the category of the subject. The Bunraku puppets exemplify this move by dividing three major indices of identity into voice, gesture, action, each performed by a different agent. It would be a mistake to call such complex images, such a complex "imaginary," a matter merely of surfaces: Barthes preempts that position by claiming that the Bunraku puppets dissolve Western antinomies - which would include surface and depth. Nevertheless, whatever play is involved in either this theater or Barthes's interpretation of it, the question of depth is not really relevant. The insignificance of a package's contents in Japan, or the emptiness of Tokyo's urban centers make the point in another way: images signify even without referents.

To flatten the antithesis between surface and depth is to marginalize the possibility of a hermeneutics. For deep play, we turn to Clifford Geertz, who cites theater and spectacle as the center of a Balinese cultural hermeneutics. It is hermeneutics which restores the traffic between surface and depth, image and global meaning, cultural representation and person.

Geertz's acknowledged debt to the methodology of literary criticism, the kind that shuttles back and forth between tenor and vehicle, the "general form" of cultural life and its concrete embodiments, coincides fairly closely with his adoption of an interpretive approach in which part and whole each serve to explicate the other. Such an approach anticipates Appiah, who places this two-way traffic within a temporal perspective. Yet Geertz's method would constitute a variation upon the formalism we already noted in

Levi-Strauss and Barthes, if it did not include at one level the concern with what constitutes a person for a given culture (a somewhat transgressive concern for contents) and at another the insistence upon the "native's point of view."[9]

One crucial instance for Geertz appears in Balinese theater, in which all aspects - masks, roles, stage and spectacle - compose "not the facade but the substance of things, not least the self" (232). Thus what we would think of as "the surface of things," the spectacle or pageant of life, is inseparable from life itself. According to Geertz, Balinese society is complex and hierarchical, organized by a system of markers in which individuals occupy representative places: "in both their structure and their mode of operation, the terminological systems conduce to a view of the human person as an appropriate representative of a generic type, not a unique creature with a private fate"(233). At this point, however, it seems that we have arrived at an inversion not so very different from what we saw earlier, and that a culture's images represent - in a deep sense - its realities. Whereas the Caduveo Indians used their face paintings to convey deep social tensions - in which case the paintings are a "vehicle" for a deeper tenor, or the outside signifier for something inner - the Balinese masks, symbolic as they seem, constitute a reality which guards against a potentially disruptive individuality. Such a claim, however, moves us closer to the Bunraku puppets, whose composite being also blurs the distinction between the "subject" and the artificial forms it inhabits. Although we seem to be caught in the very formalism we thought we had escaped, each formal instance here varies from the others as if to exemplify the perpetual motion of antinomies that empowers interpretation. Only Levi-Strauss invokes the traditional outside-inside dichotomy, whereas Geertz reverses it and Barthes invokes it only to dissolve it.

How, then, can we avoid the antithesis that informs all these cultural readings? To this point, the very act of reading positions the anthropologist-culture critic-interpreter as a spectator. Suppose, however, she were to enter the scene of action. If "From the Native's Point of View" raises antithesis to the level of "we" and "they" (with the adoption of the other's point of view a requisite for cultural understanding), "Deep Play" introduces the anthropologist interpreter into the culture and makes him in some sense a player.[10] The Balinese cockfight becomes another kind of ritual drama.

Geertz analyzes the cockfight in a small Balinese village - the fight itself, the rules for betting, its illegal status - within a double frame: that of his own visit, "malarial and diffident" (181) as a professional intruder into a small village; and that of Balinese culture, whose art forms apart from the cockfight convey a far more orderly, pacific national identity. These two frames are interlocked insofar as Geertz finds access to a cultural ritual that uncharacteristically serves as a reflection upon violence: "on its look, its uses, its force, its fascination. Drawing on almost every level of Balinese experience, it brings together themes - animal savagery, male narcissism, opponent gambling, status rivalry, mass excitement, blood sacrifice - whose main connection is their involvement with rage and the fear of rage, and binding them into a set of rules which at once contains them and allows them play, builds a symbolic structure in which, over and over again, the reality of their inner affiliation can be intelligibly felt" (219). In this self-representation, the Balinese appear as they do not want to be. "Intrusion" becomes the condition for an extension of representation into the domain of its own antithesis: the cockfight becomes a way of expressing and containing the violence that is unacceptable in daily life, except in this surreptitious form. The image is neither a cipher nor a key to Balinese life: Geertz implies that the interpreter who retains a spectatorial role (as Levi-Strauss does) can become locked into such an approach. Geertz needs to experience a culture and at the same time to treat it as if it were a literary text. The interpretive experience seems to be at once an experiential and a methodological transgression, diminishing his own "physical" otherness at the same time that it distinguishes a culture's otherness to itself. Geertz's disclaimer that the cockfight represents a "correct" interpretation of the Balinese may seem to place the cockfight in some interpretive limbo in which it is neither aberration nor direct expression. His intrusion, however, identifies another route - or detour - to interpretation, one in which (a) formal cultural expression constitutes not wish-fulfillment but the image of what one does not wish to be and (b) the interpreter shuttles back and forth between his experience of a culture's experiencing itself, and his reading of that culture as if it were a text. The latter, of course, is modeled on a hermeneutic circle, although the "tradition" he brings to the artwork consists of a relatively new and problematic mode of interpretation. Geertz's presence at the cockfight, as well as his flight from the police who come to break up the event, purchases for him a certain entree into local society. From his indeterminate position, his otherness to the society he is studying becomes secondary to the alterity of that society to itself. The object of study, the violent fight and its attendant rituals, appears under the twin rubric of negation and de-idealization. We can also add that the elaborate rituals of betting shift economic conditions to internal ones.

Barthes's analysis of the Bunraku puppets suggests that antinomy is a Western concept, one that need not be intrinsic to all modes of cultural understanding. Where *The Empire of Signs* suspends antithesis by scrutinizing the plane of representation, examining the formal properties of the theatrical image, "Deep Play" suspends it by triangulating the process of interpretation itself, dissolving the barrier between interpreter and image and arguing that what appears to be a bracketed form of experience bears a tangential but crucial relation to its culture. Nevertheless, one may question whether the entrance of the interpreter into this hermeneutic circle doesn't produce the very condition it is attempting to account for. Disinterest, as we saw, is likely to subscribe to a suspiciously limited formalism; but interest, or interpretive self-involvement, may collapse into cultural oblivion on the one hand, and on the other, the production of the very object, image or reading it professes to discover and analyze.

"We live in an old chaos of the sun" (Stevens)
At this point, let us turn to a double image that appears in a text that scrutinizes metaphors in Western philosophy, Derrida's "White Mythology."[11] Metaphor, he claims, functions as a necessary detour, a turn away from the dazzling radiance of a central truth which eventually returns, by away of an "interiorizing anamnesis" to meaning itself (268-269). This metaphoric movement, in which truth is recaptured as an interior moment, is itself cast in a double metaphor: "The sensory sun, which rises in the East, becomes interiorized, in the evening of its journey, in the eye and the heart of the Westerner. He summarizes, assumes, and achieves the essence of man...." (268). The sensory sun becomes an interior sun not only in the course of a day's journey from East to West, but in the course of a geographical journey from East to West, as Derrida observes in citing both Rousseau and Hegel on the origins of language. Here is Rousseau: "As man's first motives for speaking were of the passions, his first expressions were tropes. Figurative language was the first to be born. Proper meaning was discovered last." Moreover, "the genius of the Oriental languages" is to be "vital and figurative." This becomes one source for a Western philosophical narrative in which the loss of both vitality and figure and of sensory immediacy, of the sun itself, is balanced by a compensatory inwardness. To those who mourn a vitality embodied, so to speak, in the sun, at once the source and the image of that energy, self-consciousness, or the understanding of what is proper to man, appears as a *releve*, a sublimation. And

yet, such a metaphorics takes as its exemplary figure the heliotrope or sunflower, at once the flower that yearns toward the sun and the punning metaphor or trope that "turns" toward the sun. As Derrida points out, heliotropic metaphors, despite their claim to exemplariness, are necessarily imperfect: The sensory sun is almost impossible to describe outside of metaphor; therefore, one term of the heliotropic metaphor "cannot be known in what is proper to it" (250). By a logic of analogy, the Western journey toward what is "proper" to man is subject to the same indeterminacy as the Western heliotropic metaphor: the vital source and the sensory original is at best elusive, figuratively elided. Readers have pointed out the political irony in which such a *relevement* becomes complicit with a blanched "*white* mythology." Derrida ends the essay on what some will call a note of irresolution, others a metaphoric explosion. In one, metaphor collapses and dies into its proper term, its illustrative role finally defined as ornamental rather than light-giving. The other looks more like Keats's version of a sun myth, in which Hyperion, god of the sun, is deposed and Apollo "dies into life," a metaphoric life in which he is filled with "knowledge enormous" and plays many roles: god of the sun, medicine, poetry. To explode "the reassuring opposition of the metaphoric and the proper" is to provide for a heliotrope *releve*, a dried flower, a stone (a kind of oriental jasper). As an image/figure that contains the sensory but distances itself from the object of sense, the heliotrope properly substitutes for the mask, playing in a deep sense with the margins constructed in interpretation.

With Derrida, then, we return by way of the most abstract form of the image, the written, to a new conception of how it works. Derrida's representation echoes uncannily the modernist-postmodernist dichotomy in Appiah, in which the proper now aligns itself with the African sculpture as "Primitive," while a metaphoric plurality gestures to the open-ended reading of the *Yoruba Man on a Bicycle*. One may argue that this circle constitutes simply one more form of a Western *releve*, in which openness of interpretation arrives at its philosophical form in Derrida.

A culture of the visual image, then, includes the very factors we have surveyed: Internally, the representation of intracultural tensions, competing voices, or unconscious impulses. Insofar as they represent what one is but does not want to be, these images contain the self within the limits of art. Insofar as they constitute cultural identities, however, they exceed the boundaries of representation. At the same time, such images or dramas become the sites of theoretical contests, playing the universal against the local, the modern against the postmodern, the Eurocentric against everything that is "other" to it. What complicates these tensions still further is the ambiguous role played by interpreters, whose "presence" can break down the very cultural or theoretical antinomies embodied in these objects. Whether visually concrete or performatively dynamic, these images become locked into a metaphorical relation with their interpreters, whose tropes and biases shape interpretation. The geniality and literariness of the interpreters we have considered here, however, should not obliterate the violence implied in or diverted into the objects they set out to interpret. Caduveo masks and Balinese cockfights convey internal tensions uncovered through the active intervention of the ethnologist. The Yoruba man on a bicycle, however, rides insouciantly away from a contest of cultures in which he has thrown off the antithetical burdens of a monolithic symbolism which casts him as "Primitive" and an economics which reduces him to a decorative object. As the sites of contending interpretations, images project themselves into the voices of strong interpreters. If interpretation draws fire from difference, it also thrives on the transgressive thought suspended in figures.

---

1. Claude Levi-Strauss, *Tristes Tropiques*, trans. John Russell (New York: Athenaeum, 1972), pp. 160-180.
2. See Walter Benjamin, "The Task of the Translator," in *Illuminations*, trans. Harry Zohn (New York: Schocken Books, 1969), p. 80.
3. Jacques Derrida, "Structure, Sign and Play in the Discourse of the Human Sciences," in *Writing and Difference*, trans. Alan Bass (London: Routledge & Kegan Paul, 1978), p. 282.
4. See Walter Benjamin, "Unpacking My Library," in *Illuminations*, p. 67.
5. Kwame Anthony Appiah, "The Postcolonial and the Postmodern" in *In My Father's House* (New York: Oxford University Press, 1992), pp. 137-157.
6. Appiah is citing Sara Suleri's comment *Meatless Days*, where she is tired of being treated as an "Otherness-machine."
7. Roland Barthes, *The Empire of Signs*, trans. Richard Howard (New York: Hill and Wang, 1982), p.30-32.
8. The metaphor is Fredric Jameson's, part of his discussion of architecture in *Postmodernism, or, The Cultural Logic of Late Capitalism* (Durham: Duke University Press, 1991), pp. 101-102.
9. Clifford Geertz, "From the Native's Point of View: On the Nature of Anthropological Understanding," in *Interpretive Social Science*, ed. Paul Rabinow and William M. Sullivan (Berkeley: University of California Press, 1979), pp. 225-241.
10. Clifford Geertz, "Deep Play: Notes on the Balinese Cockfight" in *Interpretive Social Science*, pp. 181-223.
11. Jacques Derrida, "White Mythology," in *Margins of Philosophy*, trans. Alan Bass (Chicago: University of Chicago Press, 1982), pp. 207-271.

Fred Dallmayr
Modes of Cross-Cultural Encounter

These reflections were originally prompted by a historical commemoration a few years ago: the quincentennial of Columbus' discovery of America. In many parts of Europe and the New World, celebrations and public ceremonies were conducted to recall this memorable event. The same discovery, however, was also the occasion for widespread protests and counter-demonstrations, organized mainly by American Indians and their many sympathizers. These celebrations and counter-demonstrations surely offered the observer much food for thought, especially for a rethinking of the historical relation between Europe (and more generally the West) and the non-Western-world.[1] What— one was prompted to ask—have been the goals and overall effects of European or Western expansion into other continents in the past? What are the goals and likely consequences of the same expansion and penetration in our time? My endeavor in the following is not to offer a comprehensive overview of all possible modes of cross-cultural encounter between West and non-West. Instead, I confine myself here to a limited number of "ideal types" (in Max Weber's sense), types which range from outright conquest and domination over a number of intermediary stages to relatively benign and empowering forms of self-other relations. As I should add, my aim here is not purely a descriptive or classificatory one, but is also guided by normative or ethical considerations, especially the standard of mutual recognition. To this extent, the sequence of types can also be seen as revealing a moral progression or crescendo.

1. *Conquest*
Incorporation of alien territories and populations through conquest is a long-standing practice in human history. Historical accounts of ancient and medieval politics are replete with stories of invasion, forceful occupation, and

subjugation—from the Persian Wars to the sacking of Rome and the later Norman Conquest. Still, not all forms of incorporation are alike. In earlier times—apart from the Islamic expansion during the Middle Ages—conquest was chiefly the outgrowth of brute aggression guided by passion or the sheer lust for power and spoliation; by comparison, modern forms of take-over tend to be more deliberate, planned, and systematic. When bent on territorial expansion, modern civilization in the West engages in what one may call a "studied" or calculated type of conquest, a type animated by general or universal ideas and geared toward the dissemination of rational principles (including rationalizations of religious beliefs). To this extent, the Spanish conquistadors—despite amazing displays of wanton brutality—were pioneers of colonial administration and early forerunners of later "development" strategies.

In his study of "America's Spanish Heritage," G. M. Foster uses the label "conquest culture" to characterize the cultural mode imposed by the conquering power. As Foster points out, a conquest culture can be thought of as "artificial, standardized, simplified, or ideal" in that it is "at least partially consciously created and designed to cope with recognized problems." This standardized character was plainly evident in Hispanic America, given that Spanish policy was marked by "a consistent and logical philosophy of purposeful guided change that extended over a period of three centuries." The conquest culture in the Americas, according to Foster, must be clearly distinguished from the Spanish culture prevailing in the European homeland, a homeland which traditionally exhibited a high degree of diversity and of regional and local autonomy. To counteract this diversity, the conquistadors imposed on the Americas a streamlined version of Spanish politics and religion.[2] This systematic and standardizing outlook of the Spanish invaders was a major factor in the swift execution of the conquest and in the efficient expansion of administrative control over American territories; the same outlook also shaped decisively the encounter of the conquest culture with the native Indian populations. By all standards, the pace of the take-over itself was staggering. Barely thirty years after Columbus' voyage, Hernando Cortés had overrun and subdued the Aztec empire of Mexico, by capturing its traditional leaders (including Montezuma); a mere two decades later, Francisco Pizarro had conquered in a similar fashion the Inca kingdom centered in Peru. Placed under the aegis of the Spanish crown, these exploits became the cornerstones of the administrative viceroyalties of Mexico City and Lima—which, in turn, were only the launching pads for Spanish expansion throughout Central and South America. These exploits were greatly facilitated by the "studied" or calculating character of the conquest, that is, by the sense of rational-spiritual mission propelling the Spanish invaders—a mission which could in no way be obstructed or derailed by the distinctiveness of native Indian cultures and customs.

In his study *The Conquest of America*, Tzvetan Todorov offers a thumbnail sketch of the colonial mentality in its encounter with native cultures, a sketch focused mainly on General Cortés. As Todorov shows, Spanish colonizers were not unfamiliar with or callously disinterested in indigenous life-forms; on the contrary, they (at least the more far-sighted among them) made it a point to study and comprehend Indian culture—though with the aim of subjugating it more efficiently, not of appreciating its intrinsic worth. Emulating Bacon's dictum, the Spaniards keenly perceived the linkage of knowledge and power. In his entire behavior, Todorov notes, Cortés affords us "a splendid example" of this outlook:

Schematically this behavior is organized into two phases. The first is that of interest in the other, at the cost of a certain empathy or temporary identification. Cortés slips into the other's skin... Thereby he ensures himself an understanding of the other's language and a knowledge of the other's political organization.... But in so doing he has never abandoned his feeling of superiority; it is even his very capacity to understand the other that confirms him in that feeling. Then comes the second phase, during which he is not content to reassert his own identity (which he has never really abandoned), but proceeds to assimilate the Indians to his own world.

Todorov at this point offers some general observations on the (tendential) relation of European or Western culture to the rest of the world: "The Europeans exhibit remarkable qualities of flexibility and improvisation which permit them all the better to impose their own way of life."[3]

The colonizers' attitude—though on a more inchoate or unsophisticated level—was evident already in the case of Columbus and his dealings with the natives. In Todorov's portrayal, Columbus was entirely incapable or unwilling to acknowledge the distinctive difference of the Indians. Truthful to his mission and his Western-universalizing bent, he admitted only two options: either the Indians were as human beings equal to or identical with the Spaniards—in which case they were known (or knowable) and did not require a special effort of comprehension; or else they were radically different—in which case they were reduced to savages and on the same level as animate or inanimate objects of nature. According to Todorov, the Spanish-Indian confrontation was a failed encounter from the start, because it was predicated on two alternative strategies: either complete assimilation or complete rejection and subjugation. These two alternatives, he muses, are not confined to the Spanish conquest but prototypical of the behavior of "every colonist in his relations to the colonized" down "to our own day." Drawing out broader philosophical implications, Todorov finds that the two modes of "experience of alterity" are both equally grounded in "egocentrism," that is, in the "identification of our own values with values in general, of our $\underline{I}$ with the universe—in the conviction that the world is one."[4]

The story of the Spanish conquest (recounted here largely through Todorov's lenses) is instructive beyond its immediate historical setting for the future of European or Western colonialism. To be sure, none of the subsequent colonial ventures can match the original Spanish exploit in the boldness and novelty of discovery, in the starkness of cultural contrasts, and (perhaps) in the extent of physical brutality. Subsequent colonizers absorbed indeed the lessons of the Spanish precedent; but—on the whole—they sought to emulate Cortés more in his calculating foresight than in his fits of anger. In the felicitous phrase coined in *The Conquest of America*: A "new trinity" replaces or supplements "the old-style soldier-*conquistador*: it consists of the scholar, the priest, and the merchant"; among the three, the first collects information about the country, the second promotes its "spiritual annexation," and the third "makes certain of the profits."[5]

Actually, during ensuing centuries, this trinity was further modified by additional shifts of accent; progressively, the linkage of knowledge and power was rendered more subtle and circuitous—without ever losing its cutting edge. As it happened, despite its standardizing and rationalizing bent, Spanish colonialism was never quite congruent with the demands of modern rationality; as a Catholic power, Spain was never fully in tune with the central guideposts of modernity: that is, individual freedom (of conscience and belief), capitalist free enterprise, and political liberalism. Apart from historical contingency, this incongruence was one of the main reasons for the decline of Spanish hegemony (after 1588) and for the progressive shift of hegemonic leadership to North European powers and ultimately to North America. Like Spain before them, these new hegemonic powers were guided in their colonizing efforts by standardizing-universal principles or ideas, but these principles were couched no longer in the language of church dogma but in a more secular-progressive idiom (sometimes the idiom of the "white man's burden"); as a corollary, Christian faith steadily gave way to, or was fused with, overarching ideologies or "world-views." To this extent, the trinity of scholar-priest-merchant was gradually transformed into the triad of missionaries, entrepreneurs, and intellectuals.

2. Conversion

In its typical form, conquest entails the physical subjugation of alien populations and sometimes also their forced cultural assimilation; where the latter feature predominates, conquest gives way to conversion. Although often closely linked, conquest and conversion are not always or necessarily connected. History teaches that there have been conquests without any overt efforts of assimilation—although modern-style take-overs usually involve also the dissemination of general ideas (religious or ideological); conversely, there have been conversions in the absence of conquest or forced subjugation (and sometimes even as counter-moves to political and cultural domination). Although distinguishable, the two modes of outreach share in common one prominent feature: the denial of meaningful human difference. In the case of conquest, difference is actually affirmed but in a radical-hierarchical way which sacrifices mutuality in favor of the rigid schism of mind and matter, culture and nature, civilized people and savages. In the case of conversion, difference is denied through the insistence on a common or identical human nature—an identity which predestines native populations to be willing targets of proselytizing missions.

As one should note, conversion is not an inextricable ingredient of religious faith. Several of the leading world religions have been strongly averse to missionary practices. This is true among Western religions of Judaism and among Eastern religions (or quasi-religions) of Hinduism, Taoism, and Confucianism; in the latter category, only Buddhism has engaged in large-scale missionary outreach—but in a manner typically shunning conquest in favor of teaching and practical example. This leaves as missionary world religions of a militant type only Islam and Christianity. Among the two, Christianity has been historically more successful, manly because of its closer kinship with the modern spirit of individualism and progress (enshrined in the "Protestant Ethic"). While the heyday of Islamic expansion occurred during the Middle Ages and before 1492, Christian expansion started with the voyage of Columbus and later merged with the secular aspirations of Western modernity.[6]

In the case of the conquest of America, conversion was an intrinsic feature of Spanish policy from the beginning and—next to the desire for plunder— served as its chief justifying rationale. To be sure, implementation of conversion underwent important changes over time. Initially the policy was carried out by the sword, often with displays of extreme brutality and savagery. This savagery was uppermost in the mind of one of the most perceptive and affable Christian missionaries of that era: the Dominican Bartolemé de Las Casas. For Las Casas the atrocities committed by the Spanish were an indictment of the military method of colonization and a compelling motive for replacing that method with missionary endeavors more in tune with the teachings of the gospel. In his *Brevissima Relación* (translated as *The Tears of the Indians*), Las Casas offers a gripping account of Spanish cruelties: hangings, mutilations, burnings—an account which was meant as an appeal to the Spanish crown for a change of policy (and which later provided welcome ammunition to the Protestant enemies of Spain in Northern Europe). In a truly historic encounter, Las Casas entered into an intense and remarkable debate with the historian Ginés de Sepúlveda at Valladolid (in 1551). Relying in part on Aristotelian teachings, Sepúlveda justified the subjugation of the Indians on the basis of their natural inferiority—thereby submitting conversion to the logic of conquest. Politics as well as religious salvation in his view were governed by the same principle: namely, the dominion "of perfection over imperfection, of force over weakness, of eminent virtue over vice"; seen in this light, the Indians were related to the Spaniards in the same was as "children are to adults" or "women to men" or savages and "wild beasts" to civilized people.

On all these counts, Las Casas opted for a radically opposite outlook, namely, for a strictly egalitarian conception according to which all humans are equally endowed with a soul and hence equally called to salvation through Christian faith. As he expostulated in his rejoinder to Sepúlveda (published under the title *Apologia* or *In Defense of the Indians*): "Aristotle, farewell! From Christ, the eternal truth, we have the commandment 'You must love your neighbor as yourself'.... Christ seeks souls, not property." Animated by this spirit, Las Casas advocated a complete shift of strategy: specifically the abandonment of military conquest, of forced land acquisition (encomienda), and of Indian slavery. Still, despite these humanitarian pleas, Todorov is probably on safe ground when he charges Las Casas with spiritual colonialism, that is, with continued support for Hispanization or the "annexation of the Indians"—provided the latter was "effected by priests rather than by soldiers." Todorov also casts doubt on neighborly love if accompanied by missionary conversion:

Can we really love someone if we know little or nothing of his identity; if we see, in place of that identity, a projection of ourselves or of our ideals? ... Does not one culture risk trying to transform the other in its own name, and therefore risk subjugating it as well? How much is such love worth? [7]

Las Casas was not successful in transforming colonial practices—although he did manage to instill in colonial administrators the need for greater subtlety, circumspection, and (perhaps) subterfuge. Following the Reformation and as a corollary of the rise of capitalist markets, colonial hegemony tended to shift from Spain (and Portugal) to North European powers, especially to England and the Netherlands. As in the Spanish case, colonial expansion by these powers was accompanied or closely followed by missionary endeavors intent on spreading religious beliefs as well as cultural and ideological preferences. Progressively, the civilizing mission of the West came to affect the entire fabric of life (from worship to politics and economics) of non-Western populations—in a manner foreshadowing later strategies of development and modernization. In the field of religious conversion, Christian missionaries working in tandem with colonizers concentrated their efforts on Africa, India, and the Far East, often pursuing a path which navigated ambiguously between Cortés and Las Casas.

To resume a point made earlier, conversion does not always serve the purposes of colonizers or colonial rule, but may occasionally have oppositional and even subversive connotations. This has to do with a central feature of religious faith: the ability of such faith to transcend prevailing social and political conditions and hence to become a resource for liberation rather than domination. Thus, in the case of India, Mahatma Gandhi was able to invoke the Hindu notions of "*swaraj*," "*satyagraha*," and "*ramaraja*" as guideposts in his struggle against British colonial oppression. On the other hand, especially after the accomplishment of independence, various groups in Indian society disenfranchised by the prevailing caste system became willing targets of conversion to Islam and Buddhism (occasionally to Christianity), sometimes on a large scale. As Lloyd and Susanne Rudolph have reported, in 1956 at least three million and perhaps as many as 20 million untouchables were converted to Buddhism in the state of Maharashtra alone. Again, during more recent decades, entire villages of untouchables have reportedly been converted to Islam, especially in the state of Tamil Nadu. Although in all these cases the role of political and financial manipulation cannot be entirely ignored, the deeper reason for these events was surely the desire of disadvantaged people for greater freedom and respect (however elusive this goal may be under the circumstances).[8]

3. *Assimilation and Acculturation*

As we have noted, conversion is not always a corollary of conquest, nor is it necessarily restricted to the dissemination of religious beliefs. Apart from colonial expansion in foreign lands, cultural hegemony may also be exercised in a more circumscribed (including a strictly "domestic") setting and, in that case, may involve the spreading of diffuse cultural patterns or ways of life (of religious and/or secular vintage). The targets of such hegemonic outreach are typically marginalized ethnic, national or linguistic groups (sometimes composed of immigrant populations). In contradistinction from external colonialism, colonization of this kind tends to be discussed by social scientists and anthropologists under the heading of "assimilation" or "acculturation." Some broad definitions may be in order here. According to Robert Park and Ernest Burgess, assimilation may be seen as "a process of interpenetration and fusion in which persons and groups acquire the memories, sentiments, and attitudes of other persons and groups and, by sharing their experience and history, are incorporated by them in a common cultural life." While assimilation is usually applied to policies in some Western or Westernizing nations, the term "acculturation" tends to have a broader and more indefinite application, extending from domestic contacts to global interactions between the hegemonic Western culture and developing non-Western societies.

In our century, assimilation and, to some extent, acculturation have been greatly abetted and intensified by nationalism and the idea of the "nation-state." In the well-known words of Rupert Emerson:

In the contemporary world, the nation is for greater portions of mankind the community with which men most intensely and most unconditionally identify themselves. . . . The nation is today the largest community which, when the chips are down, effectively commands men's loyalty, overriding the claims both of the lesser communities within it and those which cut across it. . . . In this sense the nation can be called a 'terminal community.'

The hegemonic influence of nationalism and the nation-state, one should note, is not confined to advanced Western countries but extends to non-Western, post-colonial societies. While initially opposing the "state" as an alien, colonial apparatus, independence movements quickly adopted a nationalist rhetoric geared toward the acquisition of state power. "In seeking the mandate," Crawford Young writes, "the anticolonial leadership began the process of transforming the often-arbitrary colonial state into a nation."[9]

In the Western orbit, the most frequently discussed and conspicuous examples of cultural assimilation are the United States and Israel. In both cases, large numbers of immigrants from many parts of the world were progressively integrated or incorporated into the dominant social and political fabric. Since these examples are relatively well known, however, I shall bypass them at this point. Returning to the story of Hispanic America, assimilation became a dominant policy in the newly independent countries which emerged in the early part of the last century. By that time, Latin American societies were already strongly shaped by the cultural patterns of the Spanish (and Portuguese) homeland, patterns carried forward chiefly by "creoles" (European stock born overseas). This hegemonic patterning was intensified during the post-independence period. In the words of Crawford Young:

> *During the unstable and tumultuous years of the nineteenth century, the creole elite indelibly stamped its cultural imprint on the new states. The key culture-forming groups—lawyer, <u>caudillo</u>, intellectual, or priest—were firmly Hispanic. The nodal points of urban culture—the towns and cities—were a generalized model of the Iberian community, remarkably uniform in spatial configuration and cultural pattern from the Rio Grande to the Straits of Magellan.*

During the course of the last century, the hegemonic culture shaped by colonizers and creoles was progressively disseminated through the rest of society, especially to the mestizo, mulatto and native Indian populations—in a manner approximating the melting-pot syndrome. Usually termed "mestization," this process of assimilation extended even to areas, like Peru and Bolivia, where Indians formed a large majority at the time of independence. Only in recent times have cracks in the cultural fabric been noted by social scientists and anthropologists; as in the case of North America, analytical models based on assimilation and mestization are challenged today by accounts stressing cultural diversity and ethnic rivalry.[10]

These comments on cultural fusion require further amplification. As one should note, assimilation is not only or exclusively a policy imposed from above, that is, a process whereby a hegemonic culture is disseminated by an elite to subordinate segments of the population. Sometimes (perhaps quite frequently), the hegemonic culture holds a powerful attraction for subordinate groups eager to gain social acceptance or recognition and thus to terminate discrimination. Where such acceptance is pursued deliberately and with some promise of success, we are in the presence of acculturation through upward mobility. This phenomenon is well-known in Western societies where members of underprivileged or marginalized groups may be engaged in a struggle for higher social status (sometimes termed "*embourgeoisement*"). In the context of Indian society, the process of upward mobility on the part of lower castes or subcastes has been analyzed perceptively and in detail by M. N. Srinivas under the label "Sanskritization." As Srinivas pointed out, by means of caste associations lower status groups have often been able to break through established caste barriers by adopting elite cultural patterns, for example, by performing ritual practices associated with the higher (or "twice-born") castes, by becoming vegetarian and the like.[11]

4. Partial Assimilation; Cultural Borrowing

Cultural encounter does not always entail merger or fusion, but may also lead to partial adaptation or assimilation, through a process of cultural borrowing (and lending). For such adaptation to happen, the respective cultures must face each other on a more nearly equal or roughly comparable basis—in contradistinction to the starkly hegemonic or hierarchical relation characterizing the previously discussed cases. Partial adaptation, in any case, involves a greater subtlety in self-other relations. In opposition to the self-imposition (through dissemination) or self-surrender (through upward mobility) marking hegemonic situations, selective borrowing requires a willingness to recognize the distinctiveness of the other culture, coupled with a desire to maintain at least some indigenous preferences. The outcome of such partial accommodation can be greatly varied, ranging from partial absorption or incorporation of alien elements to compromise and mutual adjustment to a process of complex self-transformation as a result of cultural learning.

Partial assimilation and selective borrowing are not unfamiliar to Western culture. Throughout the course of Western history we find many episodes of partial adjustment and incorporation—sometimes to the point of calling into question the very notion of indigenous traditions. Through recent historical scholarship we are acquainted with the extent to which early Greece borrowed from North African and Mycenean cultures. Within the confines of the Greek peninsula, we are also familiar with the intense process of cultural exchange among the various city states—although a sharp cultural barrier was erected by all of them against the "barbarians" in the East. During the period of the Roman Republic, Greek intellectual influence was steadily on the rise: several of the famous philosophical schools, including the Epicureans and Stoics, were originally founded in Greece before being transplanted to Roman soil. With the expansion of imperial power, Rome came increasingly into contact with alien—especially Near Eastern—cultures and belief systems; despite an official policy of conquest and colonization, the repercussions of these peripheral cultures on the Roman metropolis can hardly be ignored or underestimated. To this extent, the Hellenistic and imperial periods were a time of rampant syncretism.

Accommodation and the practice of cultural borrowing continued into the Middle Ages. The rise of Islamic culture around the Mediterranean led to the wide dissemination of Muslim philosophical and scientific scholarship—which provided an enormous boost to Western learning and Christian scholasticism during the eleventh and twelfth centuries. Still a few centuries later, the fall of Constantinople triggered a large-scale exodus of Greek scholars from the territories of "Eastern Rome"—a migration which provided a strong impulse to the European Renaissance. Without question, one of the most significant episodes of cultural borrowing during the later Middle Ages was the "reception" of classical Roman law, especially of the legacy of the *ius civile*—a legacy which subsequently became the cornerstone of jurisprudence in Continental European countries (and their colonies). In more recent times, partly as a result of colonialism, cultural borrowing extended from legal codes to political institutions and constitutional arrangements. In this context, one must mention the dissemination of the British "Westminster model" first among some European countries and then throughout the Empire and later Commonwealth. In our own century, this influence has been challenged by the American presidential system—which again has served as a model for many countries both in the West and around the globe.

As one should add, cultural borrowing in the West sometimes extended far afield. In view of the broad acclaim according to 1492 and the voyages of Columbus, it may be appropriate to call attention to another explorer and voyager whose travels took him precisely in the opposite direction: the Italian Marco Polo. About two centuries before Columbus' expedition, Marco Polo set off to visit far-off China which at that time was under the dominion of the Mongol ruler Kublai Khan. The written account of Marco's travels sparked considerable European interest in the Far East, while also lending impulse to advances in "scientific" cartography. During the Renaissance and Reformation this interest subsided somewhat, being overshadowed by revived concern with classical and biblical antiquity and by fascination with the New World (America). A renewed upsurge of attentiveness to China occurred during the Enlightenment or "age of reason" when enlightened forms of absolutism emulated the bureaucratic practices of the "Kingdom of Heaven," while at the same time cultivating a taste for Chinese modes of dress, coiffure (wigs), and courtly behavior.[12]

Explorations and distant voyages are sometimes considered a European or Western monopoly; but this is far from the truth. A case in point is the extension of Buddhism to China, Japan, and other parts of the Far East—an extension which constitutes one of the most remarkable instances of cultural borrowing in human history. Borrowing and lending here were closely tied to exploratory voyages. In a well-known study, Erik Zürcher speaks of "the Buddhist conquest of China"—but this is surely a misnomer. Buddhism was brought from India to China by traveling monks who faced great hardship on their long journeys and sometimes even persecution; they definitely were not accompanied by well-armed troops of conquistadors under the command of a Cortés or Pizarro. The first Buddhist monks arrived in China in the first century (C.E.), bringing with them many sacred texts as well as Buddhist practices of meditation (*dhyana*) and concentration (*samadhi*). On their arrival they encountered an alien culture which in some ways was quite congenial to their own, but in other ways was radically different. One of the principal tasks faced by these itinerant monks was the translation of sacred texts from Sanskrit or Pali into the Chinese idiom—a task which required enormous skills of interpretation as well as a good dose of cultural flexibility and mutual adjustment. As a result of these exegetic labors, Buddhism was infused or supplemented with prevailing Taoist ideas—especially the wisdom teachings of Lao-tzu and Chuang-tzu—while Taoism in turn was amplified and transformed through the integration of Buddhist ontology and metaphysics. In the words of Heinrich Dumoulin, whose study of Buddhism in India and China carefully traces the complex interaction between elements of Indian and Chinese culture:

The transplanting of Buddhism from its native soil in India into the culture and life of China may be counted among the most significant events in the history of religions. It meant the introduction of a higher religion—complete with scriptural canon, doctrines, morality, and cult—into a land with an ancient culture of its own. . . . The use of Taoist terms for Buddhist beliefs and practices not only helped in the difficult task of translation but also brought Buddhist scriptures closer to the Chinese people. . . . The 'Taoist guise' that Buddhism donned did not remain external but worked deep-reaching changes on Buddhist thought. This encounter with the spiritual heritage of ancient China became a fountainhead that was to nourish the various schools of

Chinese Buddhism, all of which were intimately related to one another despite doctrinal differences. [13]

From China Buddhism spread quickly to Japan, Korea, and adjacent lands in the Far East; again, cultural borrowing and lending was mainly the work of traveling monks and scholars disseminating Buddha's teachings by land and by sea. Some four centuries before Marco Polo, the monk Ennin crossed the sea to China where he spent about a decade, keeping a detailed record or diary of his extensive travels through the vast country (then under the T'ang dynasty); significantly, the diary was titled "Record of a Pilgrimage to China in Search of the Law" (or Dharma). While Marco Polo was mainly a trader looking for commercial contacts, Ennin was a learned scholar enjoying considerable prestige in his homeland. Comparing the two travelers, Edwin Reischauer—who has translated Ennin's diary into English and also provided an extensive commentary—writes:

Marco Polo, coming from a radically different culture, was ill-prepared to understand or appreciate what he saw of higher civilization in China. He was virtually unaware of the great literary traditions of the country and, living in a China which was still in large part Buddhist, comprehended little of this religion other than that it was 'idolatrous.' Ennin, coming from China's cultural offshoot—Japan—was at least a stepson of Chinese civilization, educated in the complicated writing system of the Chinese and himself a learned Buddhist scholar. Marco Polo came to China as an associate of the hated Mongol conquerors; Ennin, as a fellow believer, entered easily into the heart of Chinese life. [14]

5. *Liberalism and Minimal Engagement*

In the cases just mentioned, cultural borrowing involved a prolonged, sometimes arduous process of engagement in alien life-forms, a process yielding at least a partial transformation of native habits due to a sustained learning experience. Cultural contacts, however, do not always or necessarily entail such engagement. Sometimes cultures are content to live or co-exist side by side in a mode of relative indifference; this is true mainly of contacts occurring under the aegis of modern liberalism, particularly its "procedural" variant.

Faithful to its motto of "laissez-faire" (let it be, do not meddle), modern liberalism has promoted a tolerant juxtaposition of cultures and life-forms predicated on relative mutual disinterest and aloofness. While acknowledging the need for an overall framework (to prevent chaos), liberal spokesmen typically support only a limited procedural rule-system or a government that "governs least"—while relegating concrete life-forms to the status of privatized folklore. Self-other relations, in this case, are curiously split or dichotomized: while sameness or identity is presumed to persist on the level of general principle (stylized as "reason" or "human nature"), historical cultures and beliefs are abandoned to rampant heterogeneity (tending toward segregation or ghettoization).

Most advanced Western societies are imbued in some fashion with this liberal "ethos." Curiously, the United States is often analyzed in terms of two radically opposed models: those of the "melting pot" and of liberal proceduralism; while the former model postulates the progressive assimilation of all strands into one uniform culture, the latter extols the neutrality or indifference of procedures toward any and all cultures. Although serving as an antidote to melting-pot assumptions, the second model is not necessarily more accurate as an analytical tool or more enticing as a blueprint for cultural encounter. Despite its appealing "open-mindedness," liberal tolerance tends to be purchased at a price: the price of a schism between form and substance, between public and private domains of life. Since the model of procedural liberalism is sufficiently well-known, the briefest allusion must suffice here. Among American spokesmen of the model, John Rawls, Ronald Dworkin, and Bruce Ackerman are the writers most frequently and appropriately singled out for attention. In his *A Theory of Justice* and other writings, Rawls sought to develop a conception of procedural fairness which would transcend individual or group-based cultural attachments while being anchored in the principle of "equal liberty." The latter axiom has been further elaborated and fleshed out by Dworkin under the heading of "equality principle" or "liberal conception of equality." According to Dworkin, modern government in the pursuit of equal justice must be rigorously "neutral on what might be called the question of the good life"; likewise, public policies must be "independent of any conception of the good life or of what gives value to life"—whether the conception is held by single individuals or by members of a cultural, ethnic or religious community. Taking some cues from Dworkin, Ackerman has erected neutrality into the central cornerstone of liberal constitutional theory and legal adjudication. In all these approaches, liberal proceduralism—seen as embodiment of "formal" reason—triumphs completely over historically grown life-forms (which are reduced to contingent accidents or "subjective" preferences); far from being the outgrowth of concrete cultural interaction, liberal justice appears predicated on a cultural *tabula rasa*.[15]

The shortcomings of liberal proceduralism have been frequently discussed—which again permits brevity at this point. On a logical-theoretical plane, the dilemma of proceduralism can be stated succinctly as follows: either justice is truly neutral and universal—in which case it is abstract, devoid of content, and collapses into tautology; or else it is endowed with some content—in which case it is embued with cultural distinctness (where culture denotes a way of life and not merely a "subjective circumstance"). The problems of proceduralism, however, are not only logical in character; more important are its damaging effects on cultural interaction. Under liberal-procedural auspices, differences of life-forms are either completely bracketed or else they are (more candidly) subordinated to the prevailing or hegemonic liberal culture; in either case, concrete cross-cultural engagement tends to be stifled or circumvented.[16]

6. *Conflict and Class Struggle*

Liberal neutralism prefers to leave cultural or religious differences untouched while encircling them with a band of abstractly formal procedures. In the words of Rawls, justice as fairness assumes "that deep and pervasive differences of religious, philosophical, and ethical doctrine remain" as "a permanent condition of human life." Thus, proceduralists take for granted existing contrasts between ways of life, while seeking to mitigate them through a thin consensual layer composed of shared general rules. Once this layer is removed, contrasting life-forms or beliefs face each other in unmediated fashion, which may (and often does) result in mutual repulsion and conflict. The latter result is especially prone to obtain under conditions of scarcity and where cultural groups are struggling for predominance or hegemony within a circumscribed territory. In extreme circumstances, struggle entails the transformation of cultural difference into radical otherness, with the contending parties defining themselves through mutual exclusion.

As a mode of social and cultural interaction, conflict (even of the radical sort) occupies a prominent place in the annals of human history and in the literature of social-political thought. In the account of Thomas Hobbes, conflict and mutual enmity are the chief trademarks of human relations in the "state of nature"; given the absence of a deeper sympathy, the "Leviathan" established through rational agreement has to resort mainly to power and fear (as an alternative to an always fragile cultural consensus). On a more concrete-historical level, social conflict has been accorded centerstage in the political theory of Machiavelli. An ardent admirer of the Roman Republic, Machiavelli perceived the conflictual interplay between patricians and plebeians (or between nobility and common people) as the basic source of the strength and vitality of Roman political life.[17]

To be sure, in Machiavelli's account, conflict was not construed in terms of a harsh antithesis since both of the opposing parties were seen as contributing to a common goal: the maintenance of republican freedom. The radicalization of group conflict into harsh opposition is the emblem of later economic and sociological theories—and mainly of the theory of "class struggle" as articulated by Marx. In the *Communist Manifesto*, Marx (and Engels) reduced relations between social groups to the antithesis between two main classes, one dominant and the other exploited: the bourgeoisie and the proletariat. While previous centuries had been characterized by multiple and crisscrossing relations—resulting in a mitigation of class division—the industrial revolution had finally sharpened social interaction into one decisive opposition between exploiters and exploited, an opposition which could only be resolved through revolutionary reversal.[18]

The model of radical conflict—or of self-definition through mutual exclusion—is not confined to traditional Marxism (whose influence and persuasiveness have notably receded in recent decades). Sometimes, the model also surfaces in intellectual perspectives whose premises and theoretical lineage seem at first glance far removed from the Marxist notion of class struggle—for example, in existentialism and (versions of) post-structuralism. Thus, in the work of the early Sartre, social or inter-personal relations are almost exclusively conceptualized in terms of radical antagonism and conflict. Curiously, despite a strong rejection of existentialist "humanism," post-structuralist writers occasionally approximate the Sartrean analysis. In rigorously opposing melting-pot assimilation or "totalitarian" synthesis, the accent on "difference" and multiplicity sometimes shades over into a celebration of self-other separation and unmitigated antagonism. Thus, in his *The Postmodern Condition*, Lyotard forcefully chastised the assimilationist striving for a "unified totality" or "unicity"—a striving to which even Marxism has tended to succumb (in communist regimes). Countering all unifying-holistic strategies, Lyotard perceived as trademark of postmodern or post-structuralist policy the "atomization of the social" into diverse networks of language games.[19]

In the global arena, the accent on conflict surfaces in prevailing accounts of international politics among nation-states (accounts typically foregrounding the imperatives of "*Realpolitik*"). Outside the nation-state arena—and on more legitimate grounds—conflict or struggle has been a prominent feature in the relations between Western and non-Western societies, especially between colonial powers and colonized populations. In extreme situations, these relations assume the character of that great "simplified antagonism" described in the *Communist Manifesto*, an antagonism predicated on radical otherness and mutual exclusion. Not surprisingly, the model of encounter (or rather non-encounter) prevalent in cases of conquest reemerges in these situations—but now seen from the vantage point of the colonized rather than the colonizing power. Some of the dilemmas and agonies of the anti-colonial struggle have been pinpointed by Frantz Fanon in his *The Wretched of the Earth*, sometimes in harsh and uncompromising language. "Decolonization which sets out to change the order of the world," Fanon states in his book, "is obviously a program of complete disorder." To clarify the sense of "disorder" here, Fanon invokes the biblical phrase "The last shall be first and the first last"—giving it a starkly conflictual meaning: "For if the last shall be first, this will only come to pass after a murderous and decisive struggle between the two protagonists."[20]

7. *Dialogical Engagement*

To round out this survey—in no way meant to be exhaustive—of modes of cultural encounter, I want to turn finally to a type which I consider most genuine and normatively most commendable: dialogical engagement and interaction. At this point I can return to Tzvetan Todorov from whom these pages began. In his Epilogue to The Conquest of America Todorov discloses his own normative stance or commitment: a commitment to "communication" or "dialogue," specifically "dialogue of (or between) cultures." As he writes, somewhat hopefully, it is the dialogue of cultures that "characterizes our age" and which is "incarnated by ethnology, at once the child of colonialism and the proof of its death throes." In opting for this stance, Todorov joins a host of other writers in our time who likewise endorse communication and dialogue—most notably Habermas, Gadamer, and Bakhtin; but his outlook is distinctive (for one also has to distinguish between modes of communication and dialogue).

In the work of Habermas, dialogue tends to be stylized as "discourse" and communication as "rational" communication bent on the assessment of "validity claims." As in the case of liberal proceduralism, rational discourse here involves a formalized consensus or an agreement in principle, while leaving intact concrete differences; but as in the proceduralist formula again, consensus is purchased at the price of a bracketing of such differences to the extent that they exceed discursive rules. A qualified type of idealized consensus was espoused by Gadamer in his *Truth and Method* under the rubric of an ultimate "fusion of horizons." However, as one should realize, this fusion was only presented as a regulative idea, as the distant goal point of a protracted hermeneutical engagement between reader and text—and analogously, of an interpretive-dialogical engagement between cultural life-forms. Moreover, in Gadamer's later writings, there is a steady distantiation from fusionism in favor of a stronger recognition of otherness in the context of reciprocal encounter.[21]

Among the mentioned writers, Todorov associates himself most closely with Mikhail Bakhtin's position, especially with the latter's notion of dialogical exchange. Basically, Todorov shares the postmodern or post-structuralist accent on difference; instead of opting for radical separation, however, he blends otherness with a non-assimilative dialogical engagement (which grants the other room to breathe or to "be"). Todorov speaks of a dialogue "in which no one has the last word" and where "neither voice is reduced to the status of a simple object"—or (one might add) elevated to the status of a superior subject. His own historical account of the Spanish conquest, he notes, has carefully tried to avoid "two extremes": one is the historicist temptation to "reproduce the voices of these figures 'as they really are'" and to "do away with my own presence 'for the other's sake'"; the other seeks "to subjugate the other to myself, to make him into a marionette of which I pull the strings." This precarious middle path—which is that of dialogue—ultimately derives from the human condition or human being-in-the-world which again faces two options: "one where the I invades the world, and one where the world ultimately absorbs the I in the form of a corpse or of ashes."

Using Bakhtin's terminology, the Epilogue to *The Conquest of America* speaks of a new "exotopy" which involves an "affirmation of the other's exteriority" (or non-identity) which goes hand in hand with "recognition of the other as subject" (or as fellow human being). At an other point, this exotopic relation is portrayed as a "non-unifying love," that is, as a loving engagement which preserves reciprocal freedom. It is this kind of relation that Las Casas discovered in his old age when he managed to "love and esteem the Indians as a function not of his own ideal, but of theirs." In this respect, Las Casas (and some of his peers) anticipated the attitude of the later ethnologist and—more broadly—of the "modern exile": that is, of "a being who has lost his country without thereby acquiring another, who lives in a double exteriority" or double jeopardy. Yet, exile and exteriority, for Todorov, are not synonymous with nomadism or a "generalized relativism" where "any thing goes"; for such rootless straying only leads to boredom or indifference rather than engagement.[22]

Dialogue in the sense of exotopic engagement is not solely a theoretical construct or a scholarly speculation. Although relatively infrequent, history does provide examples or episodes approximating such cross-cultural engagement. In the Western context, one of the most fascinating examples of agonal dialogue was the Christian-Jewish-Islamic encounter during the early High Middle Ages—although the encounter was largely restricted to the academic plane (which does not detract from the significance of this cross-fertilization). As we know, classical learning was reaching "barbarian" Europe during this period via Islamic and Jewish translations and interpretations; thus, Greek sources—especially Aristotelian texts—were invigorating Western thinking in Christian monasteries and universities after being rendered into Latin from Arabic and Hebrew. While relatively intermittent in the Western setting, examples of cross-cultural engagement are more numerous—and also more closely tied to practice—in the non-Western world. In the context of Indian culture, the most noteworthy instance occurred during the reign of the Moghul emperor Akbar the Great who, in the sixteenth century, established political hegemony over most of India. Although himself a Sunni Muslim, Akbar practiced respect for Hindu religion and culture, as well as for other religions, and in 1575 established a "house of worship" where Muslims of different sects, Jesuit fathers from Goa, Zoroastrians, Hindu pandits and others gathered together to discuss religion with Akbar and among themselves. Historically, intercultural engagement has been even more widespread and pervasive in the Far East. In delivering his Reischauer Lectures in 1986, Theodore de Bary presented the development of East Asian civilization as a "dialogue in five stages." As contrasted to more formalized discourses, dialogue in de Bary's use refers to a "sharing or exchange of ideas in the broadest sense," including the "effect of ideas and institutions upon each other."[23]

In the concluding part of his Lectures, de Bary reflected on the future prospects of cross-cultural relations in the global arena. As he pointed out, those prospects are dim unless cultures are willing to become more genuinely engaged with one another: that is, to undergo a mutual learning process while simultaneously preserving the distinctiveness or difference of their traditions. "No new order can endure," he wrote, "that does not draw on the legacies of the past, but no tradition, whether Confucian, Buddhist, or Christian can survive untransformed in the crucible of global struggle." As he added pointedly, this struggle or contest cannot or should not involve a striving for planetary control or even extra-terrestrial conquest; in our rapidly shrinking global village, what is needed most urgently is the cultivation of a sense of mutual responsibility and of a shared readiness to care for the well-being of this world and its people:

We have long since passed the last frontier of outward, westward expansion (the bounds of the original New World), but we have not realized that our new frontier must be conceived in terms other than further penetration into others' space. Rather we must learn to live with both ourselves and others as East Asians have been doing for centuries—by a deeper, more intensive cultivation of our limited space. . . . What we need is not new worlds to conquer, star wars and all that, but a new parochialism of the earth or planet. [24]

In his Epilogue, Todorov himself ventures some steps beyond historical narrative toward an assessment of prospects and possibilities. Our world today, at the close of the twentieth century, is no longer quite the same as that of 1492—although some frightening parallels still persist in the relentless urge for conquest and domination. Still, global configurations have changed. "I believe," Todorov writes, "that this period of European history"—that is, the period of one-sided colonization—"is coming to an end today." At least, representatives of Western civilization "no longer believe so naively in its superiority" and hence "the movement of assimilation" is beginning to run down or subside. A similar change is happening on the ideological plane where our time seeks to combine "the better parts of both terms of the alternative"—in the sense that "we want *equality* without its compelling us to accept identity," but we also want "*difference* without its degenerating into superiority/inferiority." Taking into account these various changes, the Spanish conquest of America is not or should not be seen as exemplary or as providing a binding model for cultural relations in the future; even in our more aggressive moods we are "no longer like Cortés." Thus, history is still *magistra vitae*—not in the sense of announcing an inescapable fate but of providing lessons for a learning experience. To conclude with Todorov:

We are like the conquistadors and we differ from them; their example is instructive, though we shall never be sure that by not behaving like them we are not in fact on the way to imitating them, as we adapt ourselves to new circumstances. But their history can be exemplary for us because it permits us to reflect upon ourselves, to discover resemblances as well as differences: once again self-knowledge develops through knowledge of the other. [25]

1   Regarding Columbus' voyage and its effects compare Djelal Kadir, *Columbus and the Ends of the Earth: Europe's Prophetic Rhetoric as Conquering Ideology* (Berkeley: University of California Press, 1992); John Dyson, *Columbus—for Gold, God, and Glory* (New York: Simon & Schuster, 1991); Zvi Dov-Ner, *Columbus and the Age of Discovery* (New York: Morrow, 1991; Stephen Greenblatt, *Marvelous Possessions: The Wonder of the New World* (Chicago: University of Chicago Press, 1991); and Tzvetan Todorov, *The Conquest of America: The Question of the Other*, trans. Richard Howard (New York: Harper & Row, 1984).

2   George M. Foster, *Culture and Conquest: America's Spanish Heritage* (Chicago: Quadrangle Books, 1967), pp. 10-14.

3   Todorov, *The Conquest of America*, p. 248. As he continues somewhat pointedly: "Egalitarianism, of which one version is characteristic of the (Western) Christian religion as well as of the ideology of modern capitalist states, also serves colonial expansion: here is another, somewhat surprising lesson of our exemplary history." On the conquest of Mexico and Peru see Eric Wolf, *Sons of the Shaking Earth* (Chicago: University of Chicago Press, 1962), and William H. Prescott, *The Conquest of Peru* (New York: Mentor Books, 1961).

4   Todorov, *The Conquest of America*, pp. 30, 42-43.

5   *The Conquest of America*, p. 175.

6   Todorov points to the curious historical coincidence that Columbus' voyage took place in the same year in which the Muslims (Moors)—as well as the Jews—were finally expelled from Spain. "The year 1492," he writes, "already symbolizes, in the history of Spain, this double movement: in this same year the country repudiates its interior Other by triumphing over the Moors in the final battle of Granada and by forcing the Jews to leave its territory; and it discovers the exterior Other, that whole America which will become Latin." See *The Conquest of America*, p. 50.

7   Todorov, *The Conquest of America*, pp. 151-153, 160, 168, 171. The passages from Sepúlveda are taken from his *Democrates secundo: De las justas causas de la guerra contra los Indios* (Madrid: Instituto F. de Vitoria, 1951), pp. 20, 33. For the rejoinder of Las Casas see his *In Defense of the Indians*, trans. Stafford Poole (De Kalb: Northwestern Illinois University Press, 1974), p. 40. Compare also Las Casas, *The Tears of the Indians*, trans. John Phillips (first published in 1656; new ed., New York: Oriole Chapbooks, 1972). The translation by John Phillips was originally dedicated to Oliver Cromwell as an inducement to military action against Spain and against Spanish supremacy in the New World. Actually, Cromwell needed little coaxing as he had already sent out an expedition two years earlier to attack the Spanish possessions in the West Indies.

8   Lloyd and Susanne Rudolph, *The Modernity of Tradition* (Chicago: University of Chicago Press, 1967), pp. 119-120, 137-138. The more recent conversions in Tamil Nadu and elsewhere are discussed—usually from a narrowly Hindu point of view—in Devendra Swarup, ed., *Politics of Conversion* (Delhi: Deendayal Research Institute, 1986).

9   Crawford Young, *The Politics of Cultural Pluralism* (Madison, WI: University of Wisconsin Press, 1976), p. 71. Compare Rupert Emerson, *From Empire to Nation* (Cambridge, MA: Harvard University Press, 1960), pp. 95-96; also Ronald Cohen and John Middleton, *From Tribe to Nation in Africa* (Scranton, PA: Chandler Publishing Co., 1970), and Partha Chatterjee, *Nationalist Thought and the Colonial World* (Delhi: Oxford University Press, 1987). The definition of "assimilation" is cited in Milton M. Gordon, *Assimilation in American Life* (New York: Oxford University Press, 1964), p. 62, and in

Crawford Young, *The Politics of Cultural Pluralism*, pp. 15-16. See also Edward H. Spicer, "Acculturation," *International Encyclopedia of the Social Sciences* (New York: Crowell, Collier and Macmillan, 1968), vol. I, pp. 21-25.

10   It is under the rubrics of "integration and cultural pluralism" that Crawford Young discusses the political and cultural history of the Philippines; see *The Politics of Cultural Pluralism*, pp. 327-367. For his comments on post-independence Latin America see p. 85; and for a discussion of the process of "mestization" pp. 436-438, 440-442. For recent challenges to the melting-pot model in Latin America see Rodolfo Stavenhagen, *Problemas étnicos y campesinos* (Mexico: Instituto Nacional Indigenista, 1979); Guillermo Bonfil Batalla, *Mexico Profundo: Una Civilización negada* (Mexico: Grijalbo, 1989); and Denis Goulet, *Mexico: Development Strategies for the Future* (Notre Dame: University of Notre Dame Press, 1983), pp. 50-56.

11   See M. N. Srinivas, *Caste in Modern India and Other Essays* (Bombay: Asia Publishing House, 1962); and Harold A. Gould, *Caste Adaptation in Modernizing Indian Society* (Delhi: Chanakya Publications, 1988), esp. Chapter 7, pp. 143-155 ("Sanskritization and Westernization"); also Lloyd and Susanne Rudolph, *The Modernity of Tradition*, pp. 36-49. Following Srinivas and the Rudolphs, Crawford Young discusses the case of the Nadars in Tamil Nadu and of the Fur tribe in Western Sudan; see *The Politics of Cultural Pluralism*, pp. 101-103, 107-108.

12   Regarding Marco Polo's journey see e.g., *The Travels of Marco Polo*, trans. Aldo Ricci (London: Routledge & Kegan Paul, 1950), and Henry H. Hart, *Marco Polo: Venetian Adventurer* (Norman: University of Oklahoma Press, 1967). For the cultivation of Chinese tastes in pre-revolutionary France see David Maland, *Culture and Society in Seventeenth-Century France* (New York: Scribner, 1970); and Peter France, *Politeness and Its Discontents: Problems in French Classical Culture* (Cambridge: Cambridge University Press, 1992). Cultural borrowing in the form of *chinoiserie* was rudely transformed into military conquest and colonization during the nineteenth century as a result of the industrial revolution and its insatiable demand for overseas markets. One cannot bypass here in silence the ignominious story of the forced "unequal treaties" and of the later Opium War (whereby Western colonial powers sought to foist the consumption of opium on the Chinese people).

13   Heinrich Dumoulin, *Zen Buddhism: A History*, vol. I: *India and China*, trans. James W. Heisig and Paul Kittner (New York: Macmillan, 1988), pp. 64-65, 68. As Dumoulin adds (pp. 67-68): "During this period of assimilation there was a steady progress in the adaptation of Buddhist doctrine to Chinese forms of thought, or in the integration of the Chinese way of thinking into the Buddhist religion. Buddhist notions like *prajna, tathata* ('thusness'), and *bodhi* ('enlightenment') were sinicized, while Mahayana took on the typically Chinese notion of *wu-wei* ('nonaction'). But the deepest roots of this remarkable inner affinity between the basic ideas of Buddhism and Taoism suggest a naturalistic view of the world and of human

life that inspires the Mahayana sutras as well as Chuang-tzu, Lao-tzu and other Chinese thinkers." Compare also Erik Zürcher, *The Buddhist Conquest of China*, 2 vols. (Leiden: Brill, 1959); Kenneth Ch'en, *Buddhism in China: A Historical Survey* (Princeton: Princeton University Press, 1964); and R. H. Robinson, *Early Madhyamika in India and China* (Madison, WI: University of Wisconsin Press, 1967).

14 Edwin O. Reischauer, *Ennin's Travels in T'ang China* (New York: Ronald Press Co., 1955), pp. vii-viii, 3-4. See also *Ennin's Diary: The Record of a Pilgrimage to China in Search of the Law*, trans. Edwin O. Reischauer (New York: Ronald Press Co., 1955). Among remarkable cross-cultural journeys one should also not forget the travels of the Muslim Ibn Battuta who between 1325 to 1349 traveled from Tangier to Mecca and through the Near East to India and China; see Ross E. Dunn, *The Adventures of Ibn Battuta: A Muslim Traveler of the 14th Century* (Berkeley: University of California Press, 1986).

15 See John Rawls, *A Theory of Justice* (Cambridge, MA: Harvard University Press, 1971), pp. 60-65, 126-127; "Kantian Constructivism in Moral Theory," *Journal of Philosophy*, vol. 77 (1980), p. 536; Ronald Dworkin, *Taking Rights Seriously* (rev. ed.; Cambridge, MA: Harvard University Press, 1978), pp. 272-273; "Liberalism," in Stuart Hampshire, ed., *Public and Private Morality* (Cambridge: Cambridge University Press, 1978), p. 127; Bruce Ackerman, *Social Justice and the Liberal State* (New Haven: Yale University Press, 1980), p. 11.

16 For a critique of liberal neutralism and secularism, especially from the vantage of non-Western societies, see Bhikhu Parekh, "Superior People: The Narrowness of Liberalism from Mills to Rawls," *Times Literary Supplement* (December 5, 1993), pp. 7-10; and Ashis Nandy, "The Politics of Secularism and the Recovery of Religious Tolerance," *Alternatives*, vol. 13 (1988), pp. 178-190. Compare also A. R. Desai, *State and Society in India: Essays in Dissent* (Bombay: Popular Prakashan, 1974), and Manoranjan Mohanty, "Secularism: Hegemonic and Democratic," *Perspectives* (June 3, 1989), pp. 1219-1220.

17 Niccolo Machiavelli, "Discourses on the First Ten Books of Titus Livius," chapter IV, in *The Prince and the Discourses* (New York: Modern Library, 1950), p. 119. Compare also Thomas Hobbes, *Leviathan* (New York: Dutton, 1953), chapters 13, 17-18, pp. 63-66, 87-96; and John Rawls, "Kantian Constructivism in Moral Theory," pp. 539, 542.

18 See Machiavelli, *The Prince and the Discourses*, p. 119; "The Communist Manifesto" in Robert C. Tucker, ed., *The Marx-Engels Reader* (New York: Norton & Co., 1972), pp. 336, 338-340, 344-345. In extolling industrialization, the *Manifesto* was blunt regarding the relations between advanced Western societies and Third World countries (p. 339): "The bourgeoisie has subjected the country to the rule of the towns. . . . Just as it has made the country dependent on the towns, so it has made barbarian and semi-barbarian countries dependent on the civilized ones, nations of peasants on nations of bourgeois, the East on the West."

19   See Jean-Paul Sartre, *Being and Nothingness: An Essay on Phenomenological Ontology*, trans. Hazel E. Barnes (New York: Philosophical Library, 1956), pp. 258, 260-263, 287-289, 296-297, 364; Jean-François Lyotard, *The Postmodern Condition: A Report on Knowledge*, trans. Geoff Bennington and Brian Massumi (Minneapolis: University of Minnesota Press, 1984), pp. 11-13, 15-17.

20   See Frantz Fanon, *The Wretched of the Earth* (New York: Grove Press, 1963), pp. 29-30.

21   Todorov, *The Conquest of America*, p. 250. Regarding Habermas see especially his "Toward a Universal Pragmatics," in *Communication and the Evolution of Society*, trans. Thomas McCarthy (Boston: Beacon Press, 1979), pp. 1-68, and *The Theory of Communicative Action*, vol. I: *Reason and the Rationalization of Society*, trans. Thomas McCarthy (Boston: Beacon Press, 1984), pp. 8-42. For a critical review see my "Transcendental Hermeneutics and Universal Pragmatics," in *Language and Politics* (Notre Dame: University of Notre Dame Press, 1984), pp. 115-147, and "Habermas and Rationality," in *Life-World, Modernity, and Critique: Paths Between Heidegger and the Frankfurt School* (Cambridge: Polity Press, 1991), pp. 132-159. Regarding Gadamer see his *Truth and Method*, trans. Joel Weinsheimer and Donald G. Marshall (2nd rev. ed.; New York: Crossroad, 1989), and my "Hermeneutics and Deconstruction: Gadamer and Derrida in Dialogue," in *Critical Encounters* (Notre Dame: University of Notre Dame Press, 1987), pp. 130-158. Curiously, although vindicating tradition against Habermas's emancipation from tradition, MacIntyre proposes a rationalist model of cross-cultural communication akin to Habermasian discourse; see, e.g., Alasdair MacIntyre, *Three Rival Versions of Moral Enquiry: Encyclopedia, Genealogy, and Tradition* (Notre Dame: University of Notre Dame Press, 1990), pp. 222-224.

22   Todorov, *The Conquest of America*, pp. 247, 249-251. As he adds (p. 251): "The anthropologist's position is fruitful; much less so is that of the tourist whose curiosity about strange ways takes him to Bali or Bahia, but who confines the experience of the heterogeneous within the space of his paid vacations." Regarding dialogue in Bakhtin's work compare Katerina Clark and Michael Holquist, *Mikhail Bakhtin* (Cambridge, MA: Belknap Press, 1984), pp. 9-12, 347-350.

23   See Wm. Theodore de Bary, *East Asian Civilizations: A Dialogue in Five Stages* (Cambridge, MA: Harvard University Press, 1988), pp. ix-x, 33; and, regarding Akbar, Sri Ram Sharma, *The Religious Policy of the Mughal Emperors* (London: Oxford University Press, 1940), and Emmy Wellesz, *Akbar's Religious Thought* (London: Allen & Unwin, 1952).

24   See de Bary, *East Asian Civilizations* pp. 123-124, 127, 138.

25   Todorov, *The Conquest of America*, pp. 249, 254.